IMAGES
of America

GUILFORD AND SANGERVILLE

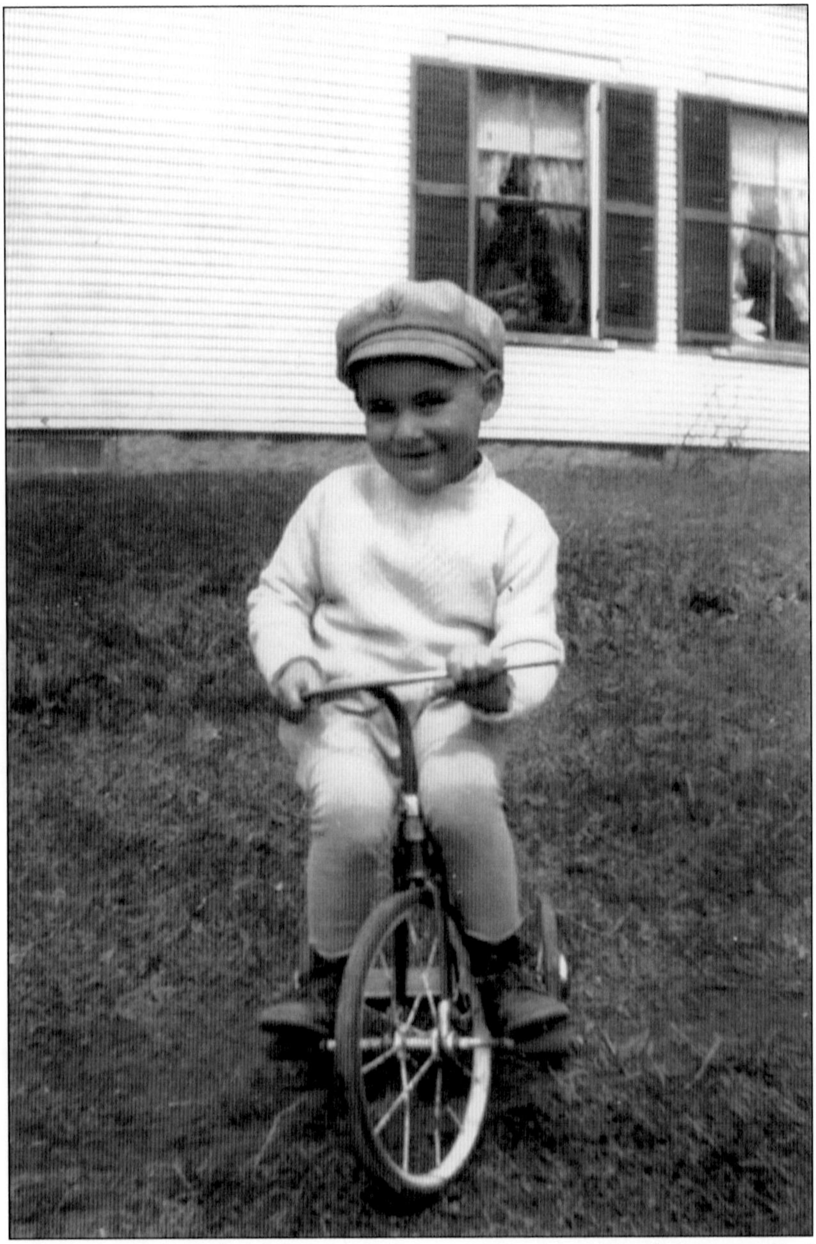

This 1938 photograph shows the author at age four, sitting in front of his home proudly displaying his brand-new set of wheels. This bicycle was a stripped-down version built for speed. Therefore, it had no fenders. Also notice the racing slicks. The home, located on South Main Street in Guilford, was owned by Del and Marcie Curtis and is currently owned and occupied by Steve and Jean Hall. (Author's collection.)

On the cover: Taken in the late 1800s, this image shows the general store of Micajah and James Hudson that was located at the top of Bank Square in Guilford. Typical of this type of store, it sold just about everything and almost every town had one like it. It also usually served as a gathering spot for the local people to meet and discuss the news of the day and local events. (Guilford Historical Society Archives.)

IMAGES
of America

GUILFORD AND SANGERVILLE

Sieferd C. Schultz

ARCADIA PUBLISHING

ISBN 978-0-7385-5511-9

Published by Arcadia Publishing
Charleston SC, Chicago IL, Portsmouth NH, San Francisco CA

Printed in the United States of America

Library of Congress Catalog Card Number: 2007929418

For all general information contact Arcadia Publishing at:
Telephone 843-853-2070
Fax 843-853-0044
E-mail sales@arcadiapublishing.com
For customer service and orders:
Toll-Free 1-888-313-2665

Visit us on the Internet at www.arcadiapublishing.com

To the pioneering spirit, hard work, and unmatched courage of those who have come and gone and left for us these two beautiful towns along the Piscataquis.

Contents

ACKNOWLEDGMENTS

Thanks go to the members of both the Guilford and the Sangerville Historical Societies, especially Thomas Blake and Carl McKusick of Guilford, and Lisa Fortier, Shirley Drew, and Alice Moulton of Sangerville. Unless otherwise noted, all images appearing in this book are from the Guilford Historical Society archives.

Special thanks to my son-in-law, Brian Woodworth, for all his computer work to help move this project along.

Special thanks also to Marion Race, whose long memory of Sangerville helped answer a lot of questions that probably would have gone unanswered.

And last but not least, special thanks to my wife, a very special person, who put up with my sometimes-cantankerous disposition while trying to get this book off the ground.

INTRODUCTION

In 1803, two men, Robert Low Jr. and Robert Herring Jr., purchased a large tract of land from Bowdoin College in what is now the incorporated town of Guilford, with part of the agreement being that they would establish homes on this land. In 1804, a number of trees were felled on lots along the Piscataquis River, and corn was planted the next year. By 1806, there were seven men residing within the area. At this time, the area was within the boundaries of Somerset County, and in October 1812, a warrant was issued by the county to organize the area into a plantation. This was done in November, and immediately provisions were made for the education of the children. Education has remained a high priority for the entire existence of the town. In 1815, Thomas Macomber was given a grant of 300 acres and, in return, agreed to stay and preach for a minimum of 10 years. He actually stayed 20.

In 1816, the town petitioned the general court to be incorporated under the laws of the State of Massachusetts and to be named Fluvanna. The Massachusetts legislature passed the warrant in February 1816 but disliked the name and changed it to Guilford. By 1819, there were 13 families living in the township. The next year, 1820, Maine was granted statehood under the Missouri Compromise and Guilford became part of Piscataquis County. According to the census at that time, Guilford had 325 citizens.

In 1818, a meetinghouse was erected in Guilford center that also served as a school and town hall until it burned in 1825. In 1824, a crib dam was built across the Piscataquis River and a sawmill was established by Robert Herring Jr., along with two other individuals. From this point on, Guilford began to grow and gradually became highly industrialized due to the abundance of waterpower available to run mills and factories. In 1825, Addison Martin opened the first store in the village, and by then, the population had soared to 500 people. In 1827, he built the first frame house, and although it has been remodeled many times, it still stands to this day and was last used as an inn and bar.

In 1834, the Guilford Free Meeting House was built on High Street by the Methodists and Universalists and was used by both until each established their separate churches within the village proper. It stood where the First Pentecostal Church is currently located.

In the ensuing years, many businesses were established, factories and mills flourished, and Guilford became a model of industry until the start of World War II, when almost anything a person could ever want was available within the town. The Bangor and Piscataquis Railroad reached town in 1871, providing both freight and passenger service to Bangor where it interconnected with the Maine Central Railroad. In 1881, a woolen mill was built on the north side of the river, and a town hall, which also contained the village high school, was erected at the corner of School and North Main Streets and saw many uses until it burned flat in 1928, a huge loss at the time.

With the advent of electricity, the power of the rivers was no longer needed to run the mills, and gradually everything was changed over to electric power, signaling the end of a very important chapter in America's Industrial Revolution.

Devastating fires and floods have plagued Guilford from the time it was settled, with floods taking out bridges and destroying property right up through 1987, when the "flood of the century" probably caused more damage than all the others put together, even taking out the historic, 130-year-old Lows bridge. Fires have been almost as bad over the years, destroying several small schools, the Turner House, the high school, the town hall, the Hardwood Products Mill, the entire Koritsky block, the Braeburn Hotel, and many private homes, with some causing loss of life, to name a few. One exception was during the 1947 drought, when huge forest fires swept the state and Guilford did not have one serious fire. The local fire chief at the time mobilized almost the entire town with roving patrols out every night to watch for even the slightest conflagration, and all the local farms were asked to keep as much water as possible at the ready. The only bad fire in this area was in East Sangerville.

Through a lot of hard work, perseverance, and sometimes a little luck, Guilford has managed to keep most of its industries, and today it is more or less the manufacturing center of the county. The town has survived many adversities over the course of its existence and continues today as a vibrant community, always looking to the future with the optimism inherited from its forbearers.

The town of Sangerville consists of 24,216 acres and was sold by the State of Massachusetts for the princely sum of 25¢ per acre, 75 percent of which was purchased by Col. Calvin Sanger of Sherborn, Massachusetts, around 1800. The other 25 percent, consisting of the southeast quadrant, had previously been allotted to Moses Hodsdon. Sanger soon purchased this also and became the sole owner of the entire town. The first settler was Phineas Ames of New Hampshire, settling near Lane's Corner in 1802. James Weymouth was next, and he settled near Center Pond. Others soon followed, and the settlement was called Amestown.

Because no major rivers flowed through the town of Sangerville, several small streams were harnessed for power and the town actually became a group of small settlements, each being mostly independent. They cleared land for farms, built their own mills, started schools, and did other things in common that were necessary for survival. The first to flourish was Brockway's Mills on French Mills Brook, named after Jesse Brockway, who arrived around 1804. At the same time the Brockway mills were being built, Phineas Ames erected a crude gristmill on Black Stream that he swapped with Sanger for three new lots. A sawmill and a shingle mill followed, and the area became known as Knowlton's Mills. At some point, Sanger sent is cousin Walter Leland to the area to look after his interests. There are descendants of both Leland and the Knowltons still living in East Sangerville. Although the mills did well, the area did not grow as fast as Brockway's, which soon had a sawmill, shingle mill, gristmill, blacksmith shop, machine shop, country store, and post office. It was also there that Sir Hiram S. Maxim was born in 1840 next door to Cyrus Brockway in the Nickerson house. Maxim was knighted by Queen Victoria of the United Kingdom in 1901.

In the northeast section, another healthy brook called Carleton Stream flowed out of Manhanock Pond and had an excellent drop in roughly one mile, allowing for the construction of four separate dams that provided a considerable amount of power. It was here that the main village came to be and was at first known as Carleton's Mills when Carleton and Dudley built a sawmill on the west bank of the stream. When the town incorporated in 1814, the entire township was named Sangerville in honor of Sanger.

In 1869, a woolen factory was completed and put into operation at the village by Moses Carr and greatly increased the prosperity of the town. He was the first real entrepreneur in town, running several businesses, and in his later years, he was joined by his grandsons Fred H. Carr and Alton L. Carr. By 1904, there were three major woolen mills thriving in the village, the

Campbell Manufacturing Company, the Carleton Mills Company that was built on the east bank of the stream opposite the sawmill, and the Sangerville Woolen Company. These mills flourished up through the end of World War II and then gradually closed. With the exception of the Carleton Mill, which is home to Numberall Corporation, the machinery was sold and the buildings were used to raise chickens for market.

Another well-known individual was Sir Harry Oakes, who was born on High Street in Sangerville in 1874. Before his untimely death in 1943, Oakes was knighted by King George VI of the United Kingdom for his many charities and was considered to be the richest man in the British Empire.

The coming of electricity changed the makeup of Sangerville forever, as waterpower became a thing of the past. The many sawmills, gristmills, and so on, fell into disuse and gradually disappeared, leaving only traces of foundations here and there for the current generations to look at and wonder about.

Religion also played a big part in the life of the early settlers, and a number of churches were built within the township over the years. The first one, built in 1834, was a union house but was soon purchased by the Baptists. Located just east of the town square at the top of the hill, it was still used as a meetinghouse and church until the late 1800s, when it fell into disuse.

Rail service reached the town in 1871, although the station was located just across the river in Guilford, as that is where the tracks were. There is one known fatality of a Sangerville citizen involving the railroad when, in 1948, a commercial bus slid into a moving engine at the State Route 23 crossing and Ann Deckerhoff, a passenger on the bus, was fatally injured.

Over the years, Sangerville built many small, one-room schoolhouses, which saw service for many years before being razed or purchased by individuals and converted to homes. An excellent high school-grade school combination was built in 1890 and served the town well until 1949, when Sangerville, Guilford, and several other towns consolidated their 7th through 12th grades into a new school in Guilford called the Piscataquis Community High School.

Although it no longer has the industrial might it once possessed, Sangerville continues to be made up of energetic, hardworking individuals who always look for ways to better their town, look to the future with optimism, and never forget their proud past.

One

Rivers, Bridges, and Floods

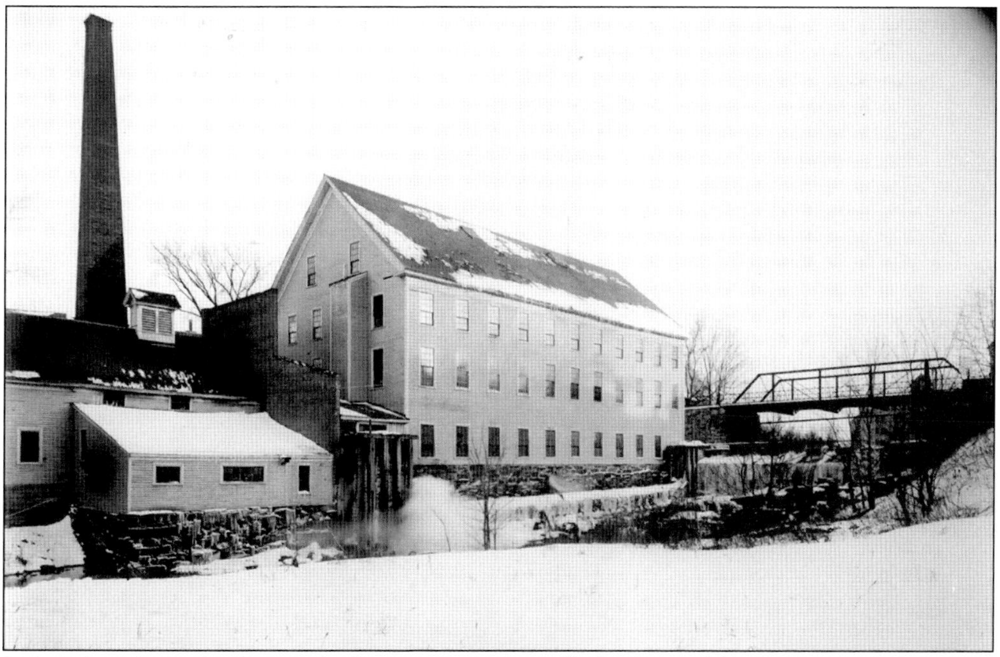

Before the I beam bridge was built in 1948, Sangerville had a steel bridge across the Carleton Stream on what is now Douty Hill Road, formerly High Street. The dam shown here is the third dam on this small stream, and it provided power for the Carleton Mill, later known as Glencoe No. 2. In 1943, the top two floors were destroyed by fire; however, the company managed to salvage the bottom two floors and continued to use the mill, even adding a spinning room above the part that was saved. Over the ensuing years, it underwent additional improvements and today is the home of Numberall Corporation.

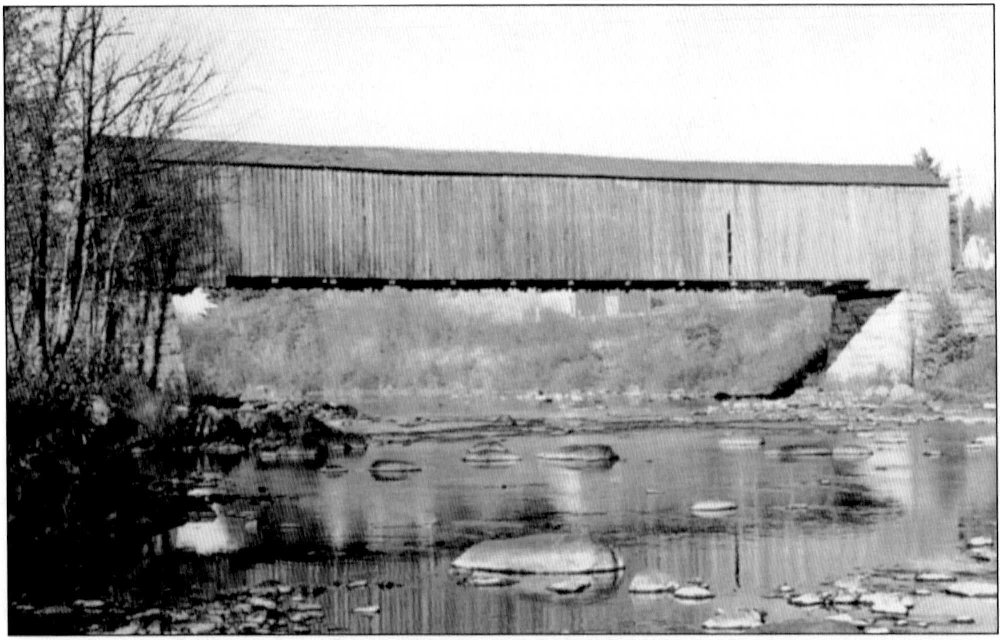

Located approximately three miles downstream from the village of Guilford, Lows bridge spanned the Piscataquis River between Sangerville and Guilford. The first bridge, built in 1830, lasted only two years, and the second one lasted 25 years before floods took them both out. The third one (above) was built in 1857, and after it was lost in the great flood of 1987, it was replaced by the state in 1990. It is one of the most viewed bridges in the state. The original construction cost of approximately $600 in 1857 was divided between the two towns. Access from the Guilford side is directly off State Route 15. From Sangerville, access was from Howards Corner, but the road has been discontinued.

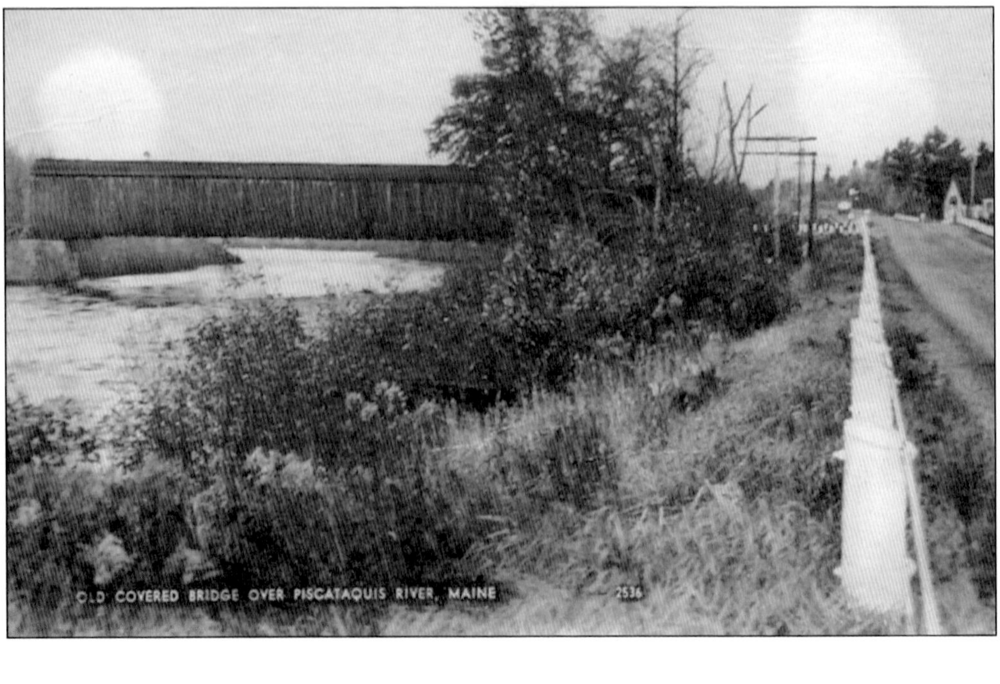

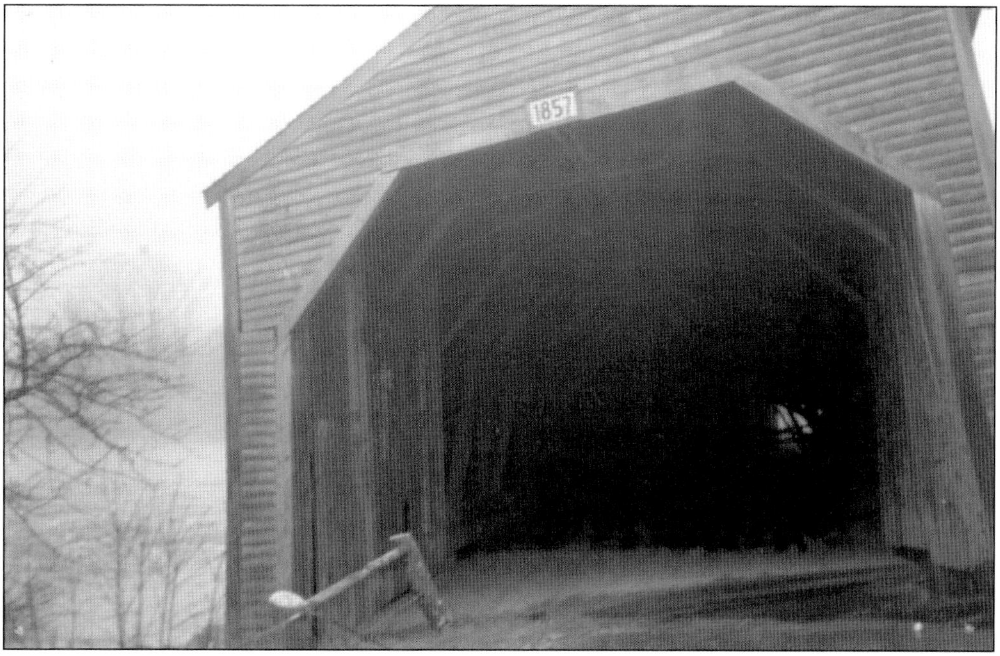

In 1987, the "flood of the century" hit Guilford and the 130-year-old Lows bridge succumbed to the ravages of the river. Here the water has risen to the point where the bridge has been lifted off its foundation and is moving with the current. (Courtesy of Dwinal Hall.)

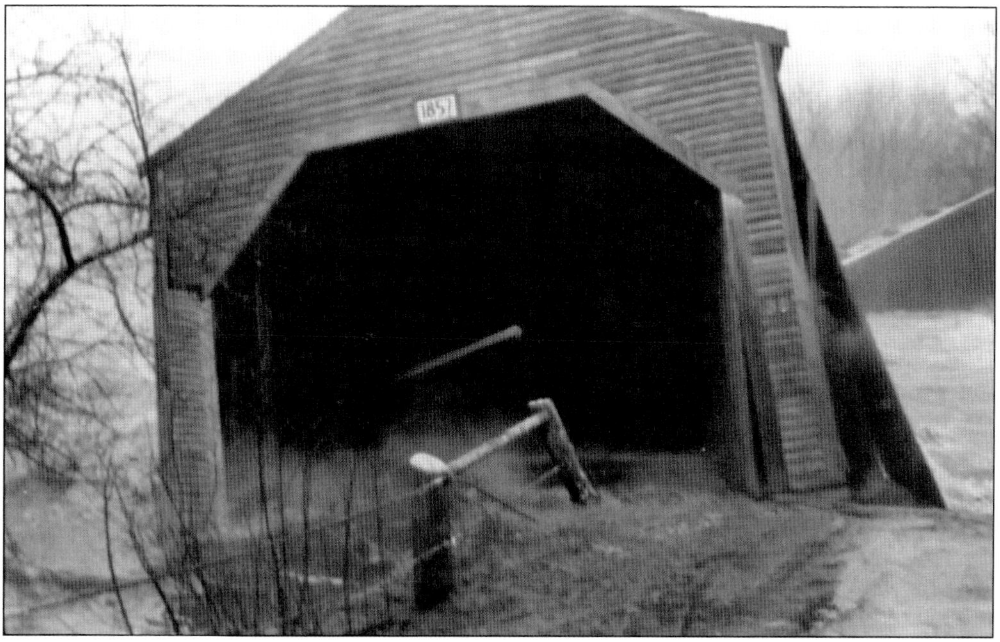

Here the bridge is completely off its foundation and has broken in half. In a matter of minutes, the two halves separated and were floating downstream. Part of the front half was caught a quarter mile down the river by trees and a bend in the river, but the rest of the bridge went over the dam in Dover. The 1857 sign seen on the front half was found 20 years after the flood. (Courtesy of Dwinal Hall.)

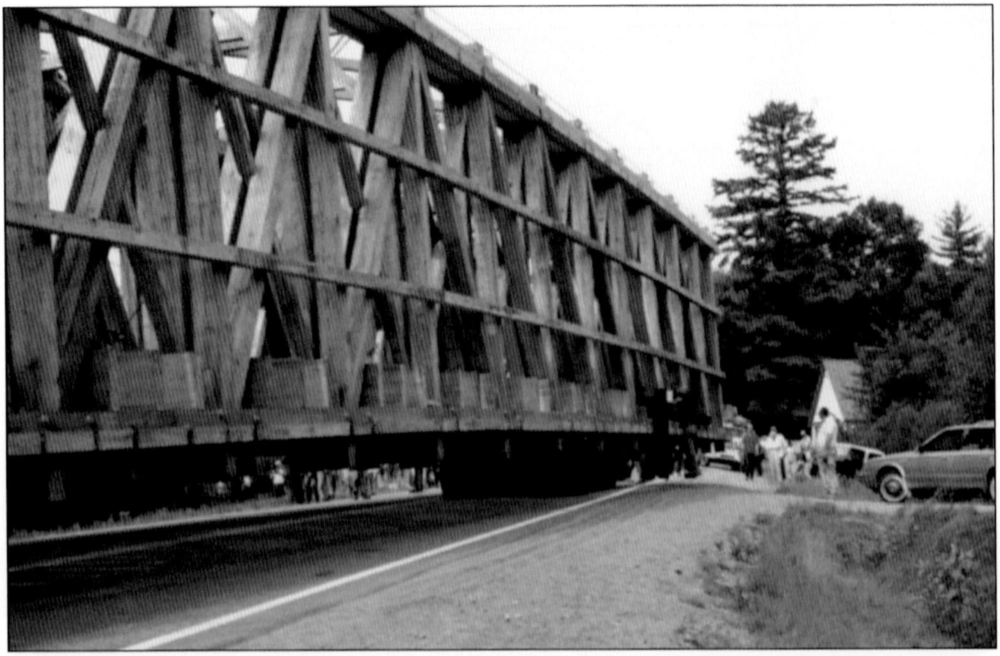

After receiving thousands of signatures on petitions, the state agreed to rebuild the bridge in 1990 and followed the original plans as closely as possible. The entire framework was actually constructed in the state highway yard about 1,000 yards west and then hauled to the site and slid across on steel beams, with the roof and sides being finished in place. It was also raised a few feet higher in anticipation of the next flood. All went well until when turning the corner from State Route 15, it was discovered that the bridge was a bit too long to make the corner. In the photograph below, the problem has been solved and the bridge is being towed across. (Courtesy of Dwinal Hall.)

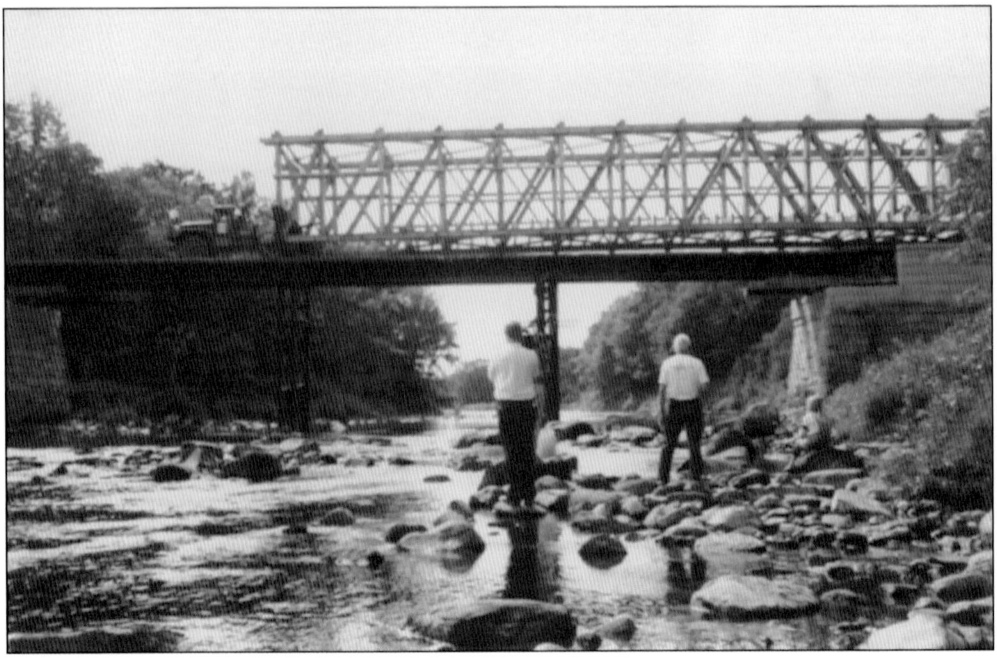

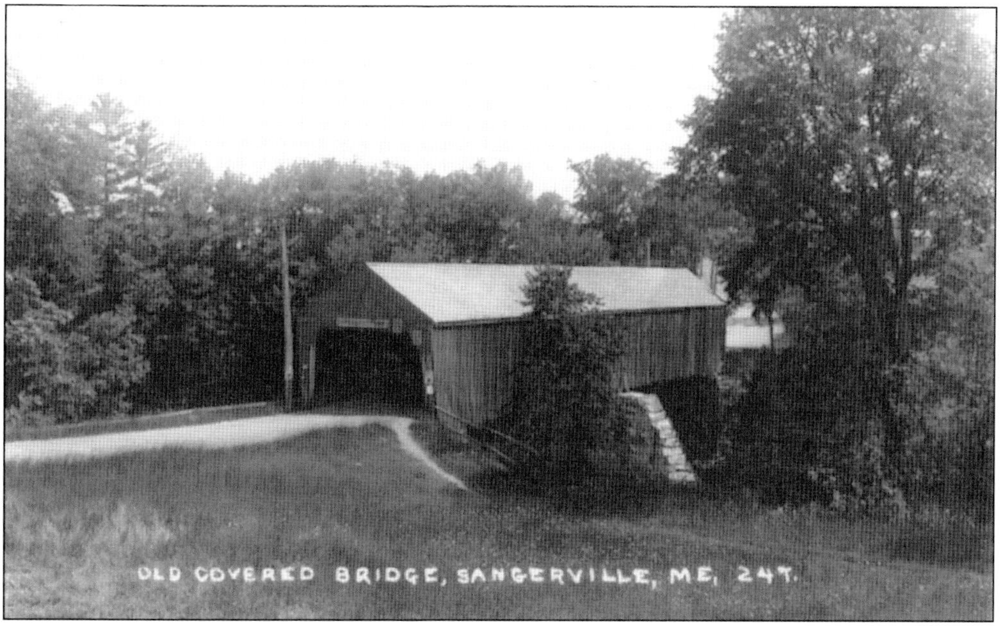

In 1828, a covered bridge was built on State Route 23 near the Sangerville Village Cemetery, but it was soon swept away by high water in 1832. After some bickering between the towns, it was rebuilt in 1835 with the two towns sharing the cost. With proper maintenance, the bridge lasted 95 years until 1930, when it was replaced by a steel bridge. By a special act of the legislature, the town portions of the replacement costs were assumed by the state. The steel bridge lasted until 2004, but because it was becoming increasingly dangerous for wider vehicles, it was replaced by the state with an I beam bridge. (Courtesy of Sangerville Historical Society.)

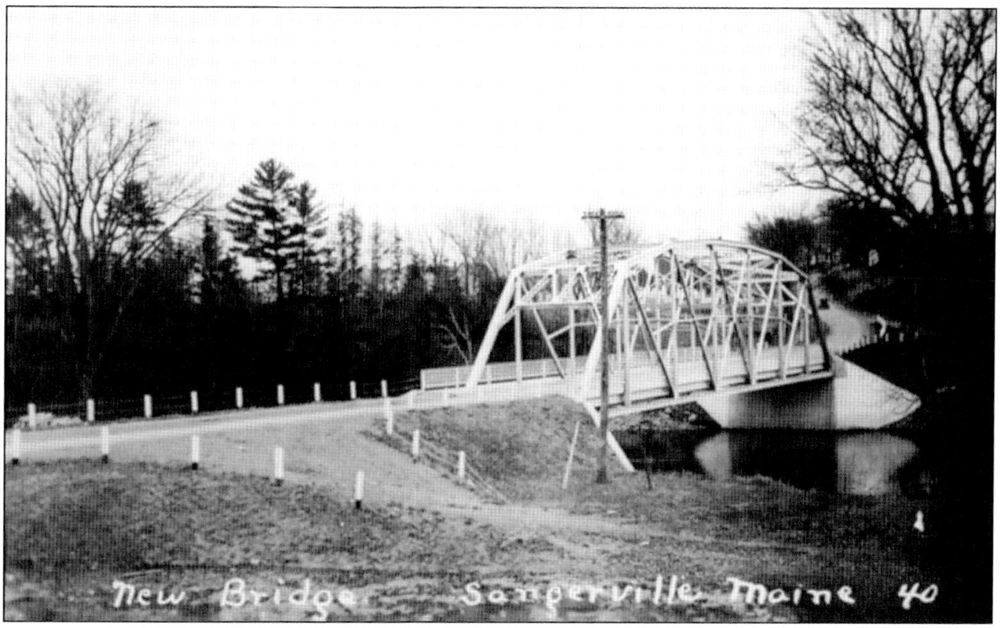

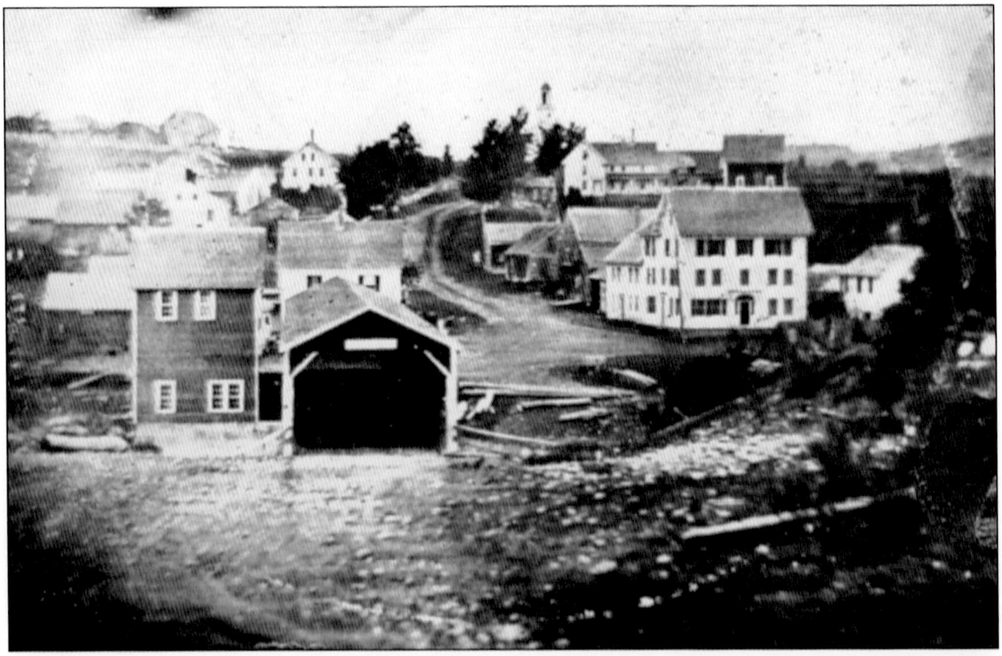

The second covered bridge in Guilford village was built in the 1830s and lasted approximately 25 years. The first one was built in 1829 and was soon washed away in a freshet. At that time, there was no dam on the river, so the bridge was much shorter than later ones. The large white building across the river is the Franklin House, which was built in 1850. This is the oldest known photograph of the village.

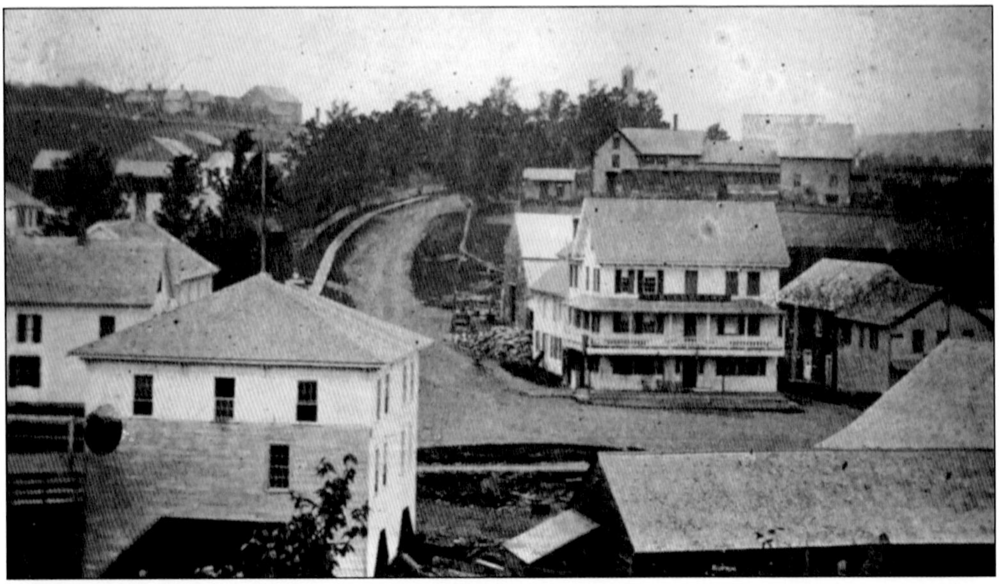

In this photograph, just downstream from the bridge, many changes have taken place in a short period of time. The Franklin House is now called the Turner House, with new porches added. The building in the left foreground is probably a gristmill judging by the millraces under the building. The building in the right foreground is unidentified.

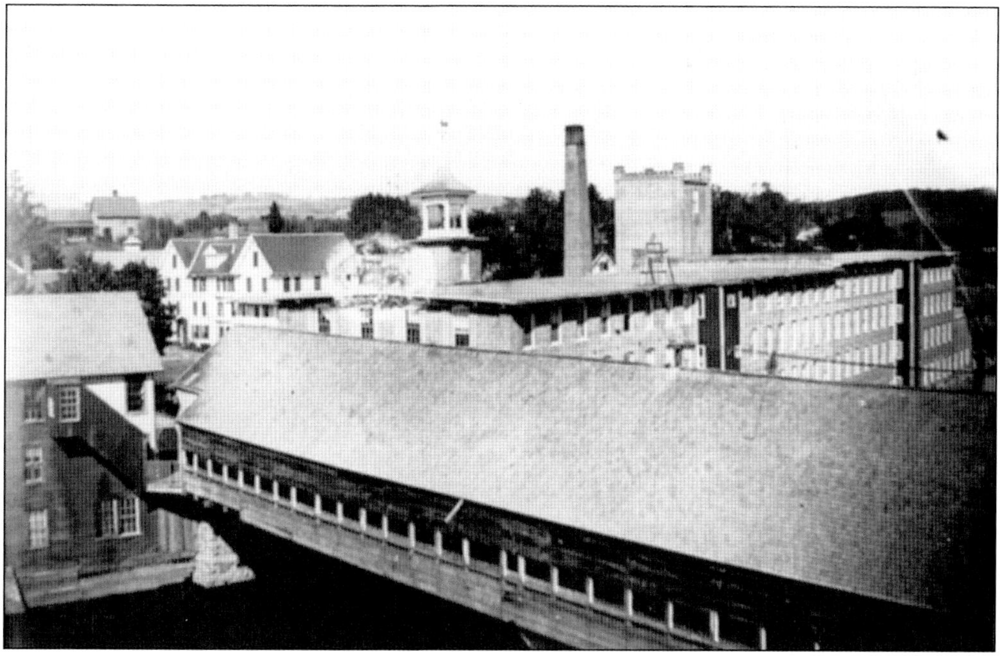

The third and last covered bridge in Guilford at this location on Main Street was built in 1855 and stood until 1907, when it was razed and replaced by a steel bridge. This bridge is much longer than the previous one due to the building of the dam about 100 feet downstream, which widened the river considerably.

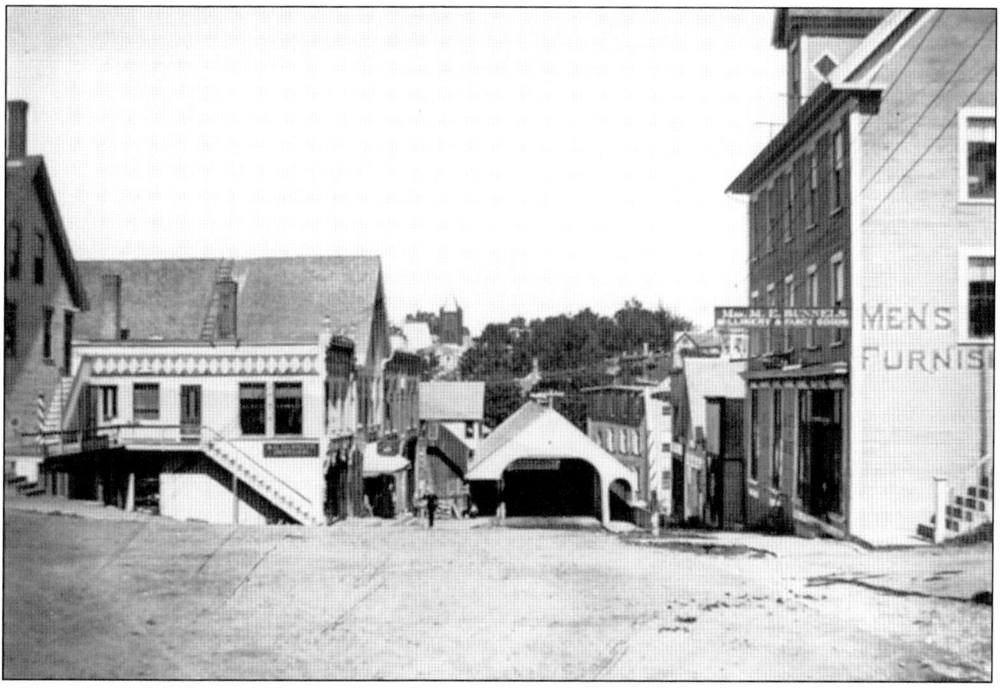

This is the southern end of the covered bridge as seen from Bank Square in Guilford. The bridge had sidewalks on both sides. One was paid for by the town and the other by Henry Hudson, a longtime resident of Guilford.

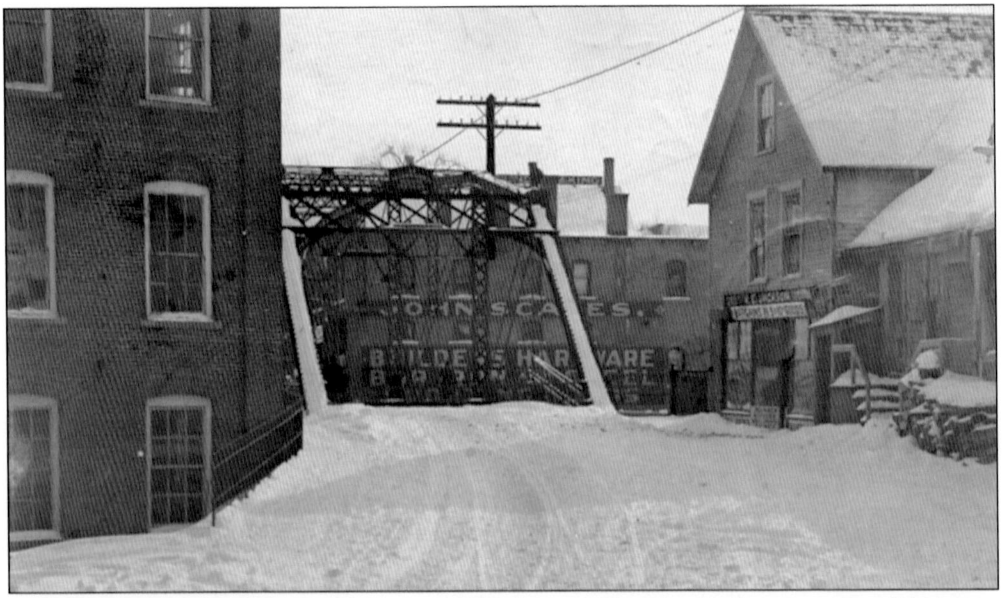

A steel bridge replaced the Guilford covered bridge in 1907. This bridge was state of the art at the time of its construction and had excellent sidewalks on both sides. A temporary footbridge was built to accommodate pedestrians during the construction. The ruts in the snow are wagon tracks, as automobiles had not arrived yet.

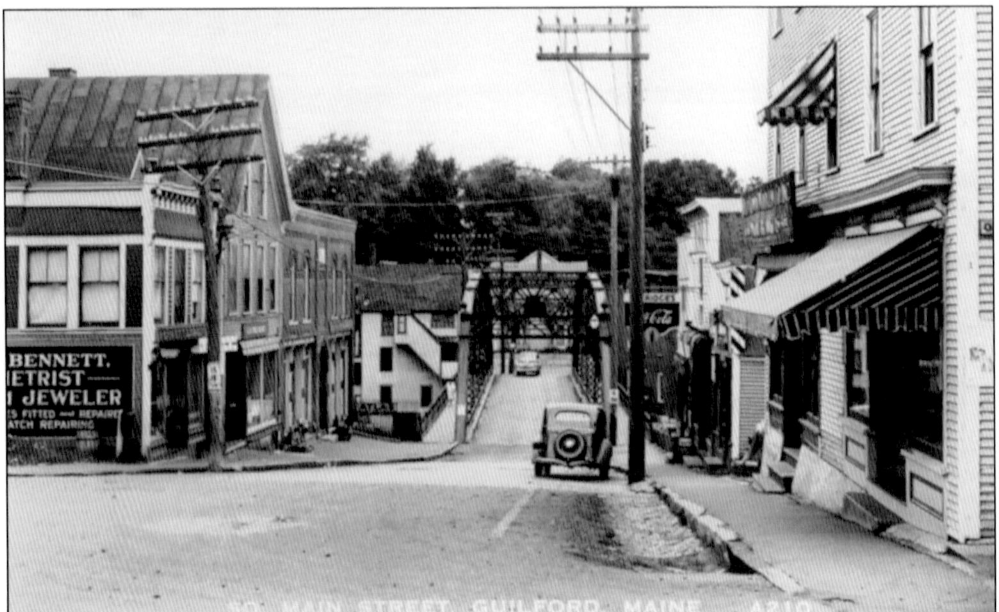

Guilford's Bank Square on the south side of the bridge was a busy area in the 1930s but was rather quiet on a Sunday morning. To the left is Bennett's jewelry store, Genthner's drugstore, and the Scales building. To the right is a laundromat, an electronics shop, a barbershop, and Eldridges candy store (better known simply as Bessie's).

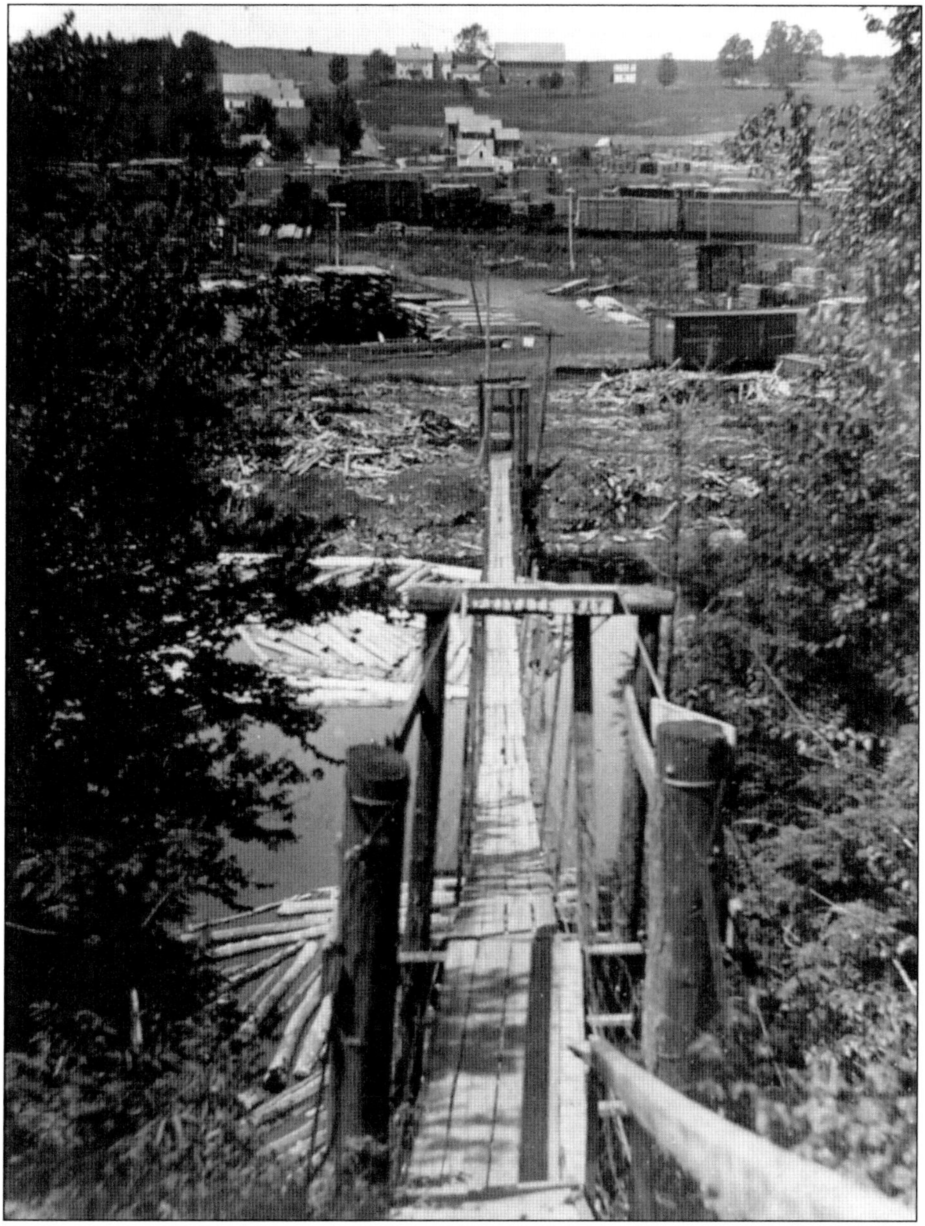

When the covered bridge was replaced in Guilford, a temporary footbridge was built across the river. When it was no longer needed by the town, it was purchased by the owner of the Guilford Manufacturing Company. He placed it across the river behind his mill just west of the Elmwood cemetery for the use of his workers, many of whom lived on the other side. This saved a lot of shoe leather until the footbridge's demise during the flood of 1923. It was never rebuilt. Large logs were floated down to the mill and corralled by boom chains strung across the river. A goodly number of logs can be seen floating and waiting to be used by the mill. Notice the large amount of railroad activity and the amount of trackage required to sustain the mill. The road going up the hill in the top left center of the picture is Winter Street, or Sawdust Alley, as it was called at the time. Across the top is High Street with the so-called company farm on the far side of the road. (Courtesy of Richard Nesbit.)

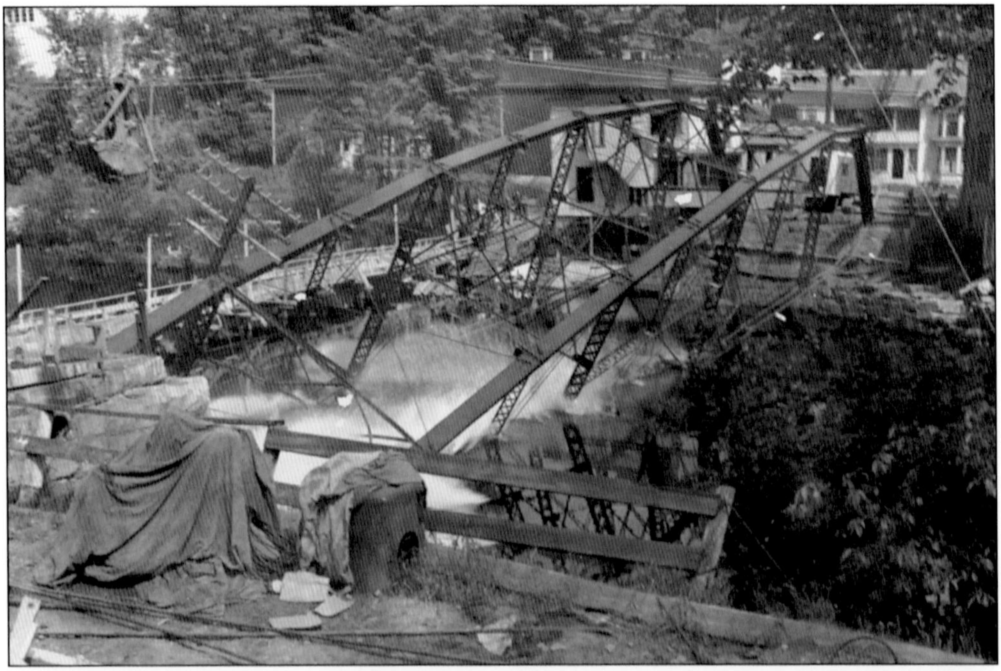

Signaling the end of an era, the 47-year-old steel bridge was dropped into the river in 1954 prior to its dismantling and replacement with the current I beam bridge. (Courtesy of Thomas Blake.)

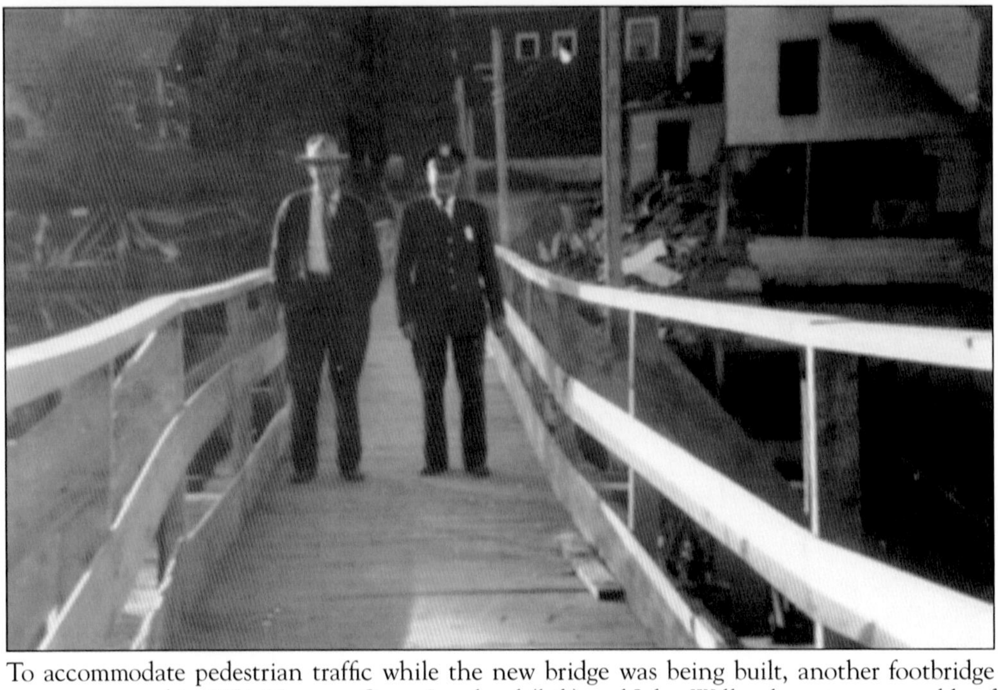

To accommodate pedestrian traffic while the new bridge was being built, another footbridge was constructed in 1954. Here are Omar Lombard (left) and John Willey, longtime constable of Guilford, standing in the middle of the bridge. The bridge was short-lived however, as another flood hit in September of that year, completely demolishing it.

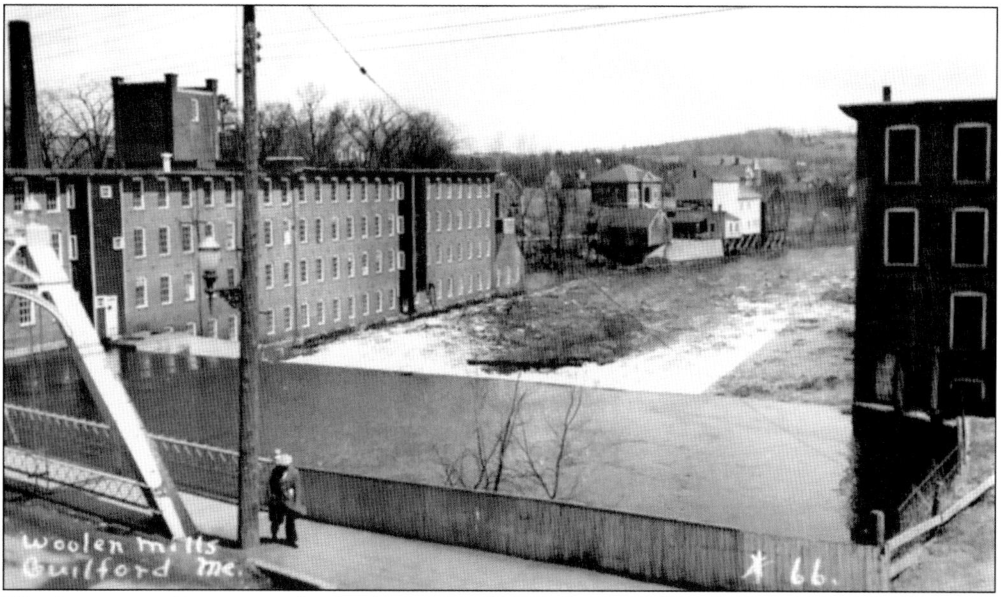

The Piscataquis River was absolutely vital to the settlement of the town of Guilford. This is a view down the river looking east over the dam. The dam initially provided the power to run two woolen mills through an ingenious combination of pulleys and belts, which ran all the machines, usually from one central drive shaft for each mill. Beyond the mills the gristmill and the public library can be seen.

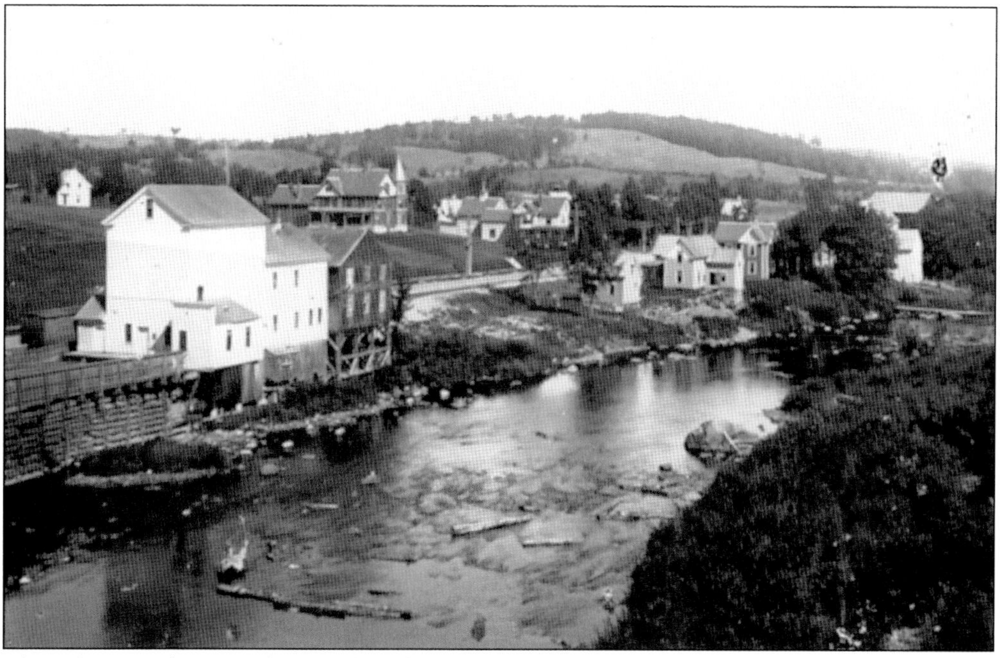

This photograph was taken farther down the river from a window of the Hussey Woolen Company in the 1920s. Palmer's Grist Mill is to the left, and the Stevens Mansion can be seen just above it. The darker, second house down on the right was the longtime home and office of Dr. Guy Dore.

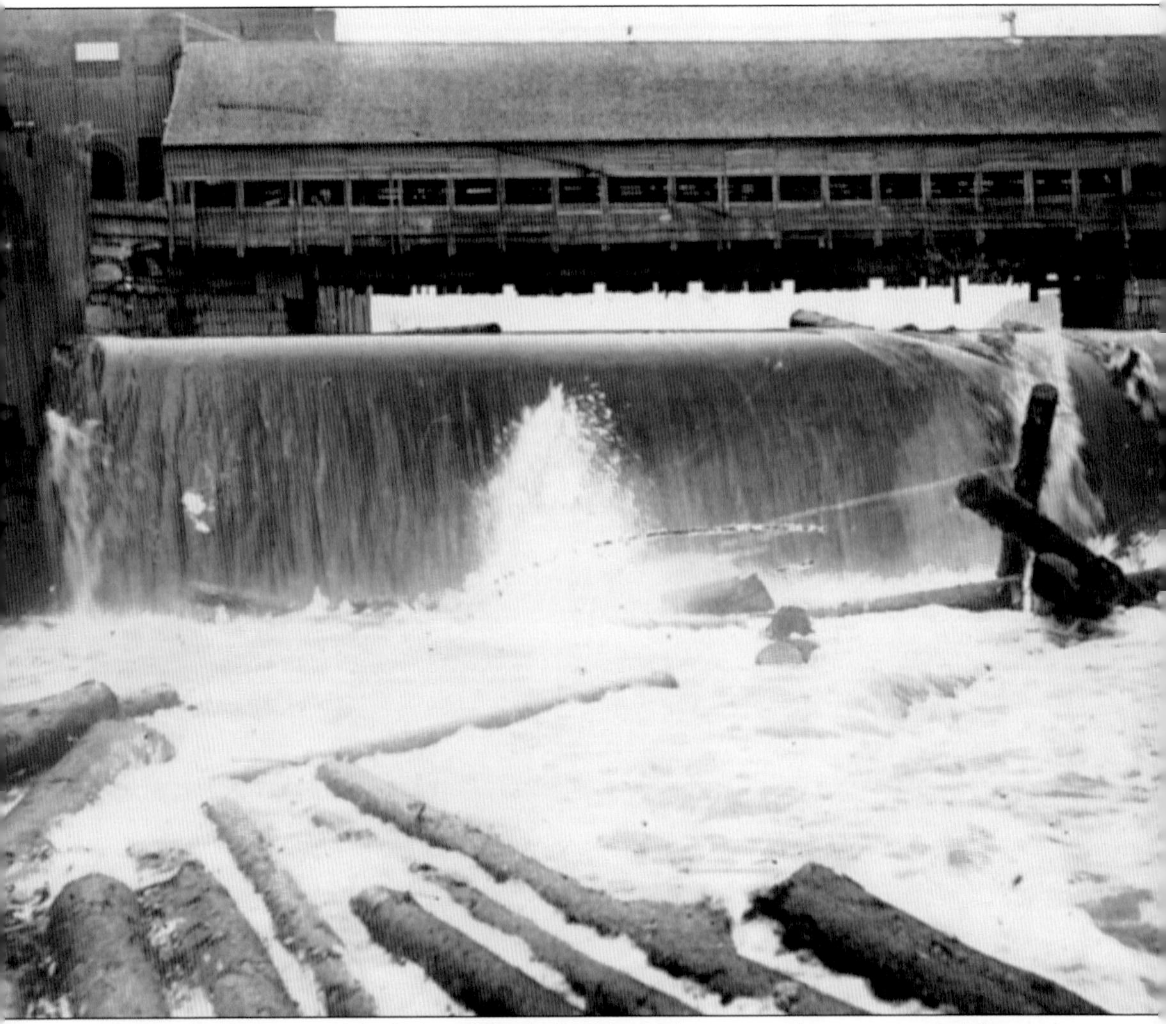

During the latter part of the 19th and first half of the 20th century, the river was vital for moving pulp and saw logs to their destinations downriver. Wood was cut all winter and stacked along the banks of the streams. After the ice went out, the logs were pushed into the stream and floated to various mills along the banks. Here are 20-foot saw logs coming over the dam in Guilford sometime in the late 1800s. At some point after 1940, the river drives were banned, a way of life was gone forever, and a lot of lives were probably saved.

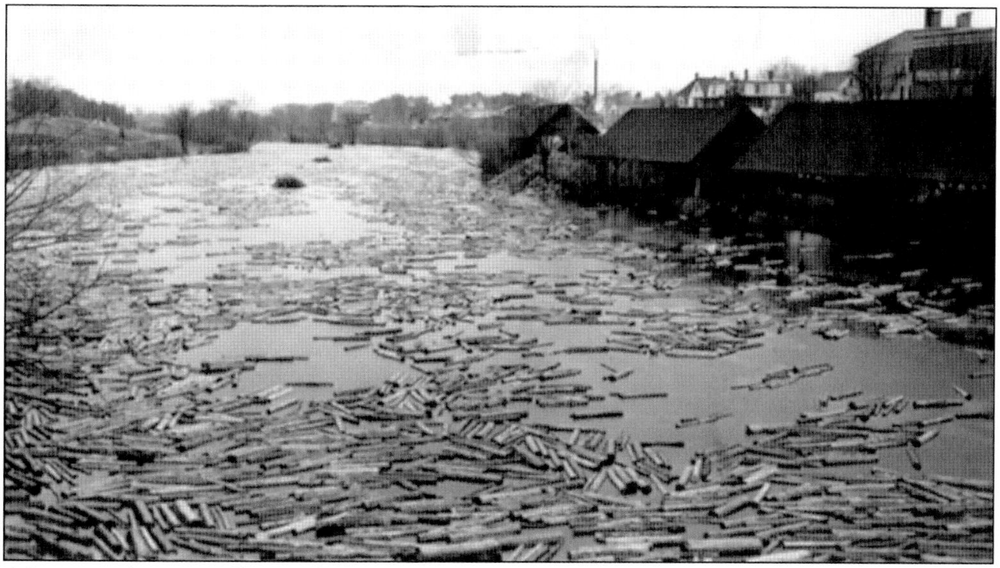

After several paper mills were built downriver, four-foot pulp logs were essential to the operation of the mills, and for a few days every spring, the river was black with the logs coming down the river and over the dam. (Author's collection.)

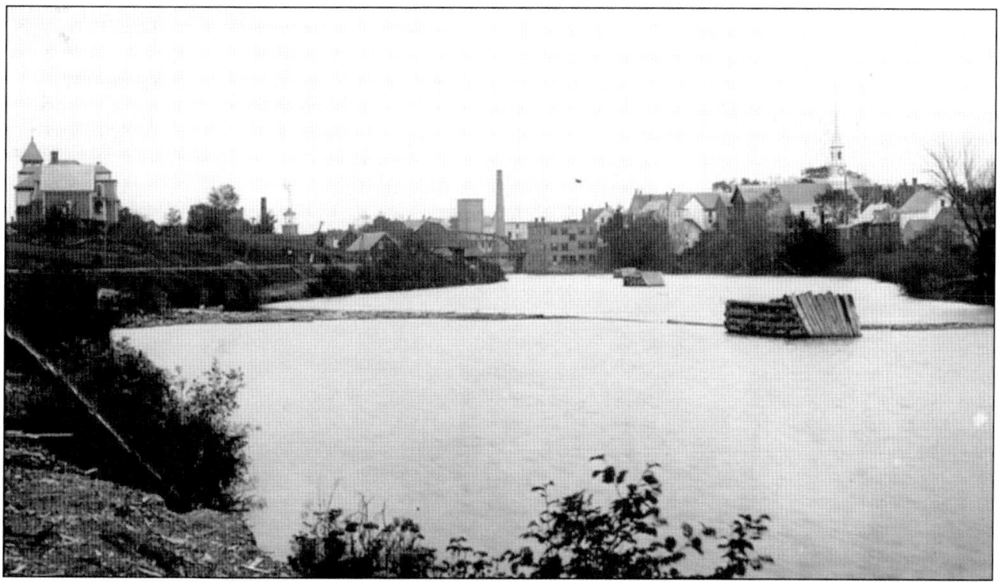

One of the ways of controlling the logs after they went into the river was through a series of boom islands and boom chains, which held the logs in place until ready to be let go. Here in 1908 is one of the islands with a chain across holding back the logs. Guilford High School is on the left, the steel bridge is in the middle, and the steeple of the Elm Street Methodist Church is on the right.

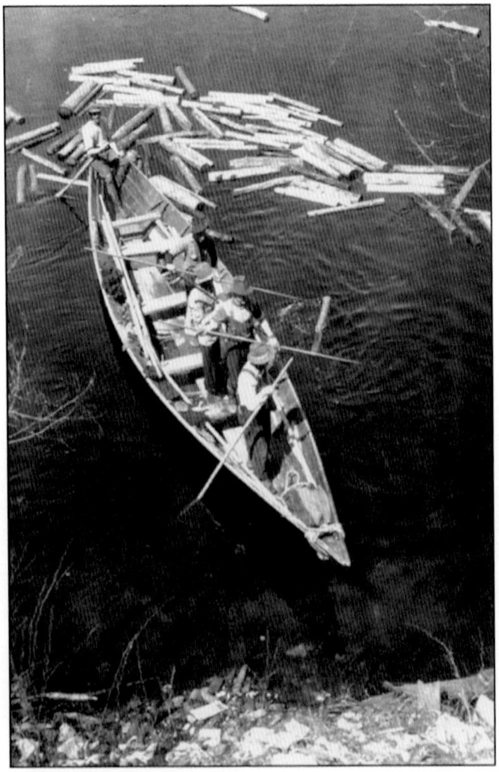

As logs made their way down the river, many of them were caught in snags, eddies, and backwaters, so men in bateaus were sent after them. Wielding long poles with iron tips, the drivers, as they were referred to, forced the logs back into the current and sent them on their way. This was extremely dangerous work, and in the city of Bangor, the Pierce Memorial was erected as a tribute to the skill and courage of these men. (Author's collection.)

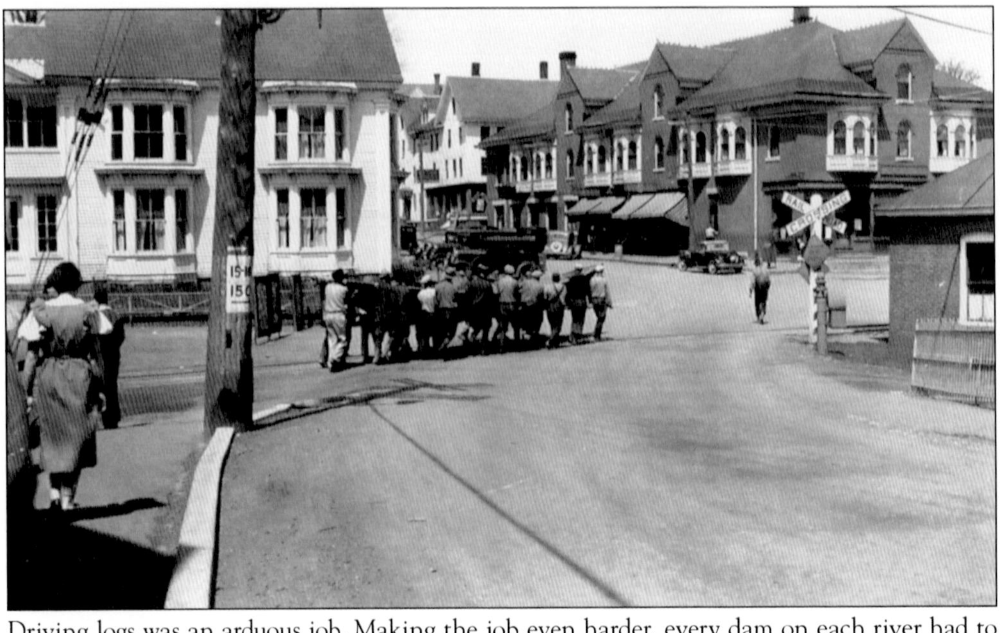

Driving logs was an arduous job. Making the job even harder, every dam on each river had to be portaged, and the heavy bateau had to be carried around the dam by the men themselves. (Author's collection.)

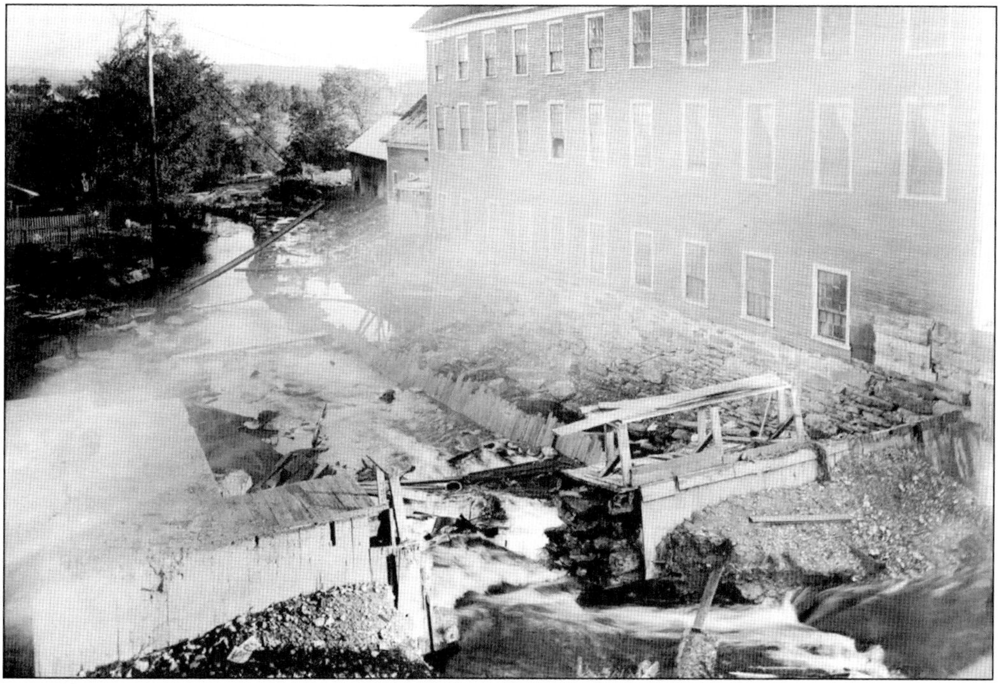

Initially the dams were an integral part of the settlement of the towns, and the first dams built were usually either crib dams using logs or earthen dams using rocks and boards. As can be seen here on Carleton Stream in Sangerville, these dams were often breached during floods and had to be either repaired or rebuilt. (Courtesy of Sangerville Historical Society.)

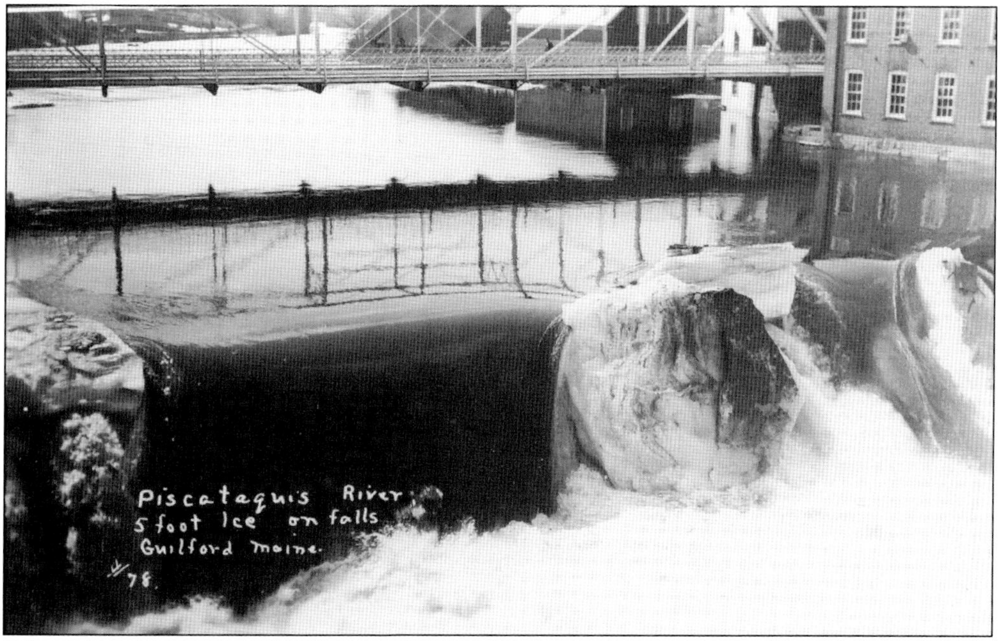

When the ice broke up in the spring, there were times when huge cakes of ice would break away and cause a lot of destruction while floating downstream. Fortunately, they would usually break apart or get hung up when passing over the dams, as seen here in Guilford.

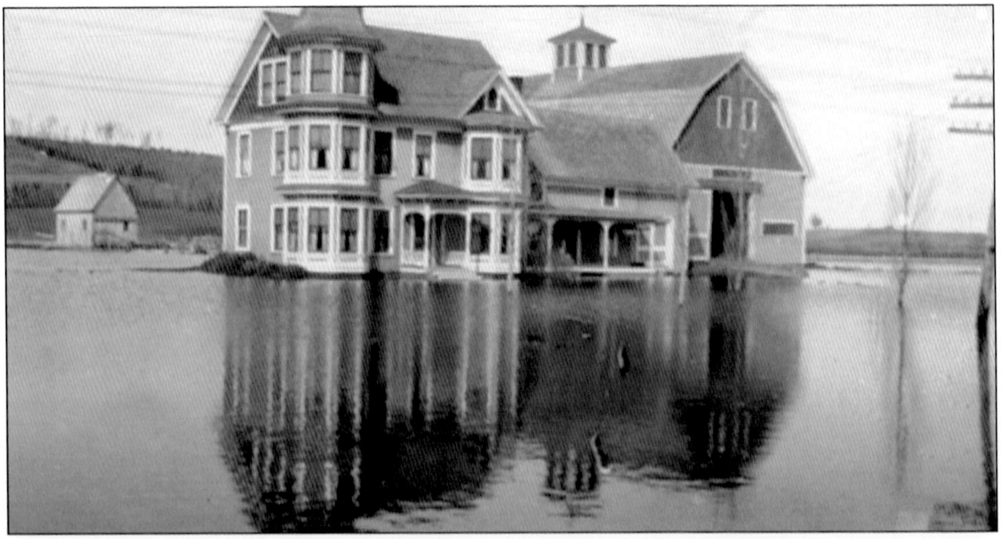

The river was a double-edged sword, and these pictures are an example of the terrible destruction wrought by floods over the years, the worst of which was in 1987. In the photograph above, the Preble Farm is underwater in 1923. This is the present location of Guilford Hardware. The photograph below looks down the railroad tracks from where the town baseball field was located and the current site of the high school athletic field. The entire area, including the ball field on the right and State Route 15 on the left, is underwater.

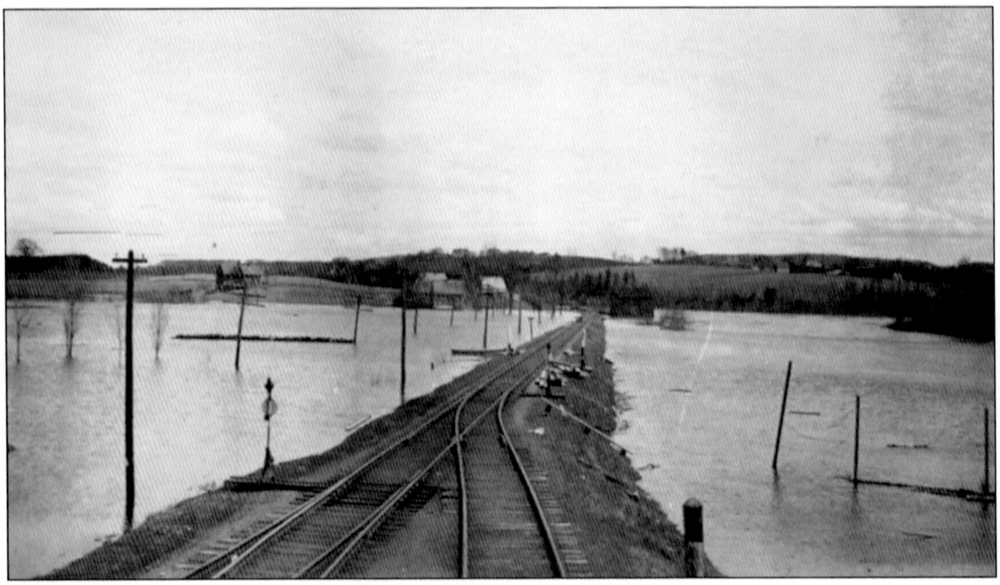

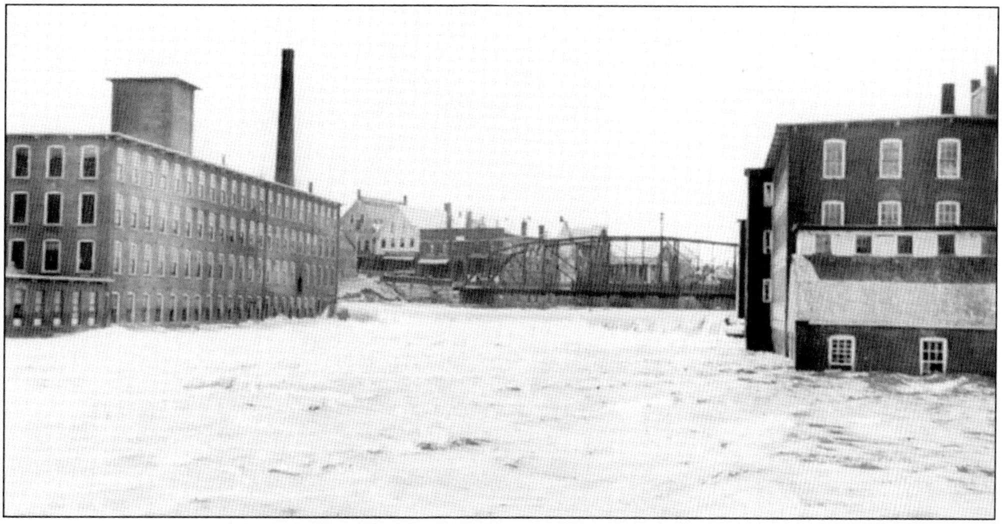

In 1934, another flood hit the Guilford area. Here is a scene looking upriver between the mills. Evidence of the dam is almost completely hidden, and water is entering the ground-floor windows of both mills.

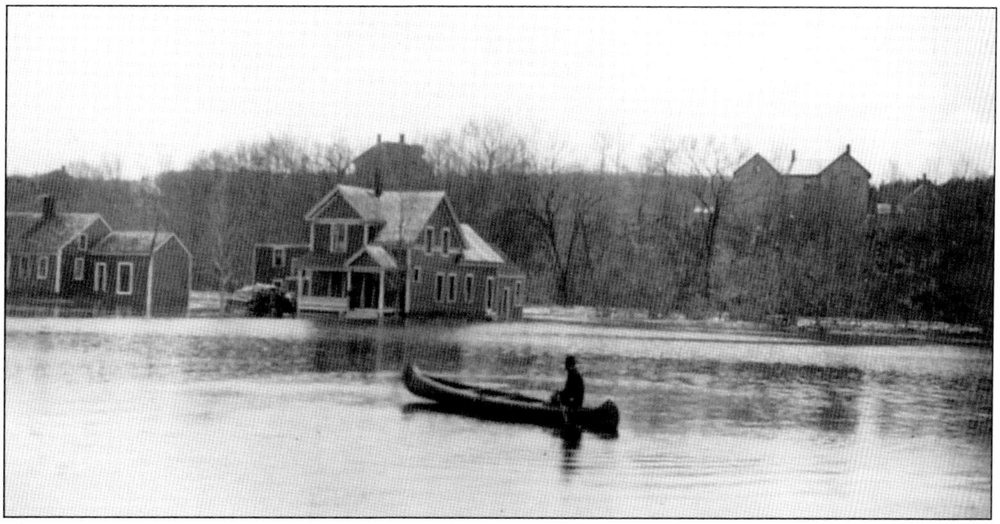

This is another photograph from the 1923 flood, showing Abe Fortin going by canoe down River Street to get to his home. The riverbed is actually behind the houses, and the houses on the horizon are located on Oak Street across the river.

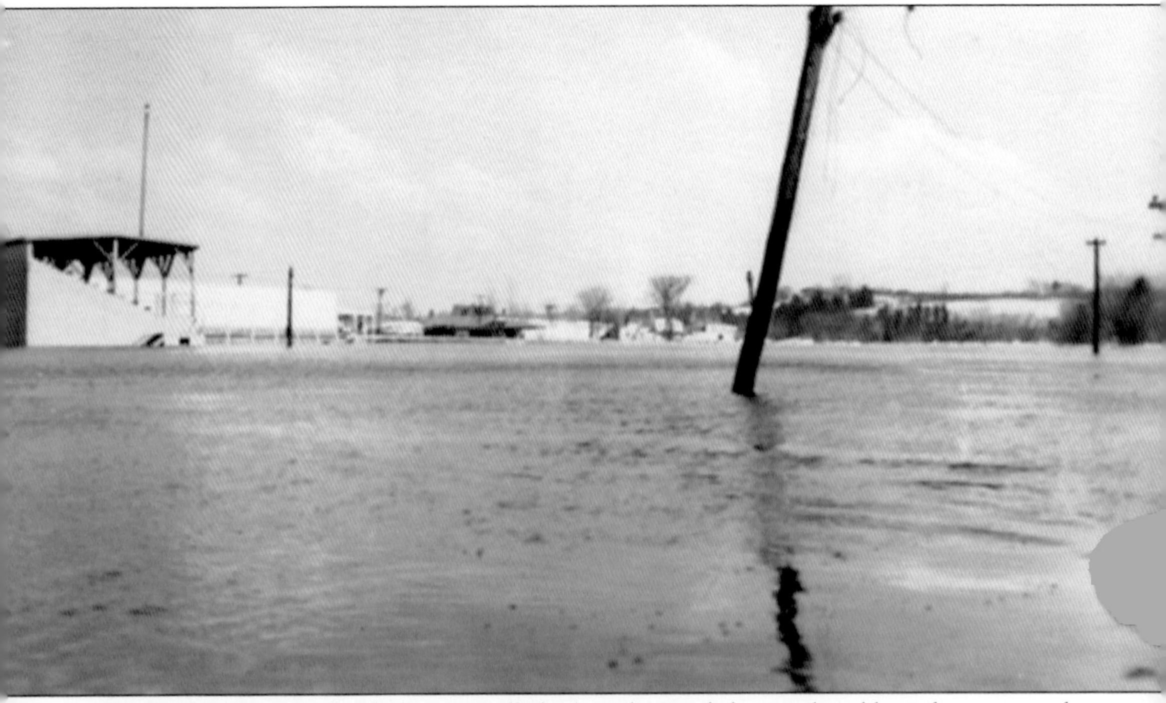

The March 13, 1936, flood was especially high and caused the usual problems for anyone who lived along its banks. Here the entire ball field is underwater again. The building to the left is the grandstand, and the structure on the left field line is the bleachers. This is the only photograph the Guilford Historical Society has of the bleachers in place.

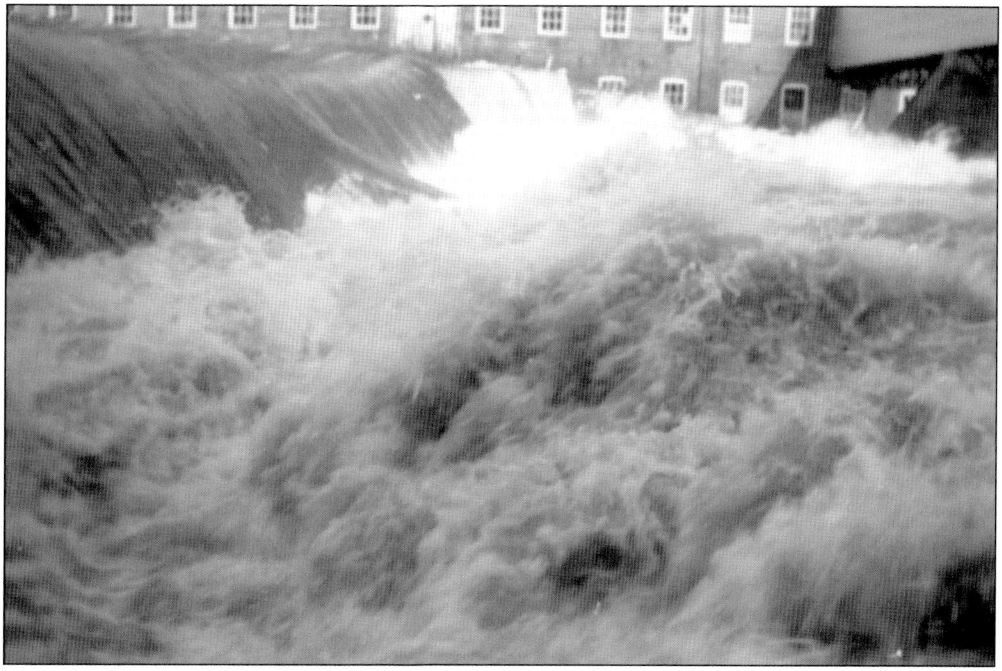

This photograph shows the water above the first-floor windows on the upper side of the dam and entering the windows on the lower side.

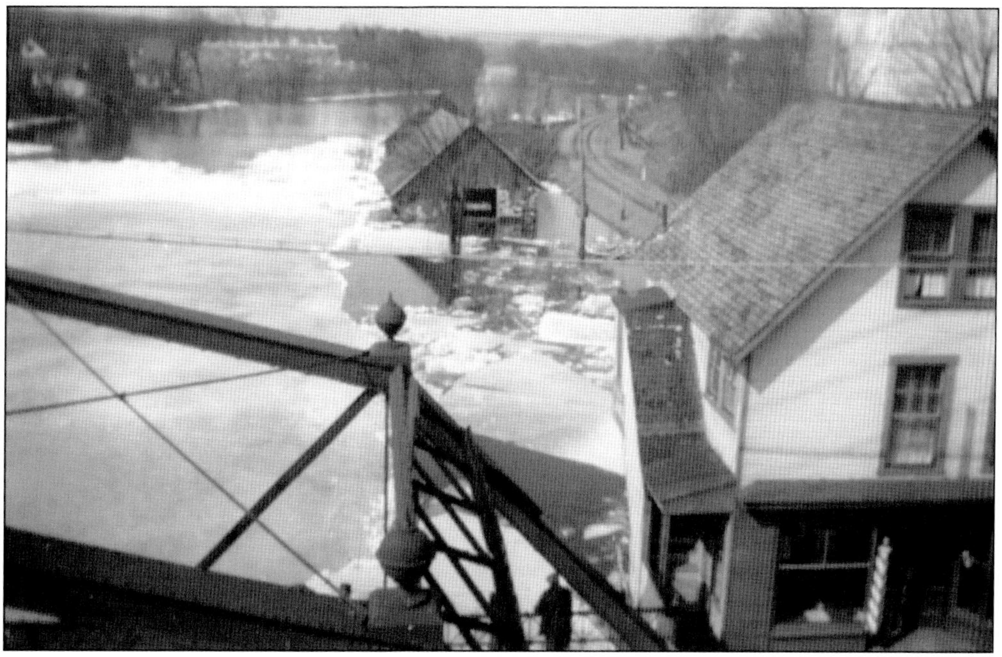

Ice jams were a big problem. They caused water to back up behind them, and when they let go, the sometimes-massive cakes of ice swept everything in their path. From the roof of the mill, one can see the start of a large jam with the cakes pushing their way over the banks of the river.

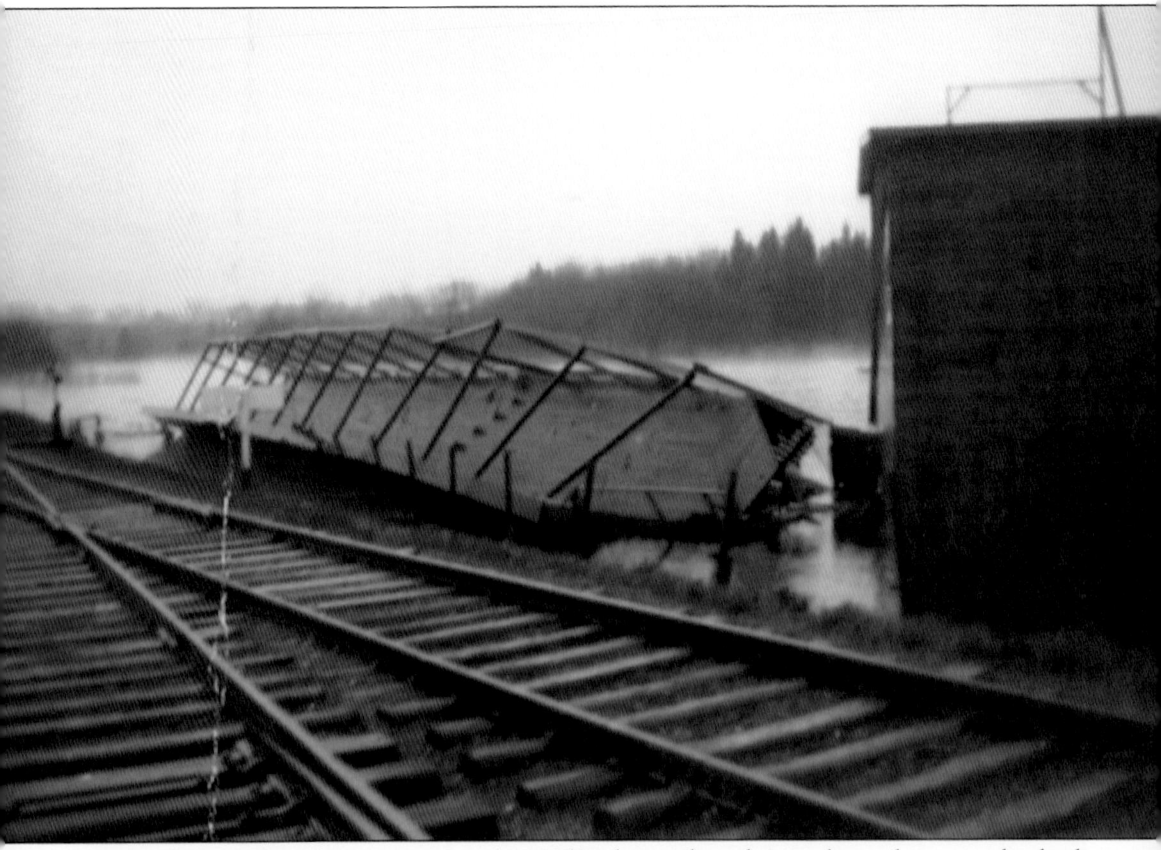

This photograph, taken sometime after 1950, shows that the ice has taken out the back framework under the bleachers at the ball diamond, and the stands have fallen over backward. The grandstand seen on the right was also heavily damaged and was razed not long after.

Two

FACTORIES AND WATERPOWER

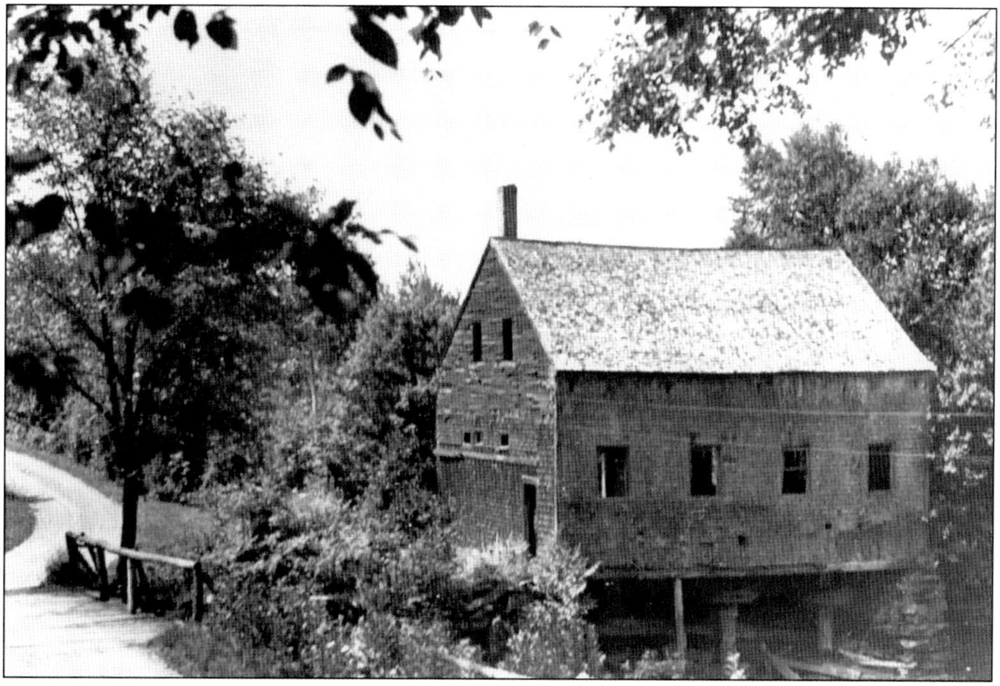

As the settlers cleared their land and planted crops, there was an immediate need for gristmills. They sprang up in every little settlement where there was a stream, such as here on Black Stream at Knowlton's Mills in Sangerville. Later a sawmill and a shingle mill were built just upstream from the falls and bridge. Although Phineas Ames built the first gristmill at this site, it soon became the property of the Knowlton brothers, who had built a farm a short distance away. (Courtesy of Sangerville Historical Society.)

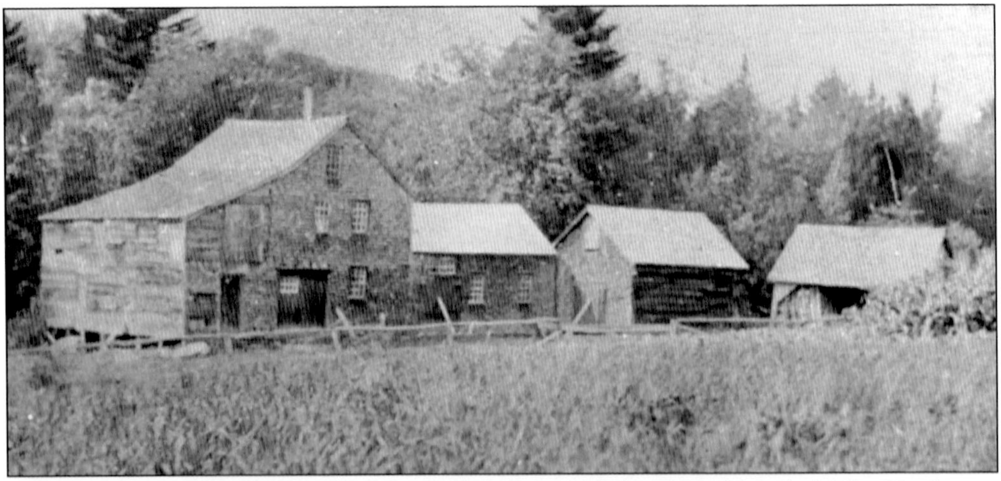

Another Sangerville settlement was at Brockway's Mills where French Mills Creek was used to power a gristmill, sawmill, and shingle mill. When originally settled, this was the fastest-growing settlement in town, having its own school and post office. (Courtesy of Sangerville Historical Society.)

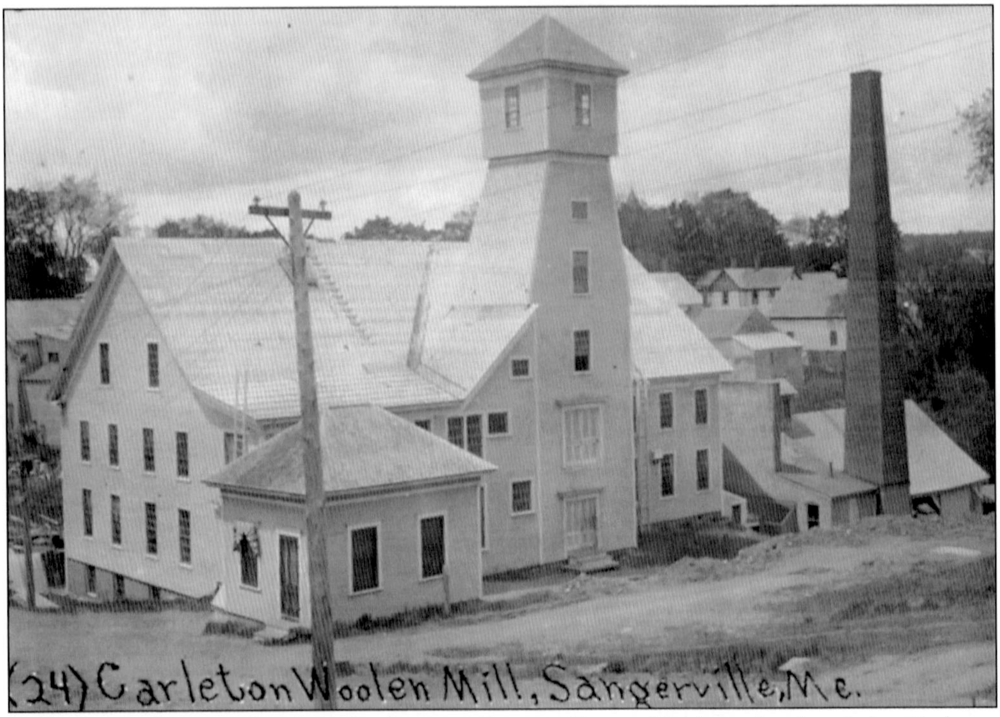

What finally became the central village of Sangerville straddled the banks of the Carleton Stream, which was located in the northwest quadrant of the township. There were three major mills located on the stream within approximately one half mile. The Carleton Mill shown here is the second mill downstream and is powered by the third dam. This is the only mill to survive in any form and today is home to Numberall Corporation. (Courtesy of Sangerville Historical Society.)

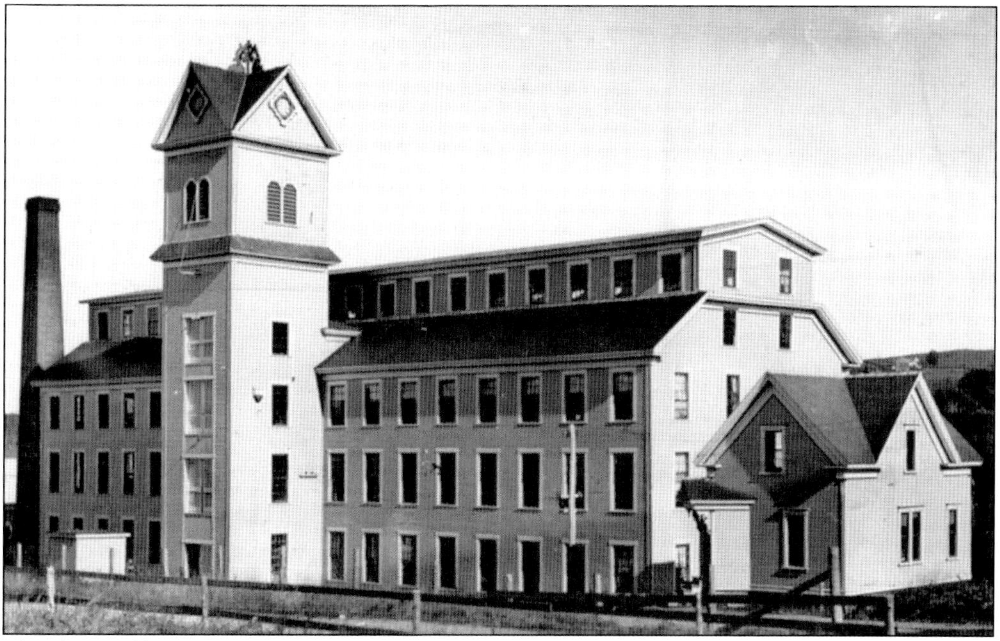

The last mill on the stream was the Campbell Mill, which later became the Dumbarton Mill. Shortly after World War II, it closed its doors to manufacturing and was used to raise roasting chickens for several years until it later burned down. (Courtesy of Sangerville Historical Society.)

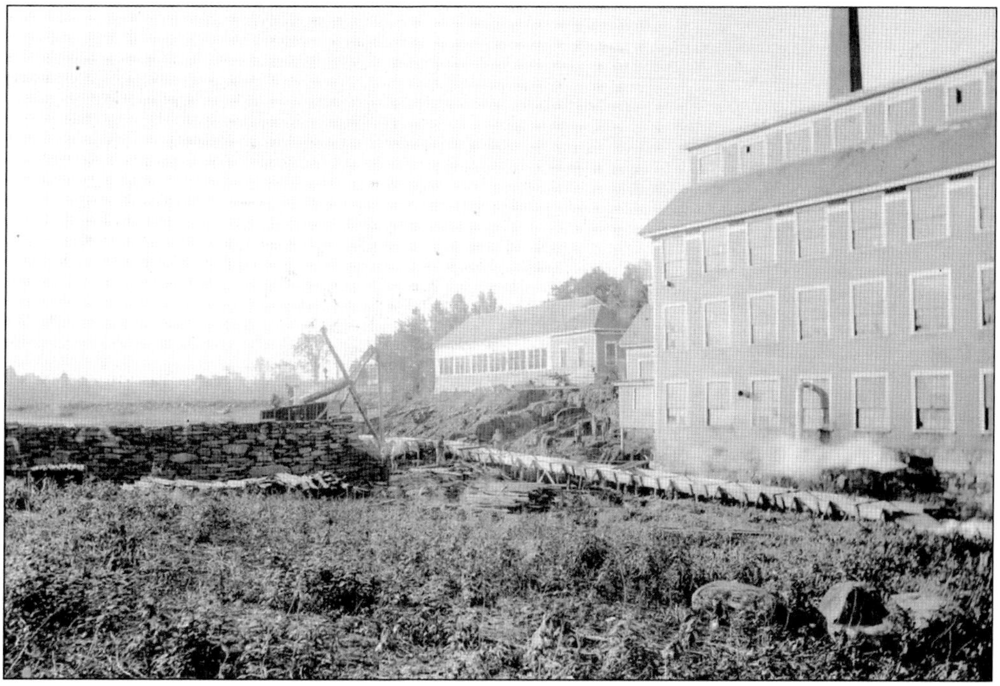

Here is an excellent example of the erection of the simple rock dam and the sluiceway that supplied waterpower to the Sangerville Woolen Company mill on the Carleton Stream. This mill later became Glencoe No. 1. (Courtesy of Sangerville Historical Society.)

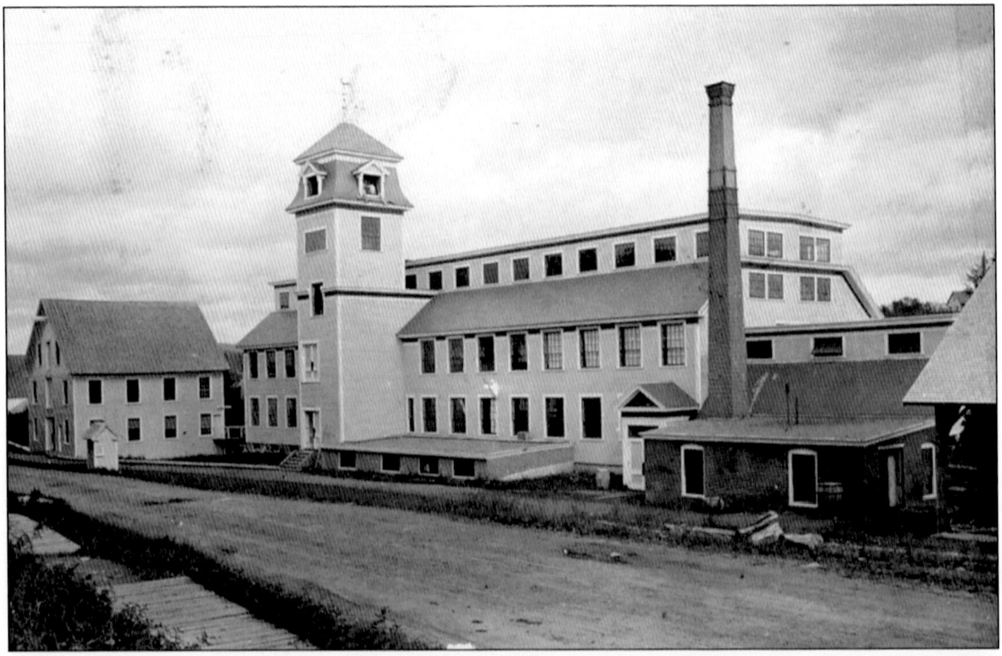

This is a later view from the street side of the mill pictured on the last page. The second dam powered this mill, which also ceased operation shortly after World War II. For a while, it was used to raise chickens and later housed the Dover Stove Company. (Courtesy of Sangerville Historical Society.)

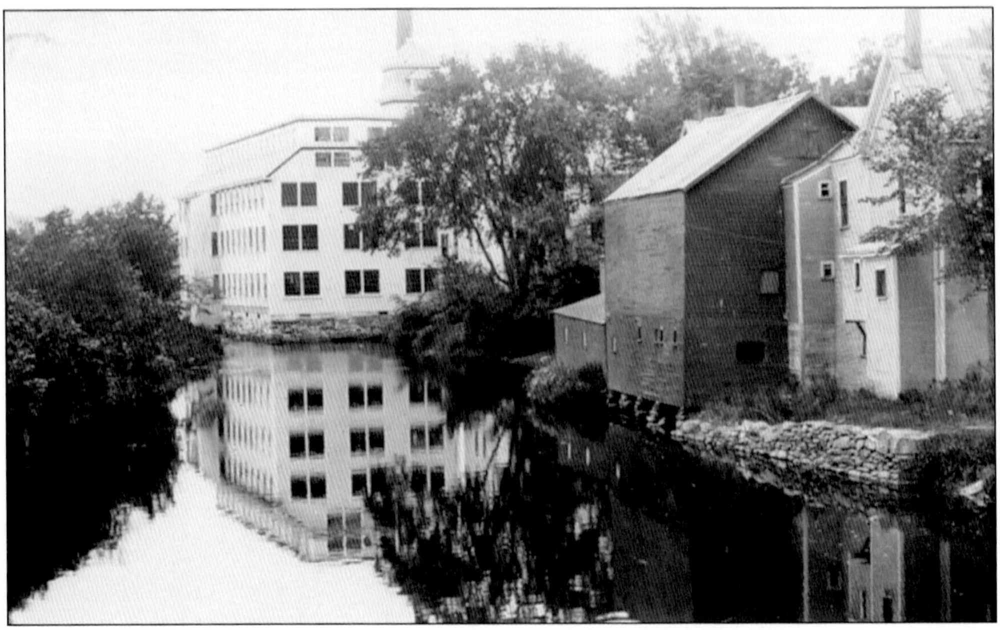

The Sangerville Woolen Company had restrooms built out over the stream and human and industrial waste went directly into the water. Almost all the commercial properties along the stream did the same, resulting in terrible pollution. (Author's collection.)

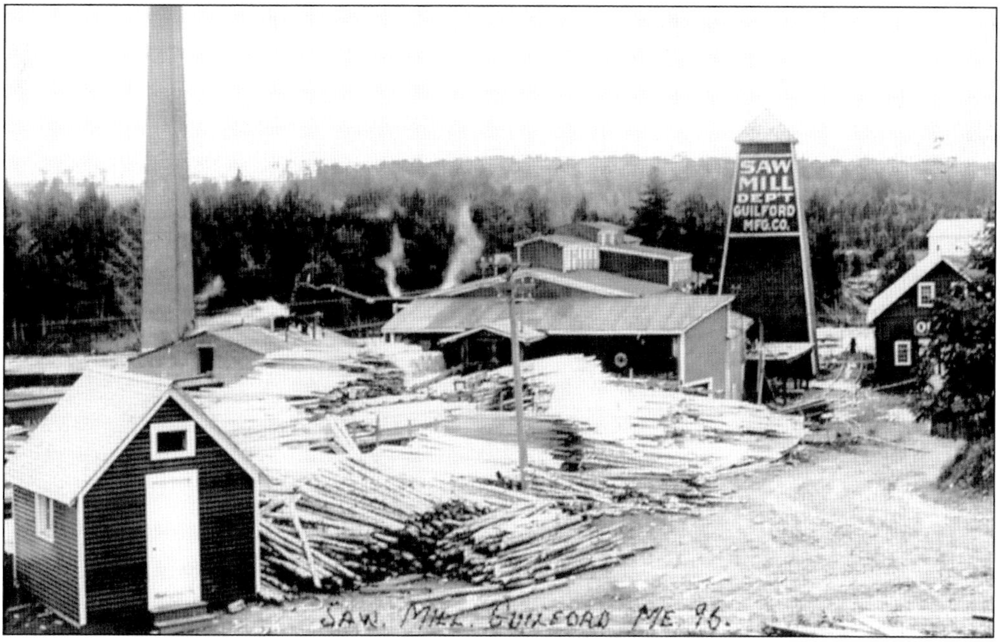

In 1896, the Guilford Manufacturing Company's sawmill department was a sprawling complex located on School Street just west of its box and shook mill. Logs to feed the mill were floated down the Piscataquis River from towns and logging operations upstream.

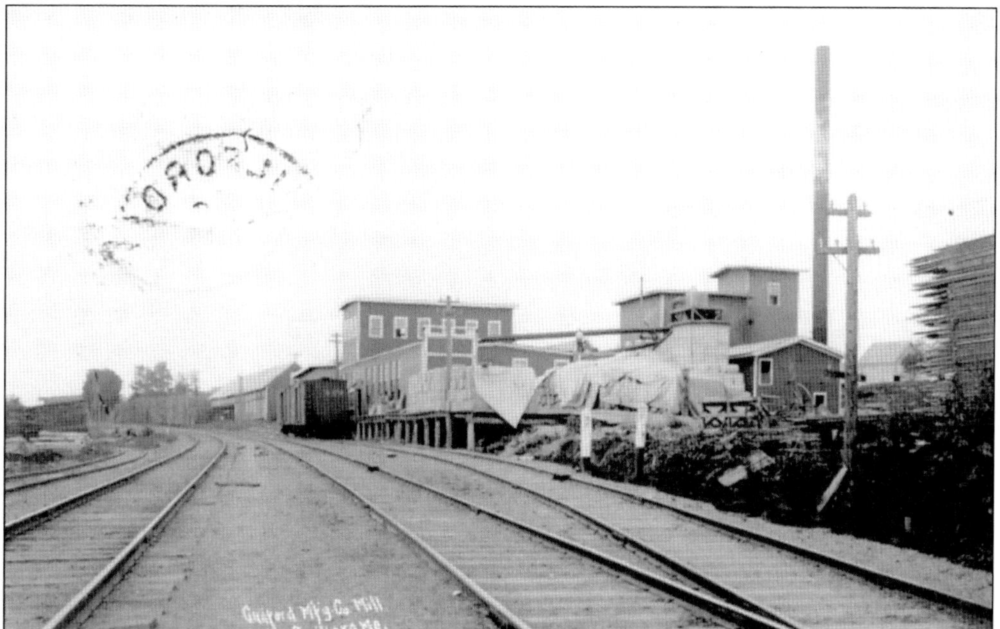

The back side of the mill was a busy place in 1908. Almost all shipping was done by rail and required a lot of siding and car storage tracks. After cars were loaded, they were parked in the storage yard until picked up by the railroad.

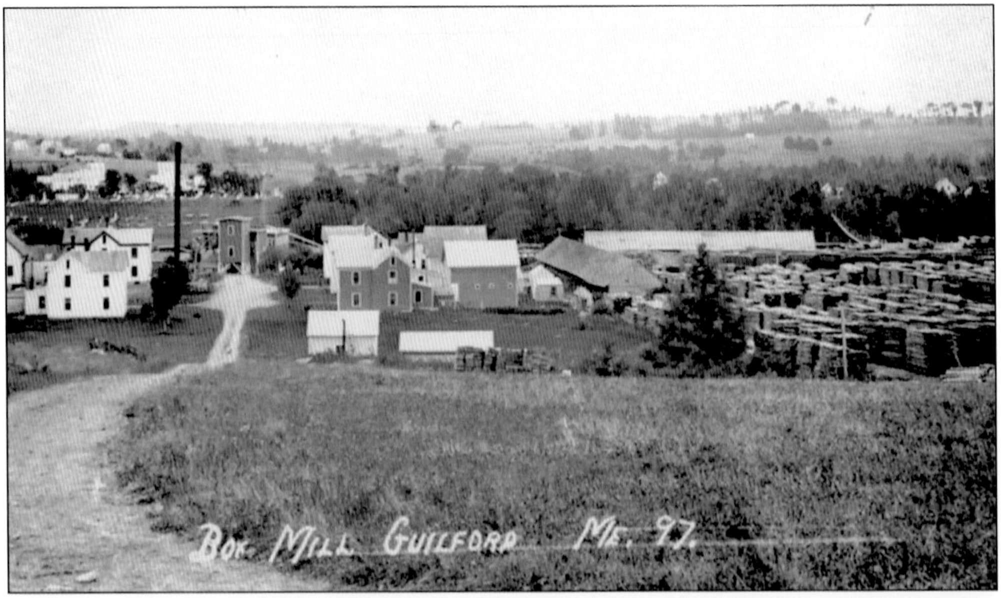

This view of the box mill and yard complex is from High Street looking down Maple Street in Guilford around 1920. The two houses on the left still exist today, but those in the center are gone, and the footbridge seen on the far right was taken out by a flood in 1923.

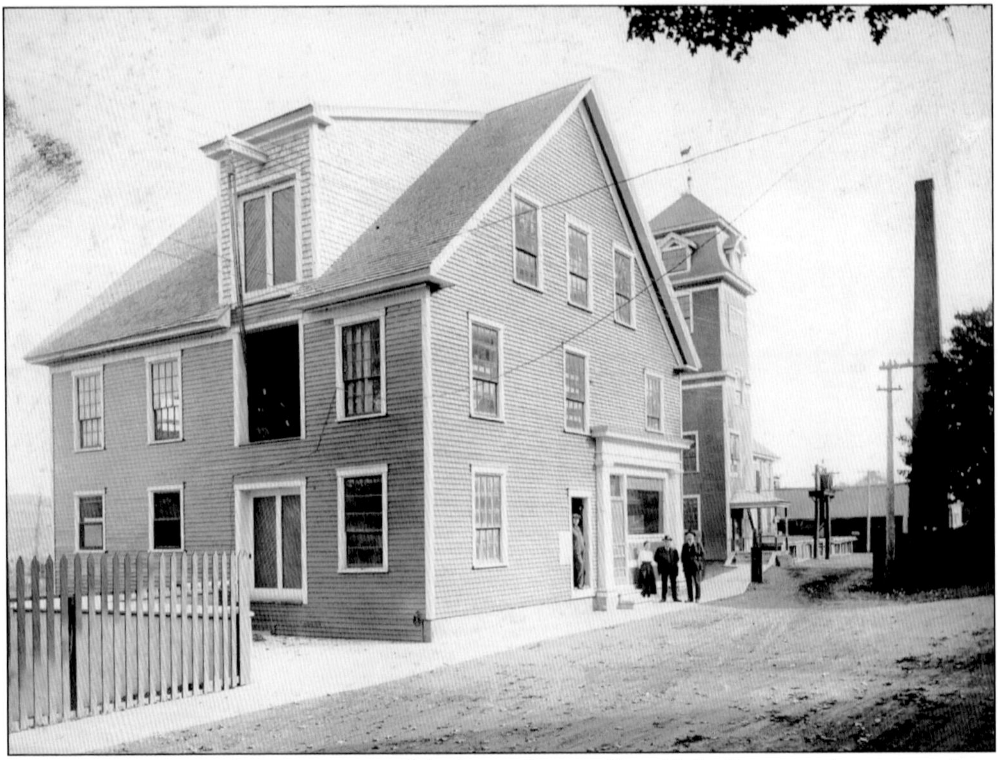

The Sangerville Woolen Company mill had a modern, well-staffed office complex, as seen here in the late 1800s. Located on South Main Street, it was neat and well kept and was considered an excellent place to work. (Courtesy of Sangerville Historical Society.)

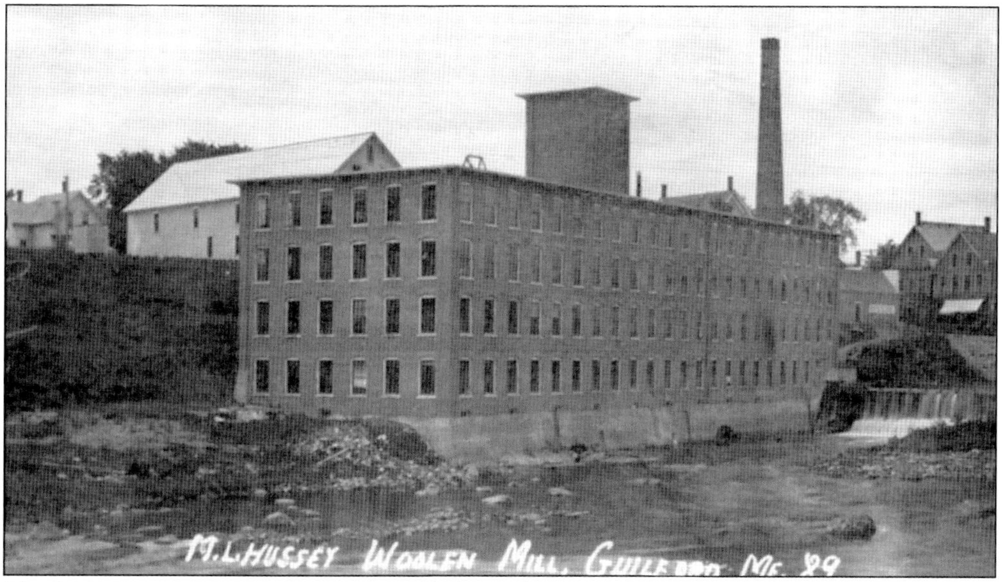

The M. L. Hussey Woolen Company mill, shown here in 1918, was located on the south side of the river just east of the bridge in Guilford. Originally powered by the river, the outlet for the water can be seen about 50 feet below the dam.

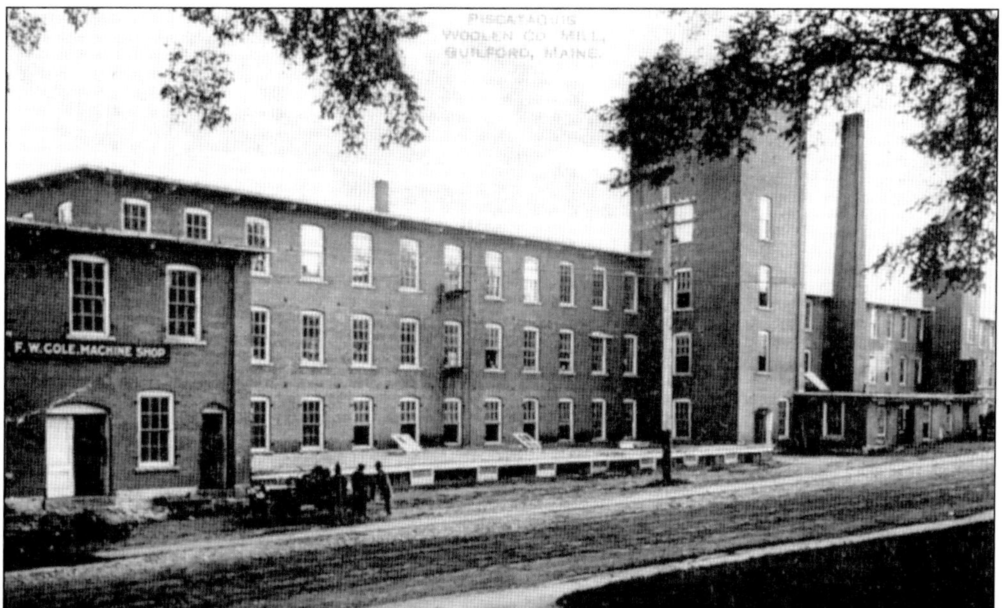

The Piscataquis Woolen Company mill, shown here in 1912, was a large factory located on the north side of the river, just across the stream from the M. L. Hussey mill. The railroad tracks can be seen beside the mill, and the F. W. Cole Machine Shop is on the left.

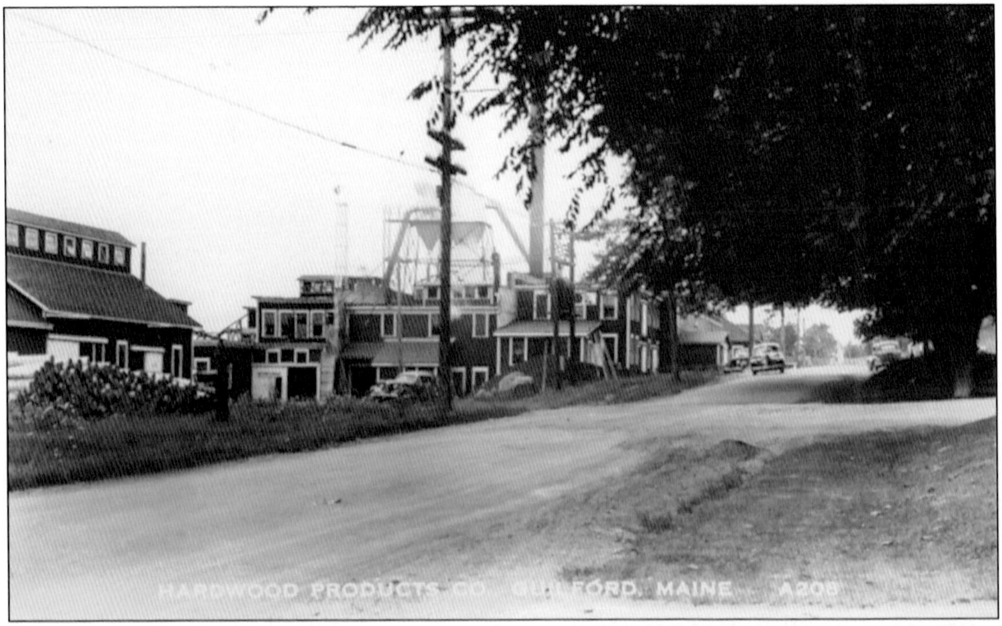

In 1926, the Minto Toothpick Company of Saginaw, Michigan, lost its supplier and decided to relocate. Selecting Guilford as an ideal location, the owner, Lloyd Cartwright, purchased the Guilford Manufacturing Company plant on School Street. Moving his manufacturing operation here, he changed the name of his mill to the Hardwood Products Company, but it was always referred to as "the pick mill" for many years. The above photograph shows the mill in the late 1930s, and the photograph below shows the raw product, which was four-foot birch logs stacked in one of the yards.

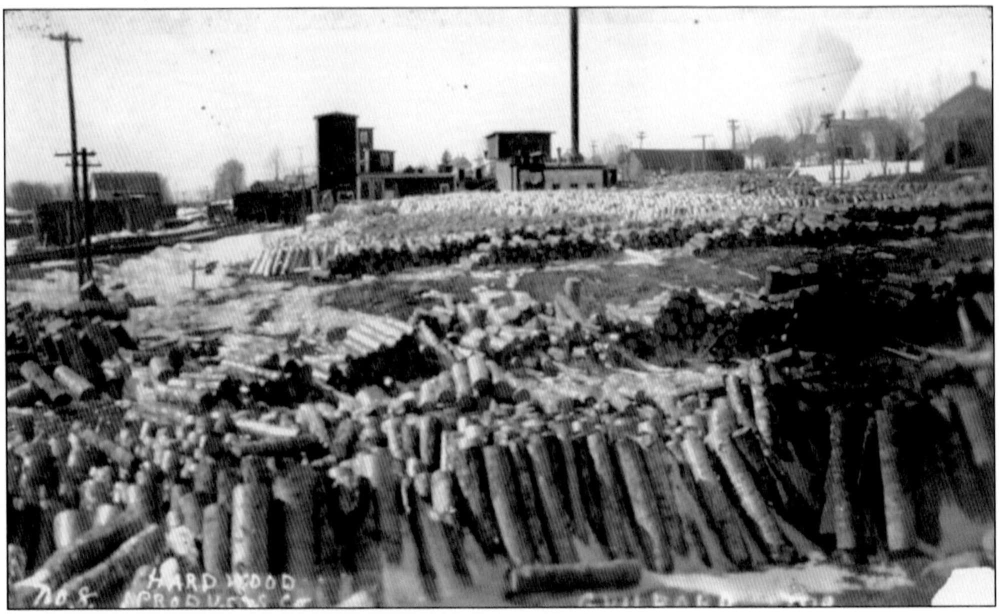

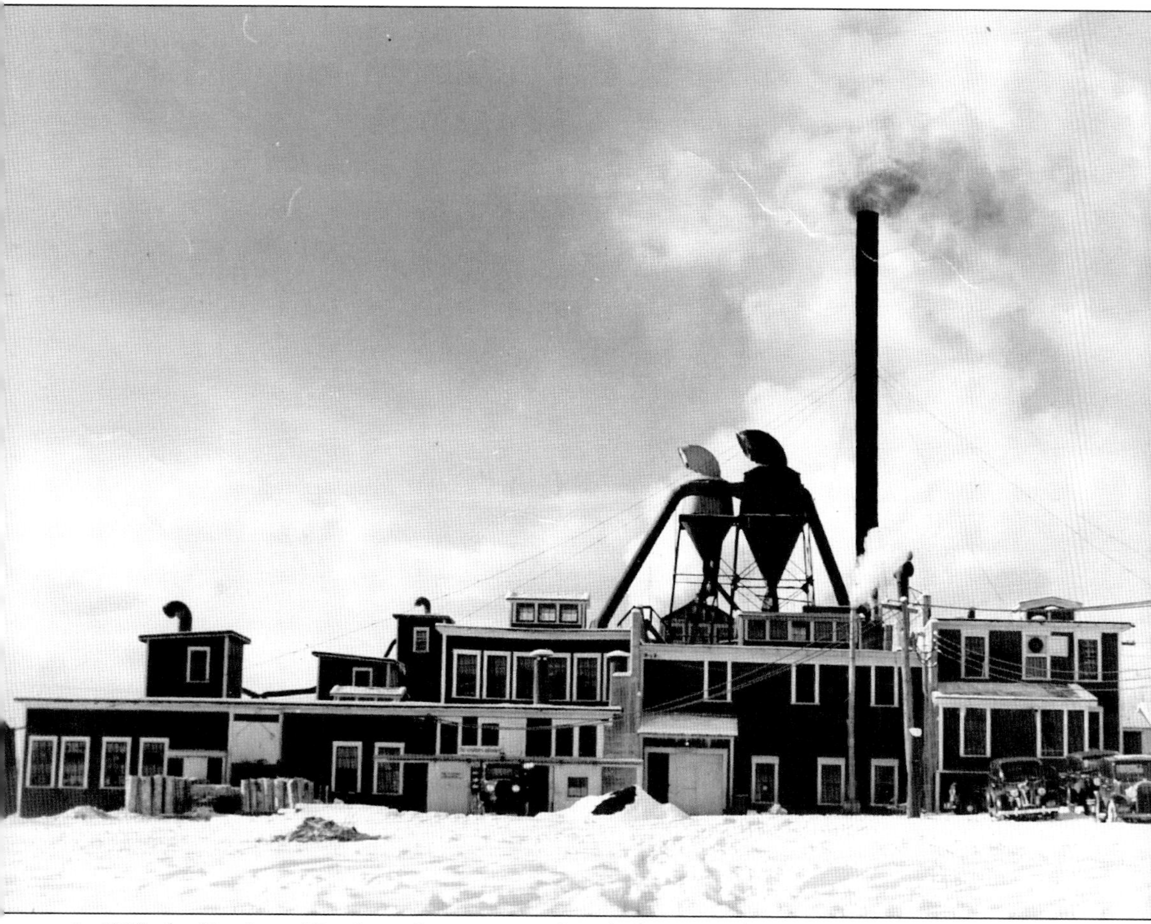

In 1938, the Hardwood Products Company employed a large number of people and ran two shifts. Each shift was nine hours long, five days per week, plus four hours on Saturday, for a standard 50-hour workweek. Before the advent of plastics, the mill produced a variety of products, including candy sticks, cocktail forks, tongue depressors, and ice-cream spoons. Sheets of birch were cut from four-foot logs from which the various products were stamped out, sorted, dried, and packed into boxes for shipment. The mill could provide specialty items if desired, such as branding the customer's name onto the various products. This was done by special branding machines that lightly burned the logos onto the products. Rebuilt after the horrendous fire of 1958, the company now turns out a large variety of medical products along with its regular lineup.

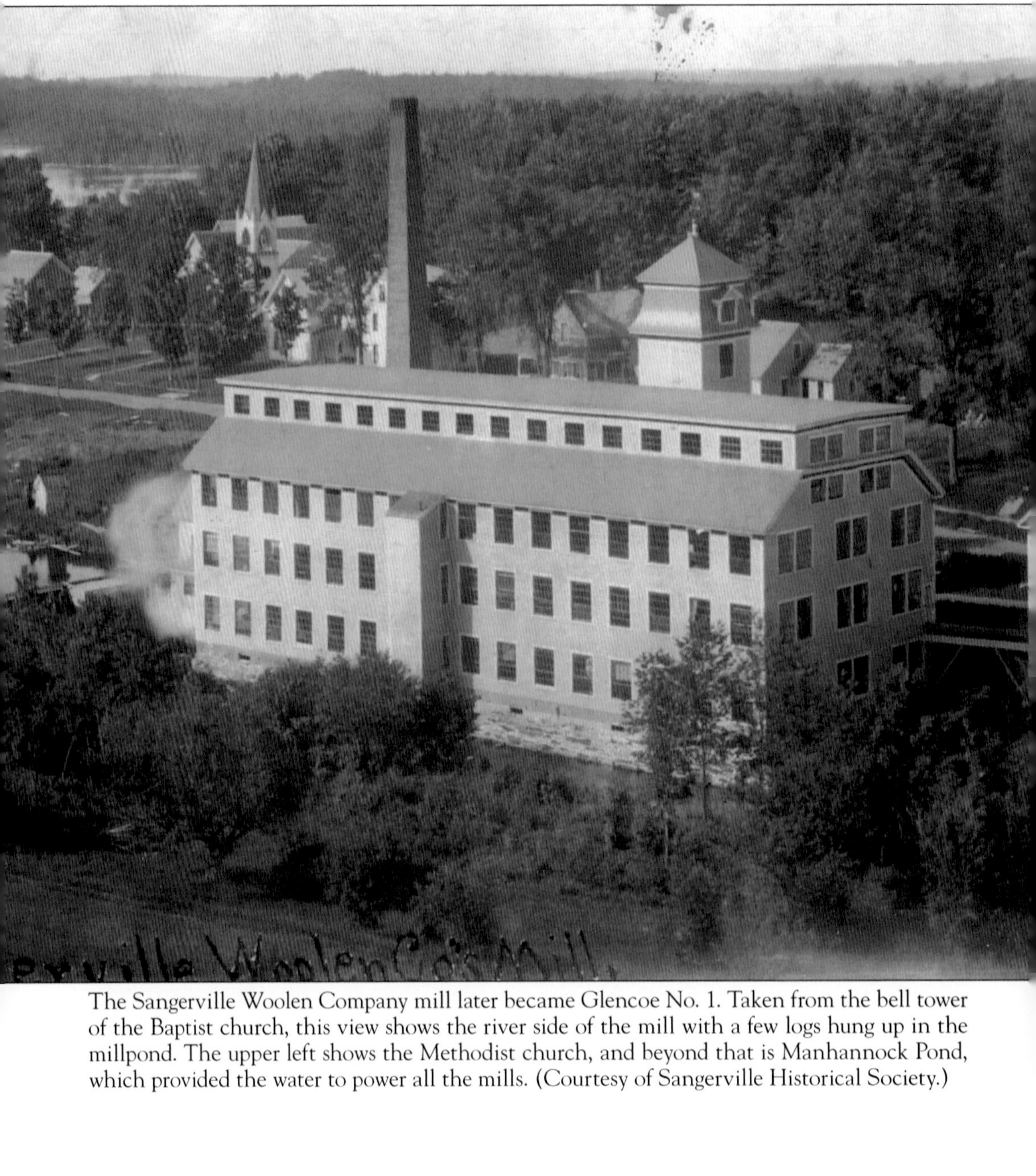

The Sangerville Woolen Company mill later became Glencoe No. 1. Taken from the bell tower of the Baptist church, this view shows the river side of the mill with a few logs hung up in the millpond. The upper left shows the Methodist church, and beyond that is Manhannock Pond, which provided the water to power all the mills. (Courtesy of Sangerville Historical Society.)

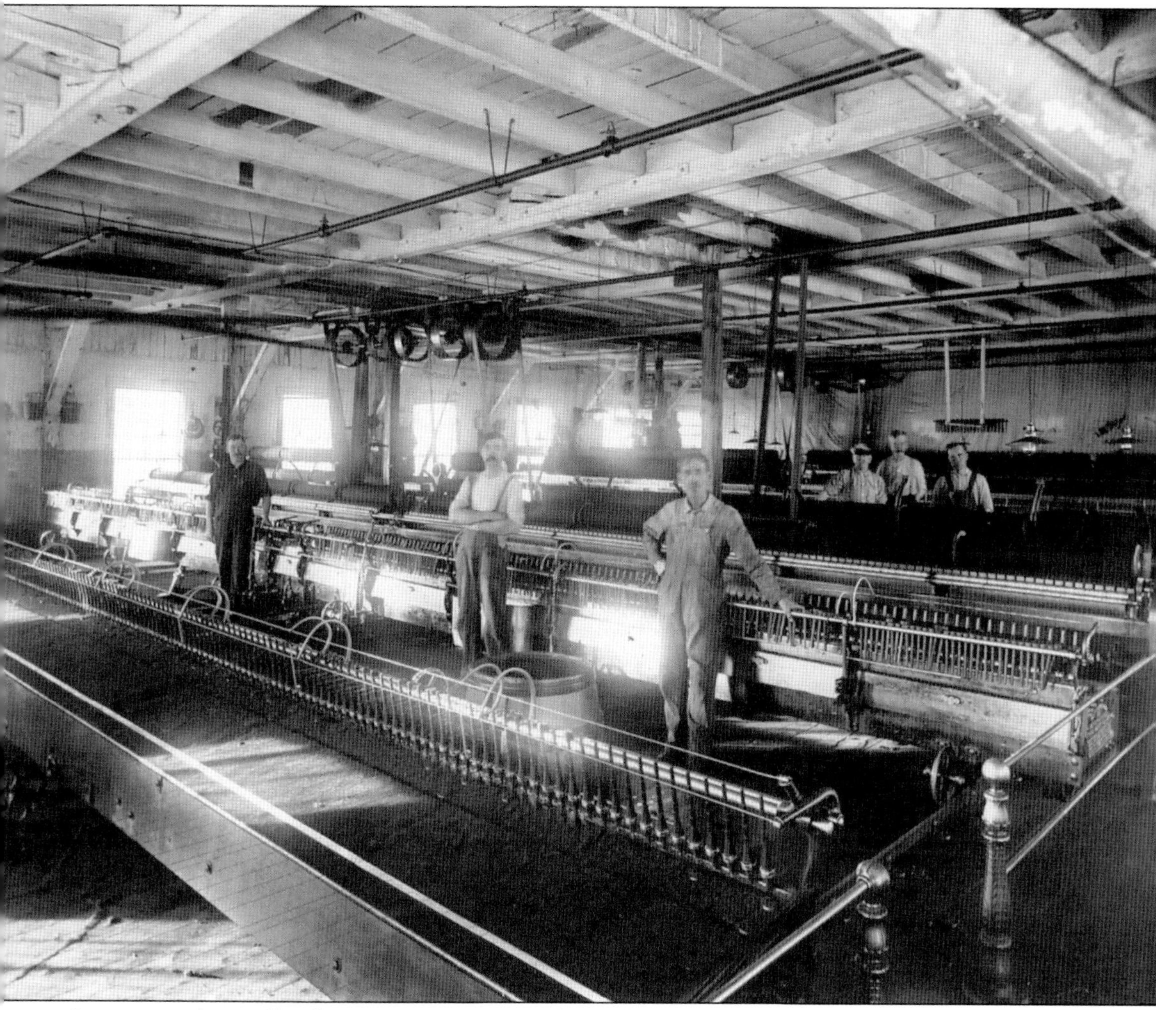

Just as in other mills, the spinning room was located on the top floor of the Carleton Woolen mill, where the previously carded wool was spun into yarn and onto bobbins. The machines were referred to as jacks or mules and moved in and out as they spun the yarn. The men were employed to watch them, and whenever a thread broke, they would quickly move to reconnect it. When the bobbins were full, they would stop the mules and remove the full bobbins. Then a young lad hired to fill sticks would replace them with empty ones. After electricity came into use, power outages were dreaded while the machines were running as this usually broke just about every thread on the machines. (Courtesy of Sangerville Historical Society.)

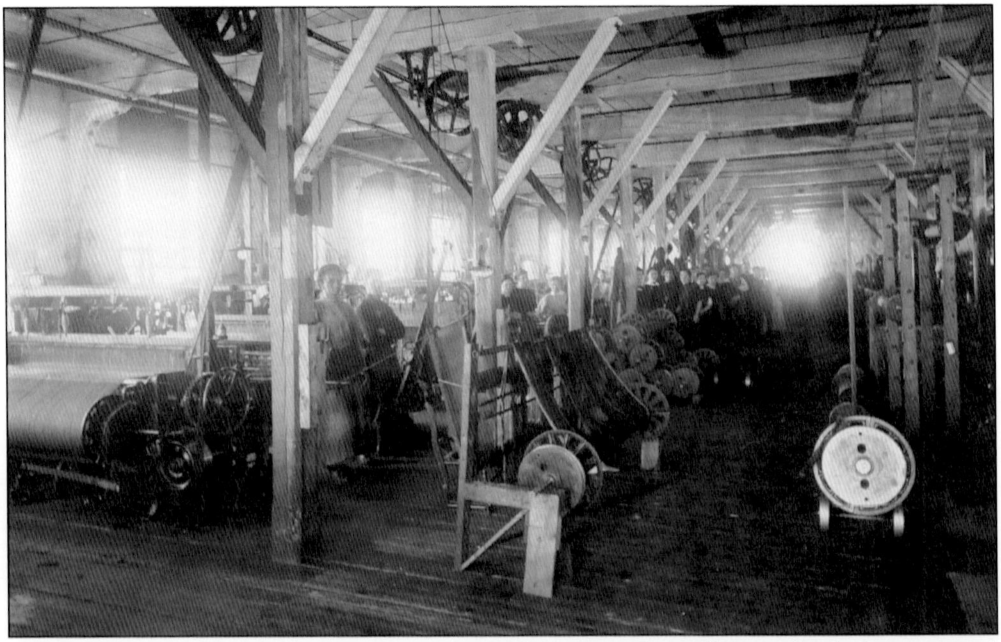

The ingenious way in which waterpower was used to power the mills was clearly demonstrated in the weave room and spooling room of Glencoe No. 1 in Sangerville. Everything was run from one vertical central shaft up through the center of the mill, usually four stories, and turned by the force of the water. From this central shaft each floor had either one or two horizontal shafts that usually ran the full length of the floor. From these, belts ran each machine, the speed of which was determined by the size of the pulleys on the vertical shaft and the machine itself. Idler arms were used to shut off each machine individually when necessary. The looms and the carding machines were almost always run by women, with men responsible for keeping the machines running and fixing any malfunctions that might occur. Giant wool bins were located on the first floor.

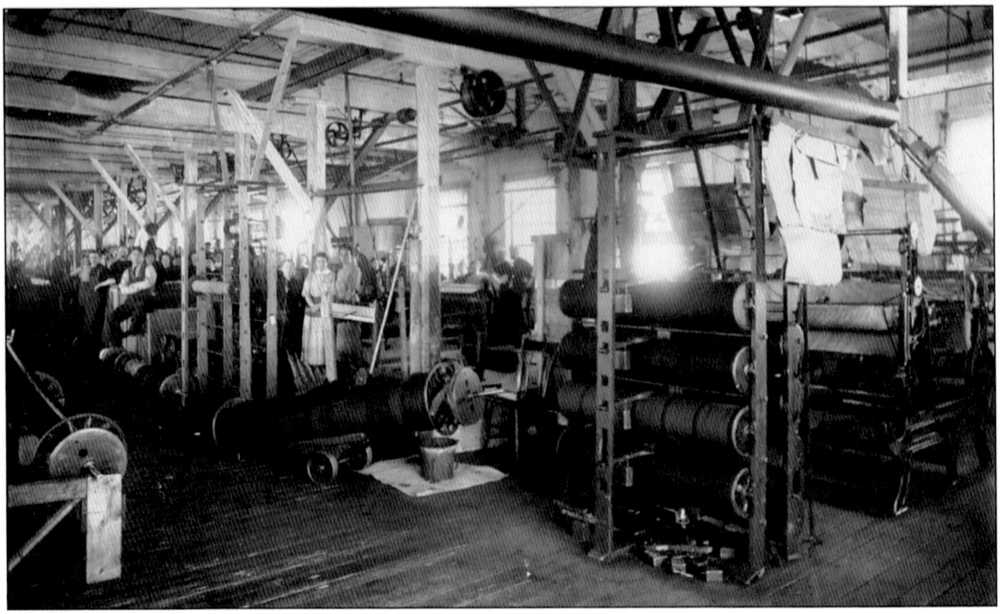

Three

BUSINESSES THAT WERE

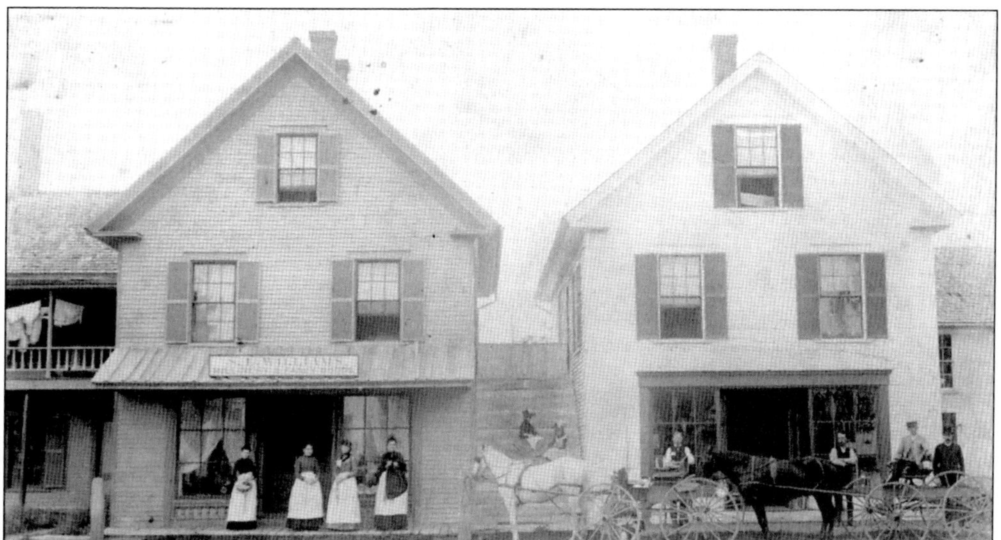

In the late 1800s, Mrs. S. L. Williams operated a millinery and fancy goods store on the north side of Elm Street in Guilford where the Davis Brothers Furniture store is currently located. Over the years, a number of businesses managed to come and go here, including Dr. O'Brien's dental practice on the second floor. The building on the right was once home to the Elm Street Theatre, the first in town to feature movies with sound, or talkies, as they were referred to at the time. A variety store, a drugstore, a video shop, and a small pub followed the theater.

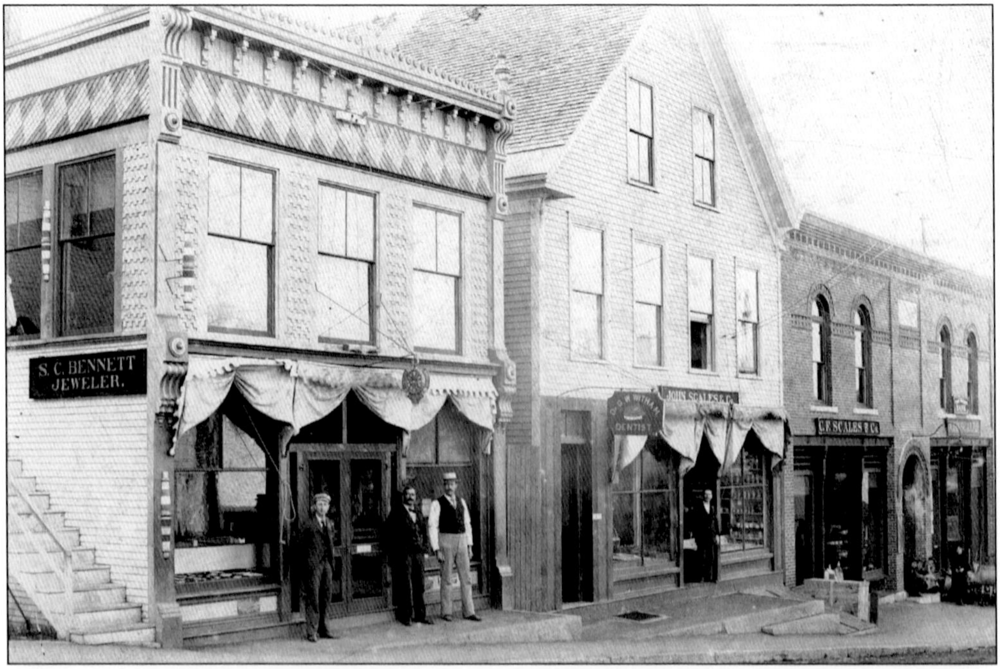

The Scales block and adjoining buildings at the southern end of the bridge housed a variety of businesses, including the First National Bank on the second floor. The individuals shown here, from left to right, are C. S. Bennett, Alex Edes, George Turner, and E. Genthner.

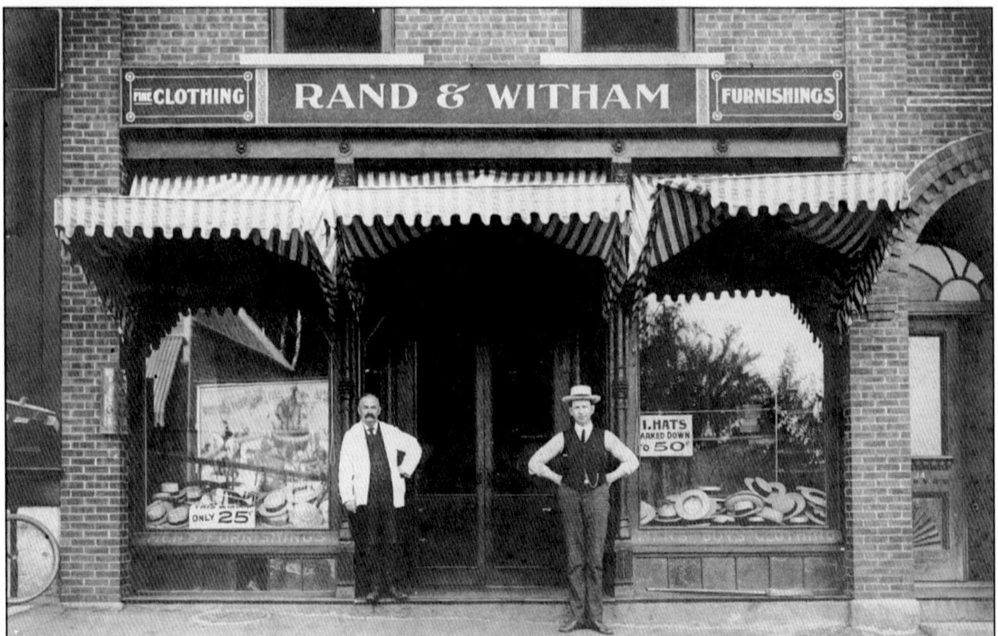

The Rand and Witham store, located in the Scales building, predominately sold men's clothing plus some household furnishings. It was partially owned by dentist E. W. Witham, who had his practice on the second floor of the building next door. This undated photograph shows Edes on the left with an unidentified individual.

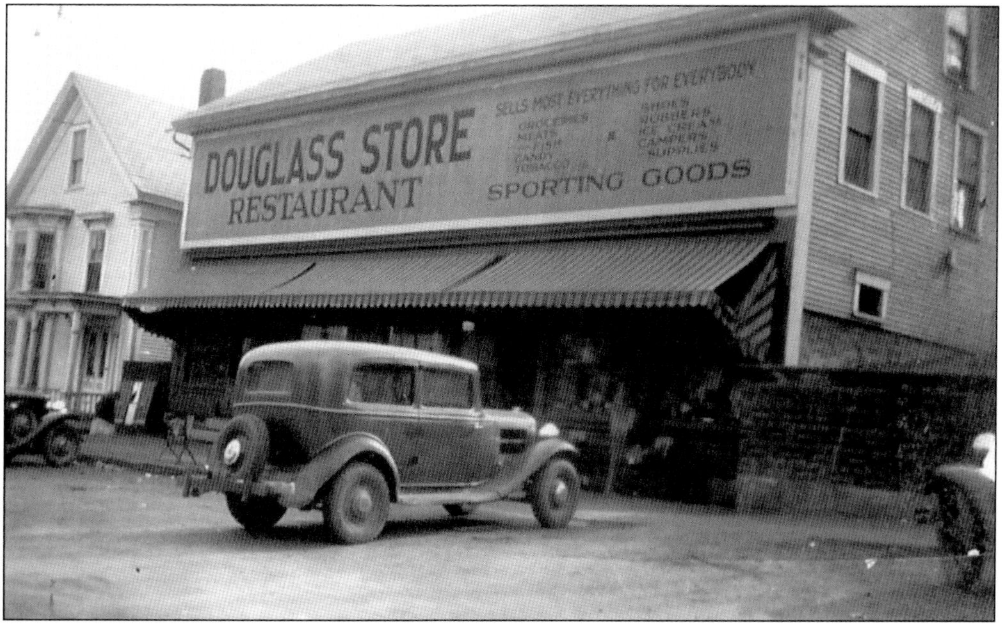

In 1832, George Douglass started the Douglass store in Guilford center. In 1854, it was moved to the village and became H. Douglass and Company after his son took over. Over the years, it sold just about anything, and by the mid-1930s, it even had a full-service restaurant. The store closed its doors in the late 1930s, and the chain known as First National Stores moved from its quarters on Elm Street into the vacated space. The First National did well there and stayed in business into the 1970s. The site has been occupied by Griffin's store since around 1980.

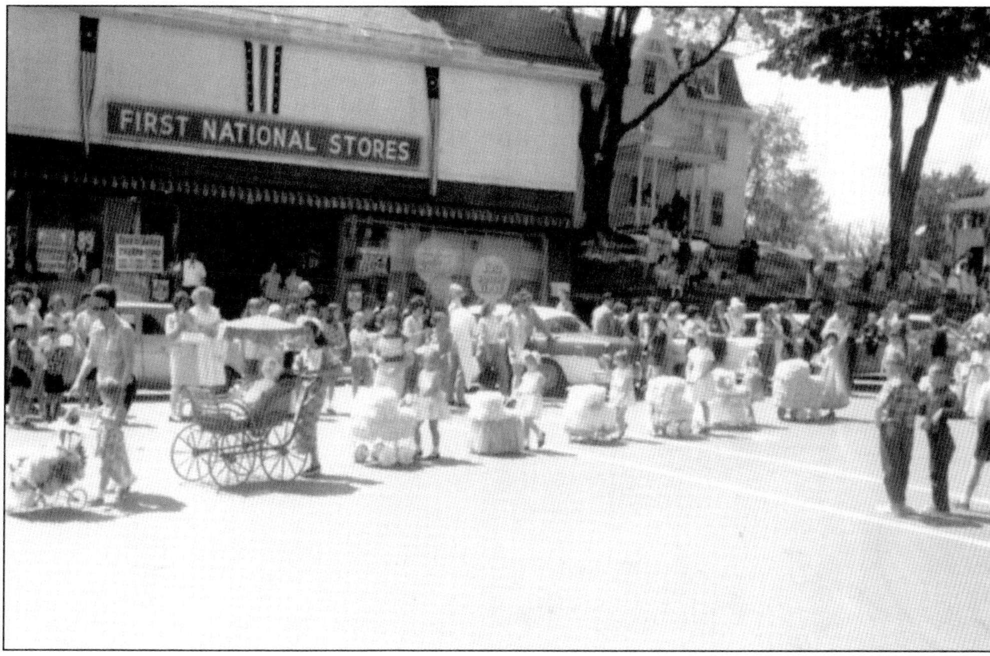

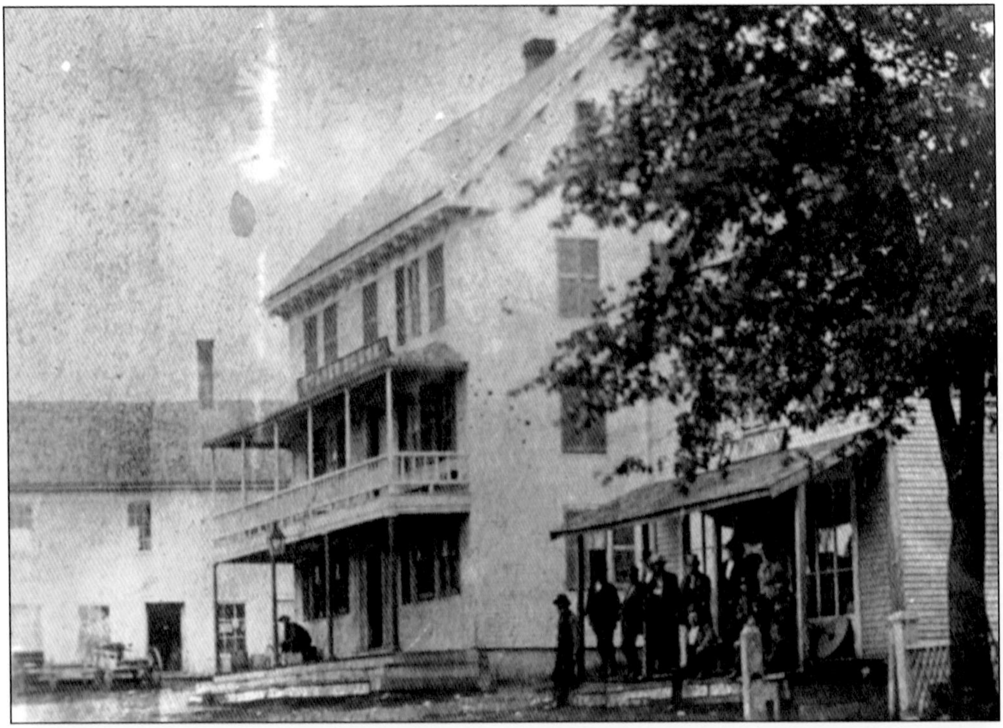

In 1856, J. K. Edes opened his clothing store on Water Street in Guilford next to the Turner House. Originally a wood frame building, it was later rebuilt in brick. The disposition of the frame building is not known. The brick building, however, has had a fabled career. First it was home to J. K. Edes and Son dry goods store, and then the T and K grocery store, a bowling alley, and lastly the original home and birthplace of Bert's Bees, a multimillion-dollar, world-wide company now headquartered in North Carolina.

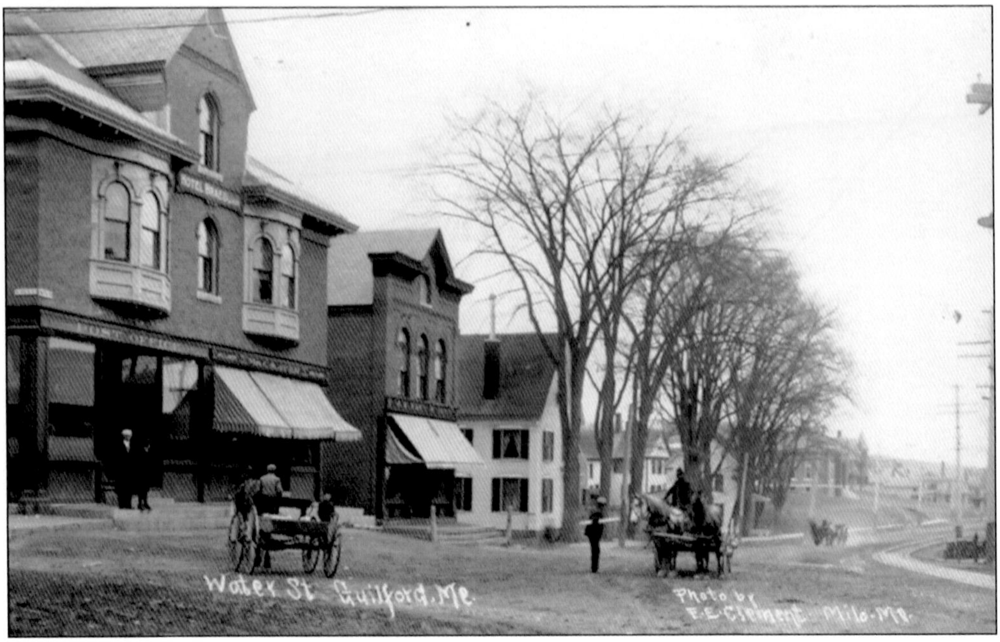

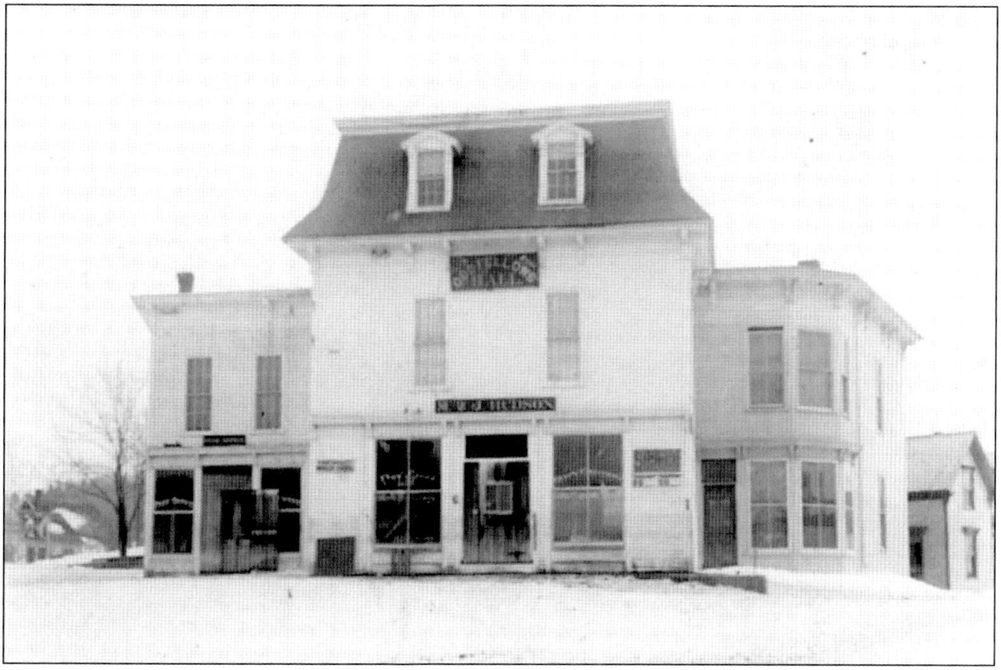

The M and J Hudson store was located at the intersection of South Main Street and Hudson Avenue in Guilford on the bottom floor of the Odd Fellows hall. The wings to the left and right were added to the original building shortly before the entire building was lost to fire in 1902. A short time later a new three-story brick building was erected to replace it. The new building was built on the same footprint except that the rear was slightly longer. The upper floor contained the Odd Fellows hall and Masonic temple, while the second floor held the telephone exchange for quite some time. The first floor housed the French and Elliott IGA store and later Worthen's Market. It was razed in 1998 to make room for the Rite Aid pharmacy.

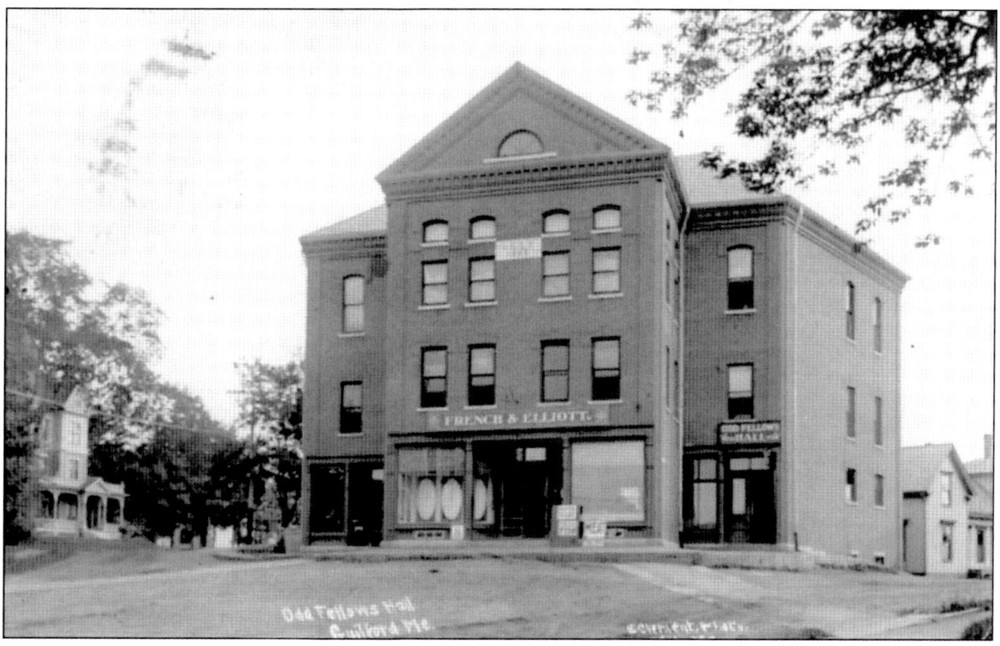

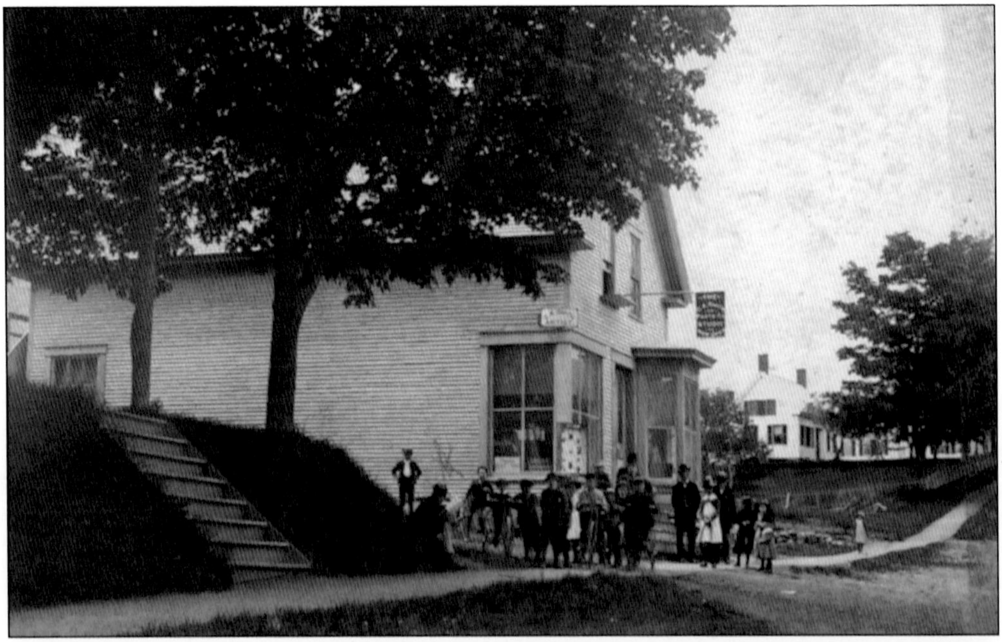

At the present location of the Guilford Historical Society on North Main Street, Addison Martin opened the first store in the village in 1825. It later housed, among other things, the Straw and Martin Insurance Office, the First National Bank (for six months), and the Blake Insurance Agency before being purchased by the society.

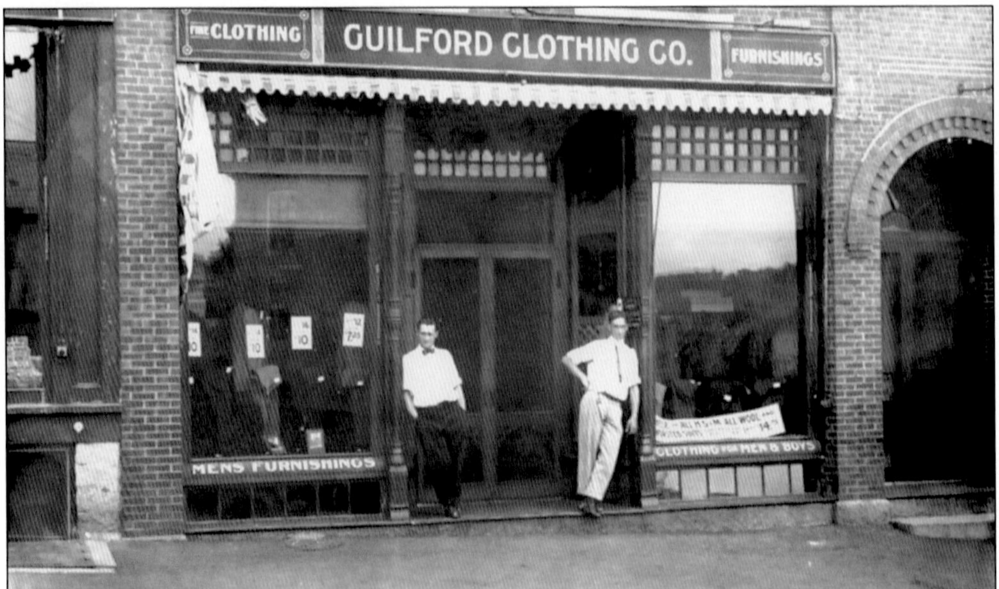

During the 1920s and 1930s the Guilford Clothing Company did business in the upper half of the Scales building on South Main Street in the quarters previously occupied by the Rand and Witham company, changing little but the name and the awnings.

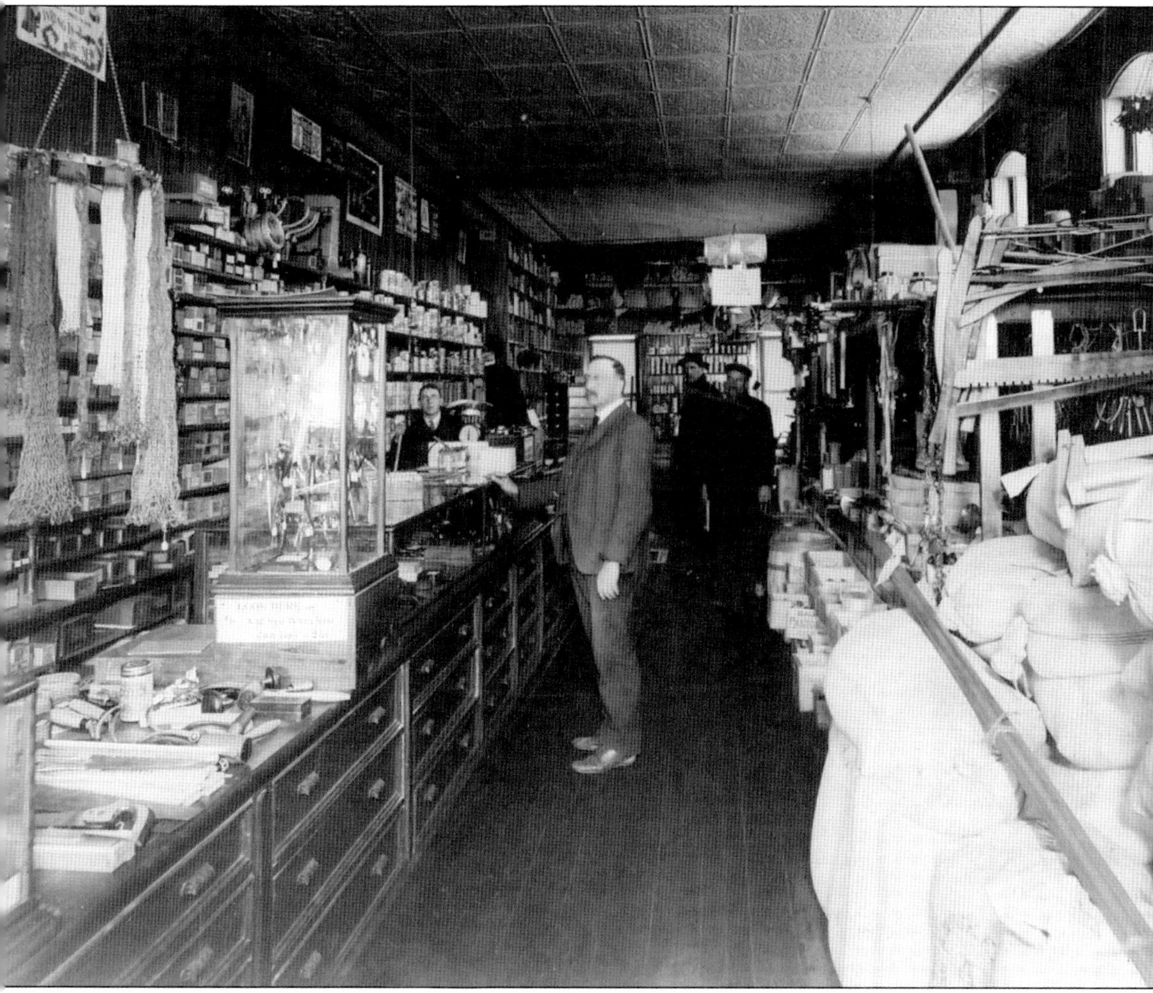

The John Scales store, located in the Scales block, was a large, full-line hardware store. This undated photograph of the interior gives an indication of the vast array of merchandise that was available. The windows on the right looked out onto the river. The individual standing in the center in the suit is believed to be John Scales.

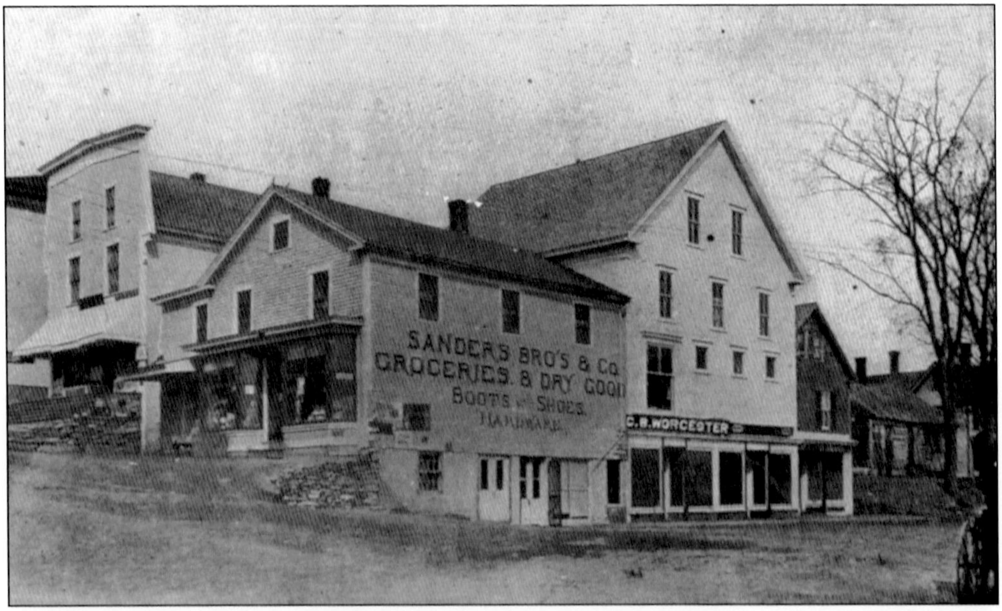

In 1857, Alden N. Sanders opened Sanders Brothers store on Main Street in Sangerville on the northwest corner of the town square. In 1899, the store sold items such as molasses and vinegar in a jug, salt pork cut to order, coffee ground while the customer waited, hardware, jewelry, and just about anything else one could think of. The Sanders Brothers store closed in 1942 due to the ill health of Sander's son Charles, who had taken over. The building's basement was used by C. C. Worcester's Alpine Candy Kitchen, and Vena E. Sanders, pictured in the doorway, maintained a millinery shop for many years. Next to her store was the U.S. post office. The building was razed in 1950. The next store up the hill is the M. L. Stott dry goods store. It is now the American Legion hall. (Courtesy of Sangerville Historical Society.)

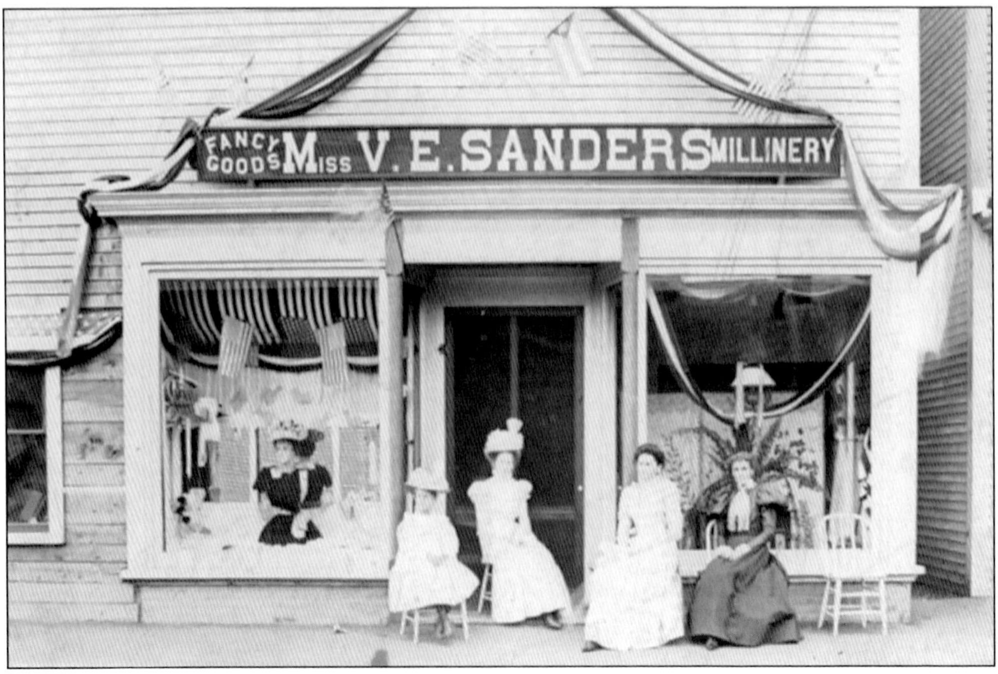

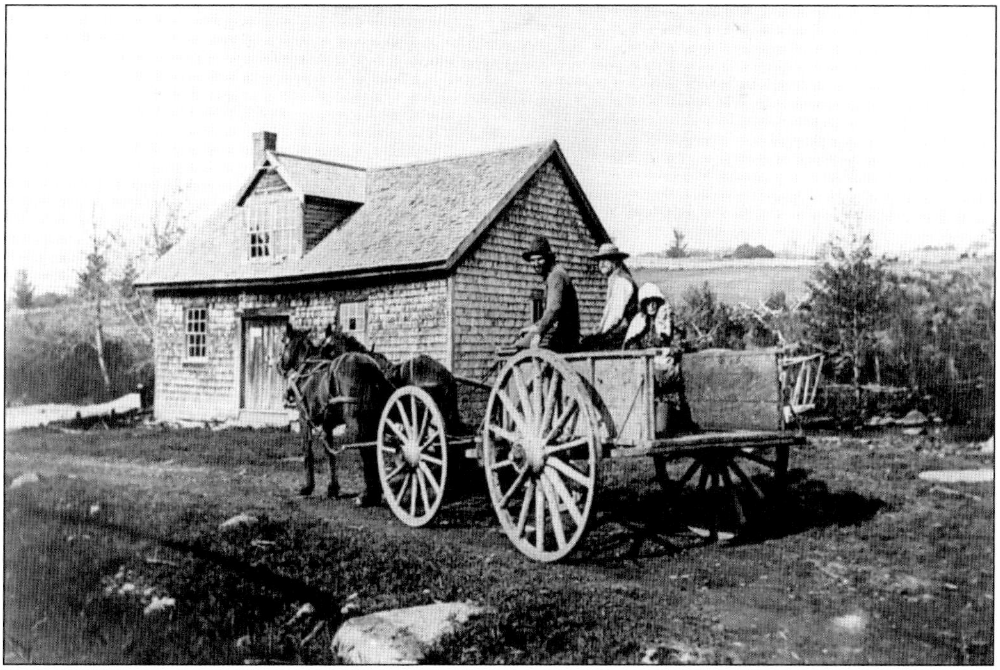

In the mid-1800s, Brockway's Mills near south Sangerville was a busy little settlement with a general store and post office in addition to its mills and farms. With the exception of a few farms, very little remains. (Courtesy of Sangerville Historical Society.)

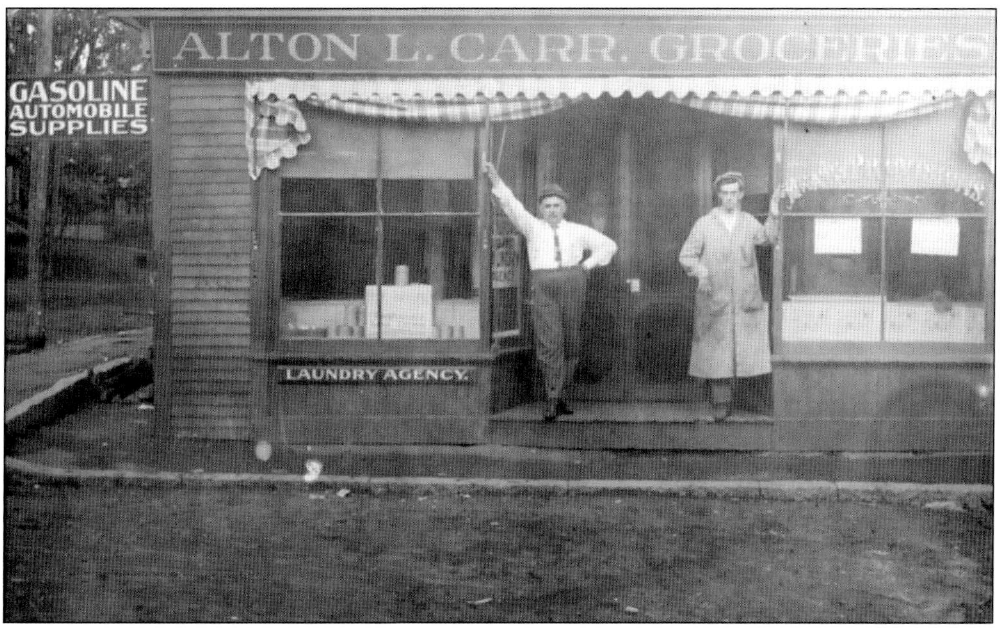

On the northeast corner of the town square in Sangerville, W. A. Hill purchased a former feed and grain store and converted it to a grocery store. It was later purchased by Alton Carr, who added a gas pump and rented space in the rear to Bert Smart for a meat market. (Courtesy of Sangerville Historical Society.)

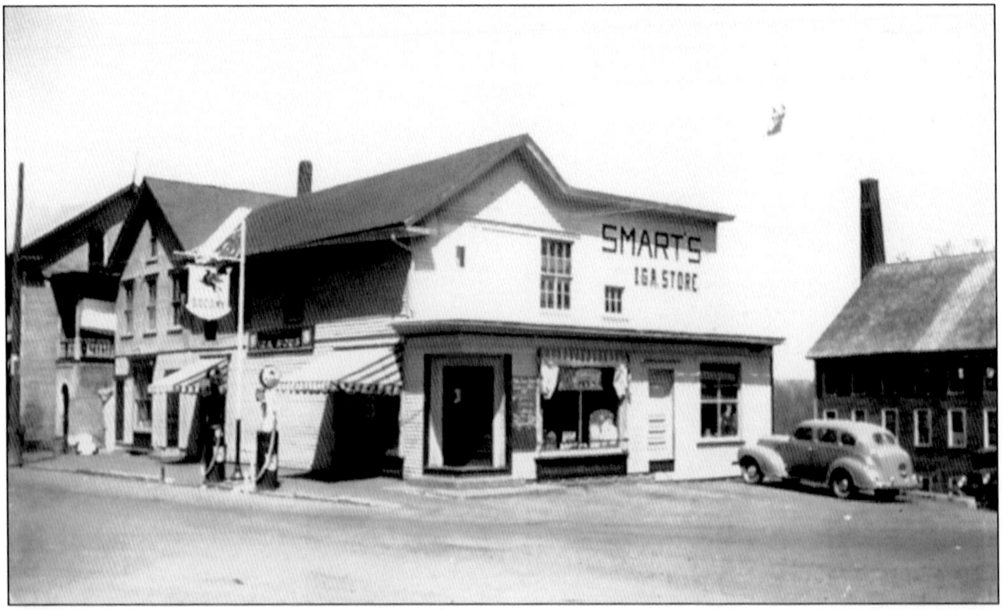

After the closing of the Sanders Brothers store, Smarts IGA was the main store in town to purchase groceries, meats, and perishables. It was owned and run by Millard Smart and his father, Bert, who tended the meat department until his retirement. Here one could also bring a jug for vinegar or molasses and have it filled from barrels in the basement. (Courtesy of Lisa Fortier.)

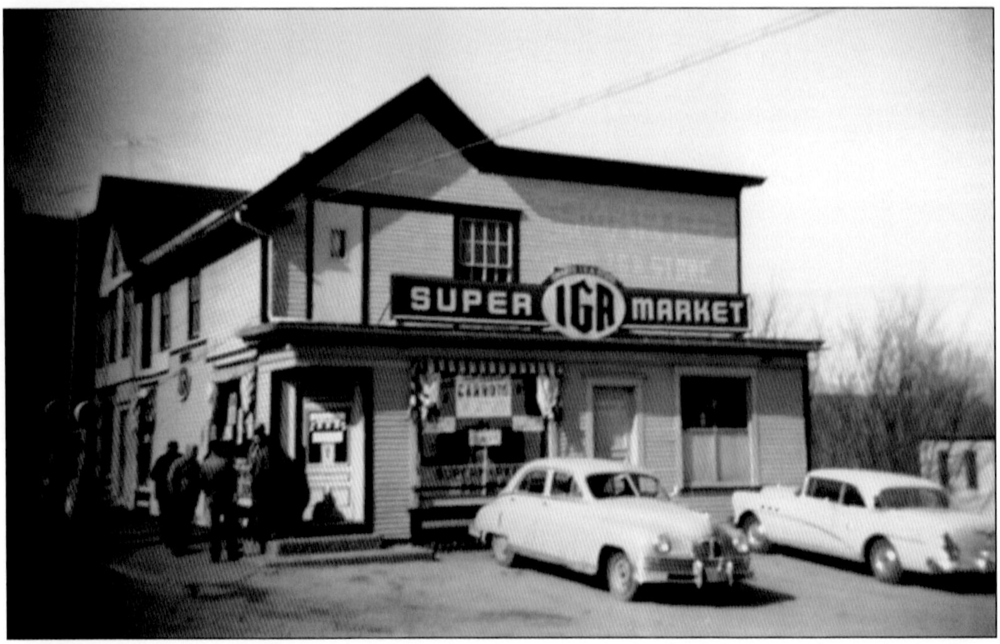

In 1961, the store was purchased by Willard and Louine Starbird, who changed very little about how it was run. Located on the northeast corner of Main Street, it was the usual gathering place for men on summer evenings. After the store closed for the night, the steps provided a place to sit, and the weighty problems of the world and country could be discussed at length. The store burned down in 1973. (Courtesy of Lisa Fortier.)

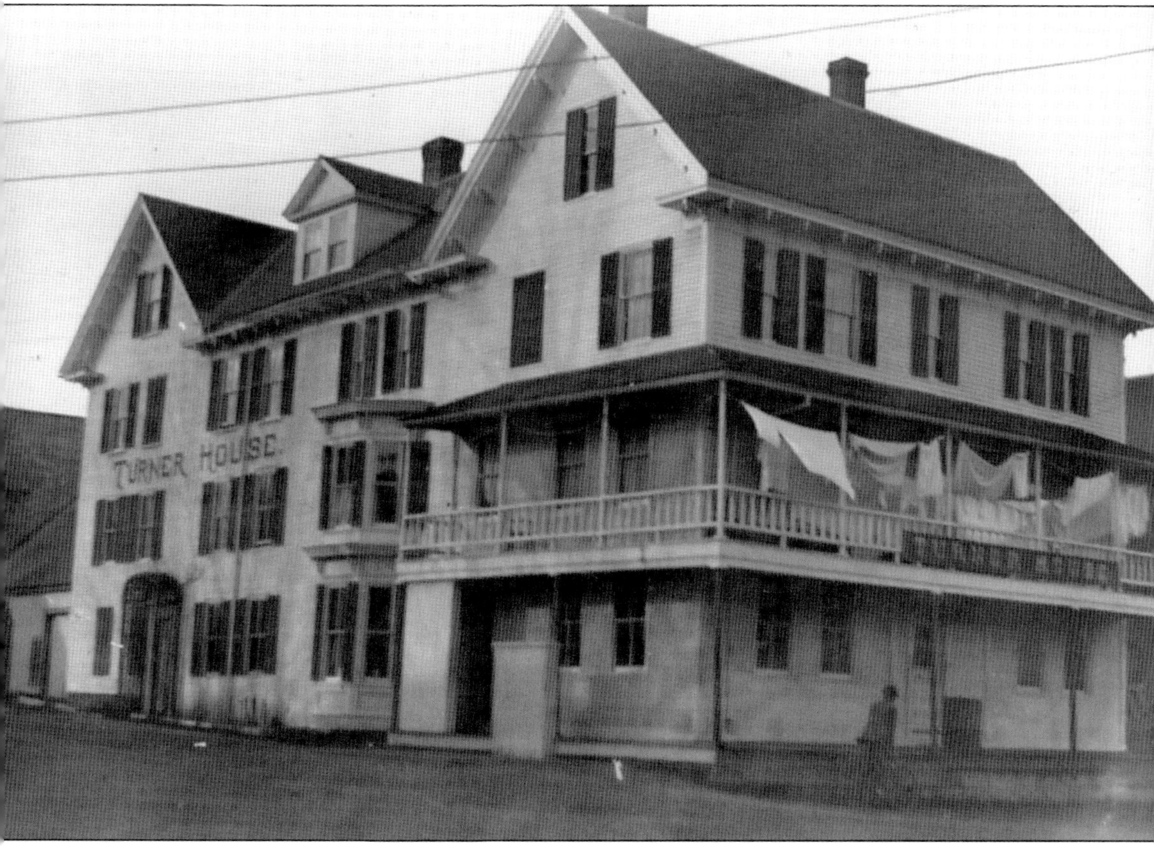

The first lodging place of any consequence in Guilford was the Franklin House at the corner of North Main and River Streets. In the mid-1800s, Zadoc L. Turner purchased it and made many improvements and upgrades, including installing porches facing the street on the first and second floors. Before the coming of the railroad, stagecoaches stopped here on a regular basis and stables were provided to care for horses for those staying the night. With the advent of the railroad, the hotel still maintained a livery and ferried its guests to and from the station as a regular service. The Bangor and Piscataquis railroad station was a little over a quarter mile away on Water Street. In 1903, a disastrous fire destroyed the stables and much of the hotel itself. What could be salvaged was moved up the street a few hundred feet to make room for the new Braeburn Hotel. A part of this building still exists to this day.

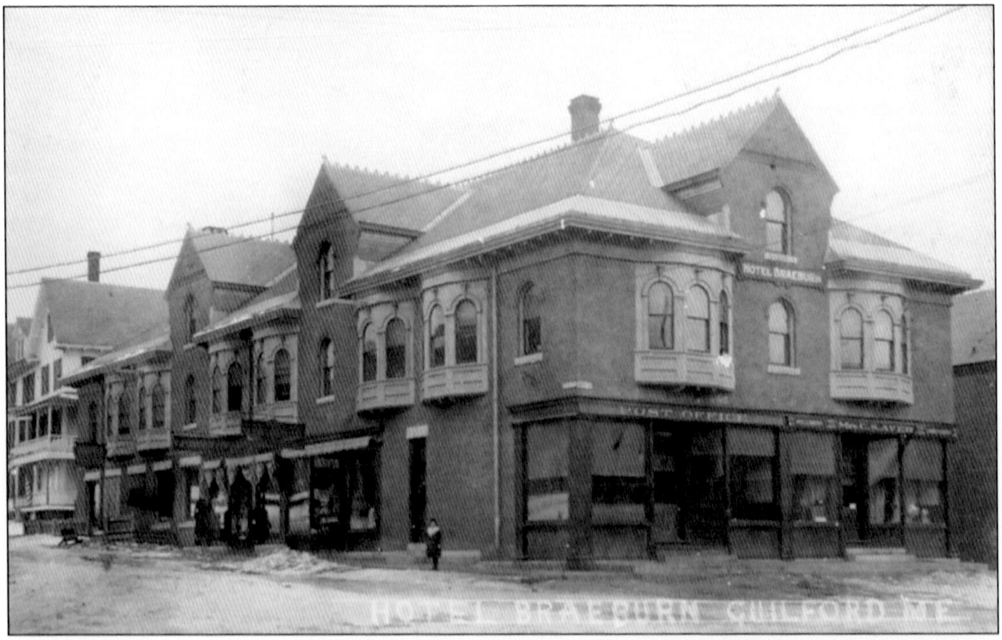

After the disastrous fire destroyed a good portion of the Turner House, a new, completely modern, brick hotel was erected on the old lot. Named the Braeburn Hotel, it was considered at the time to be one of the finest in the state. It lasted about 100 years. Pictured from left to right in the above photograph around 1920, the first floor housed the lobby and dining room, Jackson Company Men's Clothing store, a drugstore, the U.S. post office, and Mrs. C. S. Ayers Millinery Shop. In the photograph below, Fred Wheeler stands behind the reservation desk in the hotel lobby in 1928.

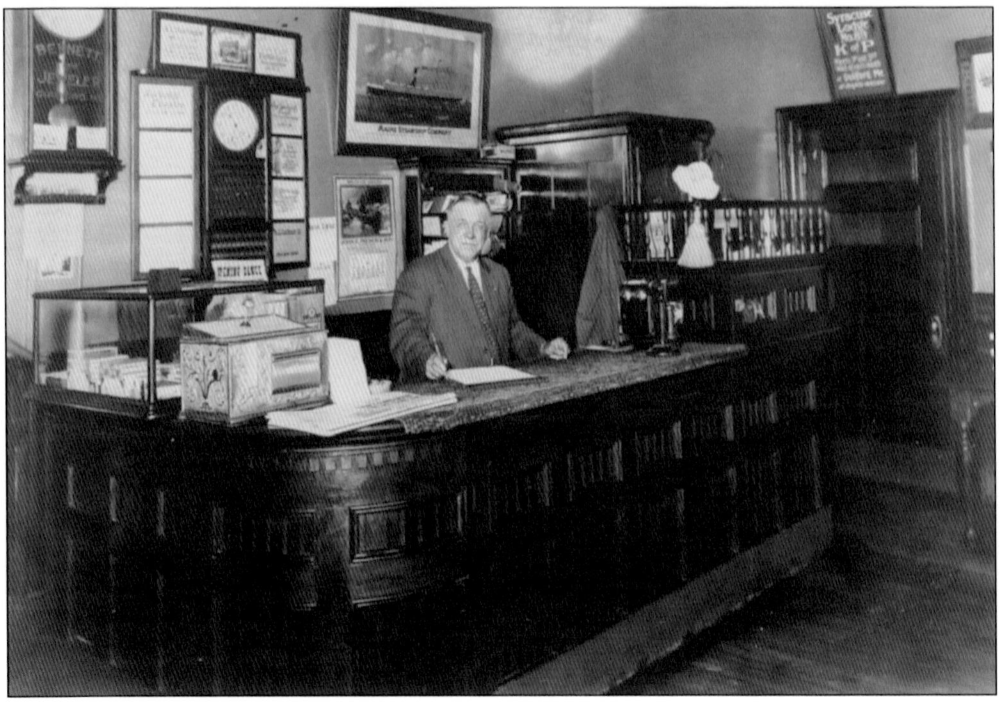

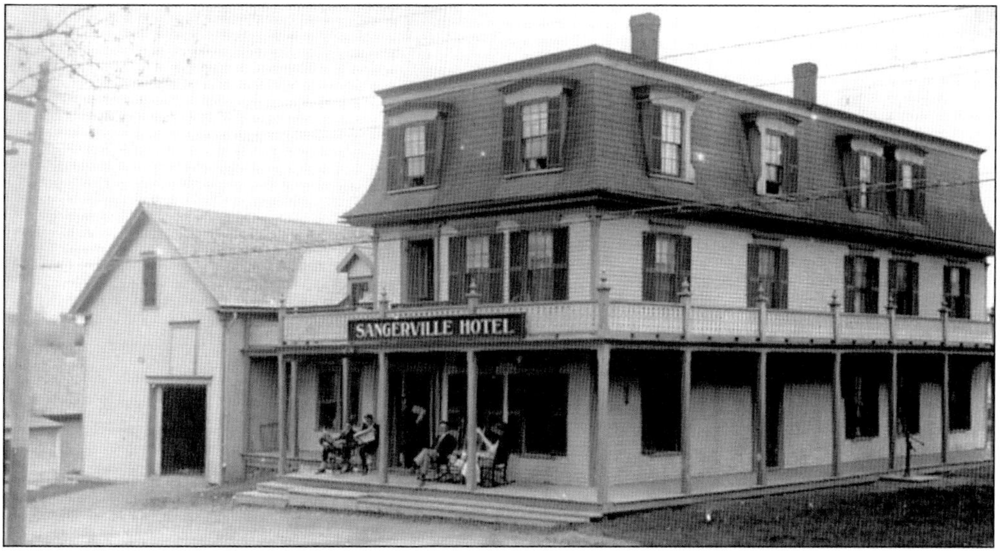

In Sangerville, lodging could be procured at the Sangerville Hotel located at the top of the hill on the west side of town. The rooms were well appointed and had hot and cold running water in the bathrooms. A livery was maintained, and guests were provided with transportation to and from the train station that was about a mile away. The building was later used as an apartment house and was destroyed by fire in 1978. (Courtesy of Sangerville Historical Society.)

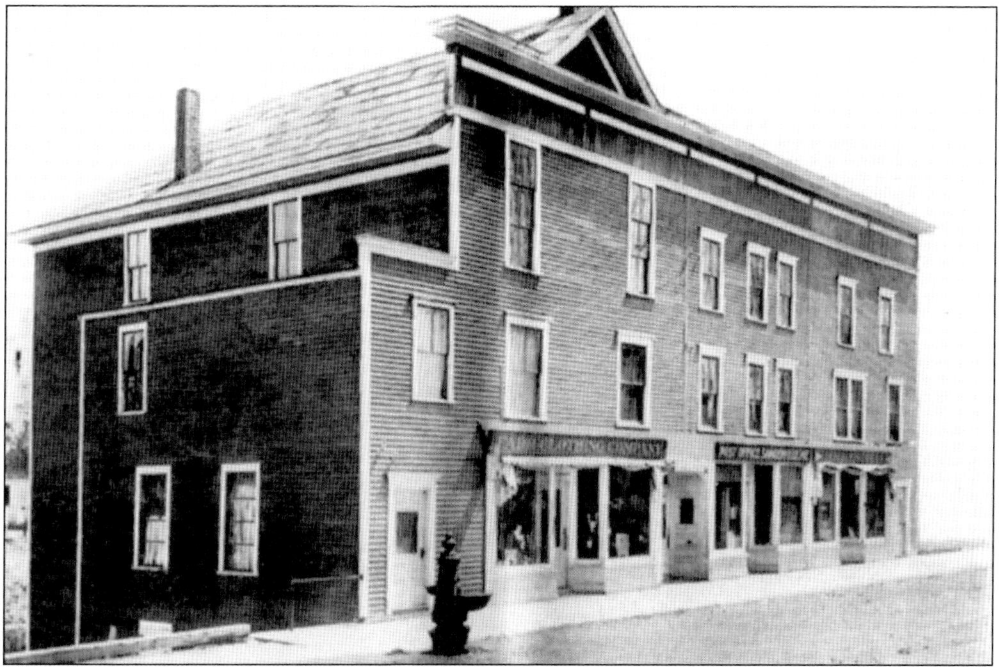

One of the finest commercial buildings in Sangerville was the Carr block on Main Street. Seen here around 1910, it housed the Farr Clothing store, the U.S. post office, and Les Seabury's Candy and Ice Cream store. On the second floor was an amusement hall that was later used as a silent movie theater and many nice apartments. The third floor also contained apartments. The building was razed in 1955. Note the horse watering trough in front. (Courtesy of Sangerville Historical Society.)

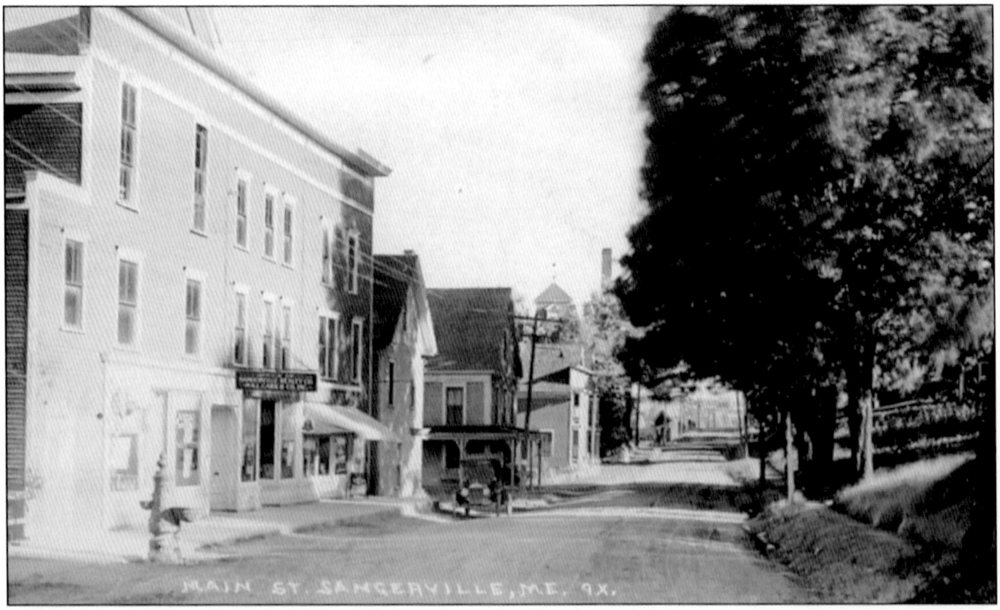

A view of the Carr block on South Main Street shows Littlefield's Boarding House (the building with a porch) and livery stable. The next building beyond that was always referred to as the "beehive." Sangerville Realty Company and A. L. Carr Company maintained offices in the Carr building. (Courtesy of Sangerville Historical Society.)

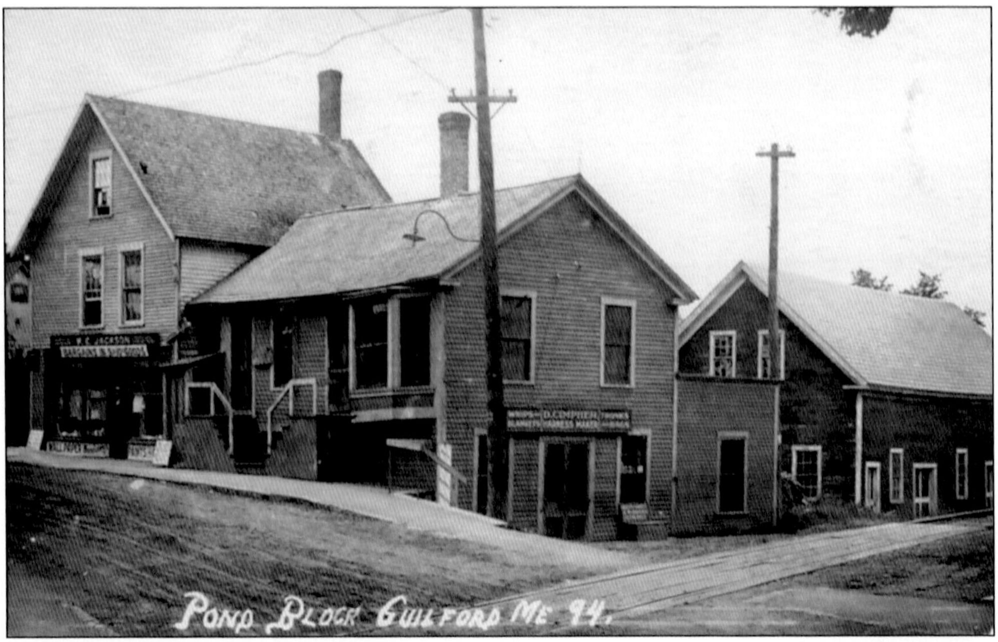

At the north end of the Guilford bridge was Jackson's Clothing store, a law office, and Cimpher's Harness Shop. The tracks of the Bangor and Aroostook Railroad are in the foreground. Heavy planks were laid between the rails to facilitate the movement of horses and carriages over the tracks.

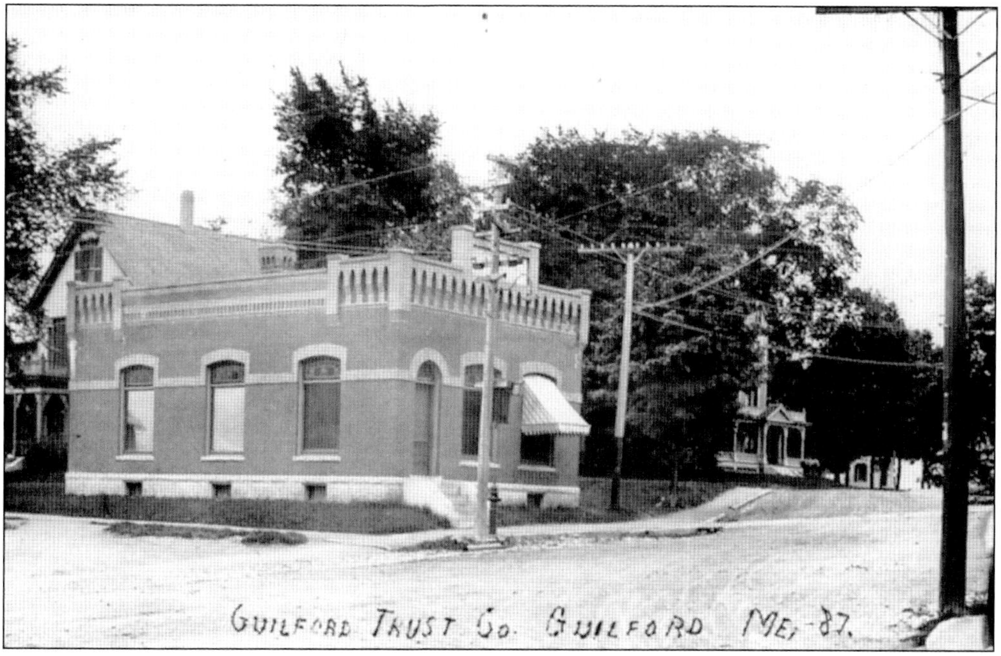

At the corner of Hudson Avenue and Oak Street in 1902, the first bank building was constructed in Guilford. It had previously been housed for 10 years on the second floor of the Scales building. Originally incorporated as the First National Bank in the 1892, it was later reorganized as the Guilford Trust Company, and a branch opened in Greenville. The photograph below, taken around 1940, shows the new addition on the right.

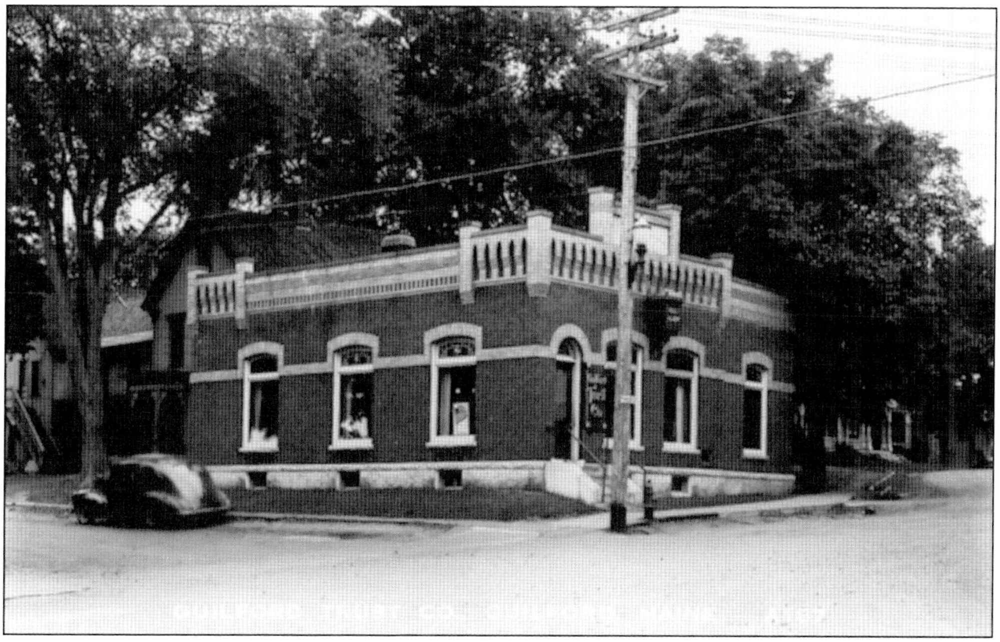

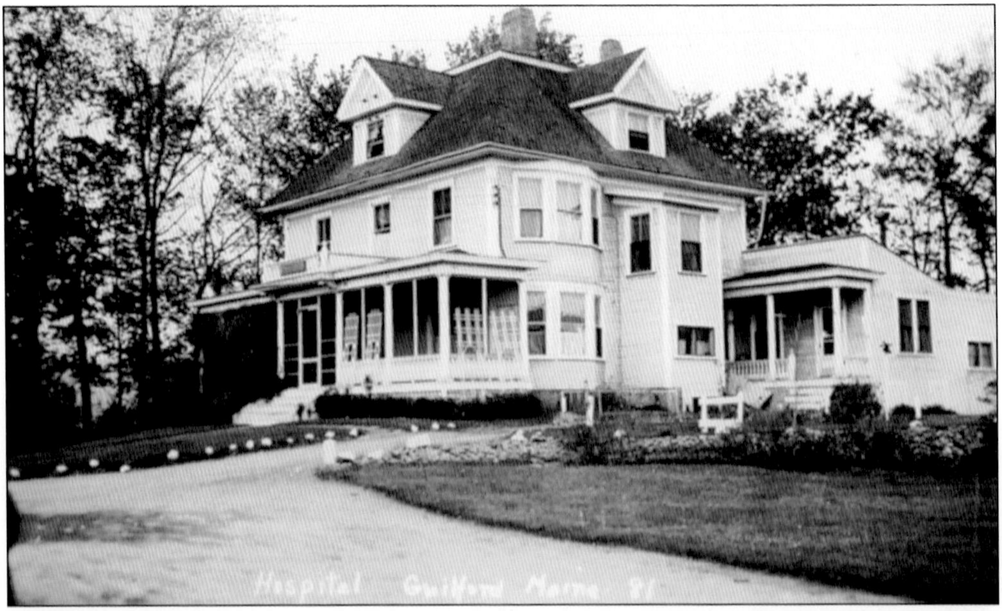

In 1921, Louise Chase purchased the homestead of Charles P. Turner, which was located at the end of Oak Street; and in October, she opened the Guilford Hospital. The house was remodeled to suit the needs of a modern hospital, with private rooms, both men's and women's wards, and a well-equipped operating room. The hospital operated into the 1940s.

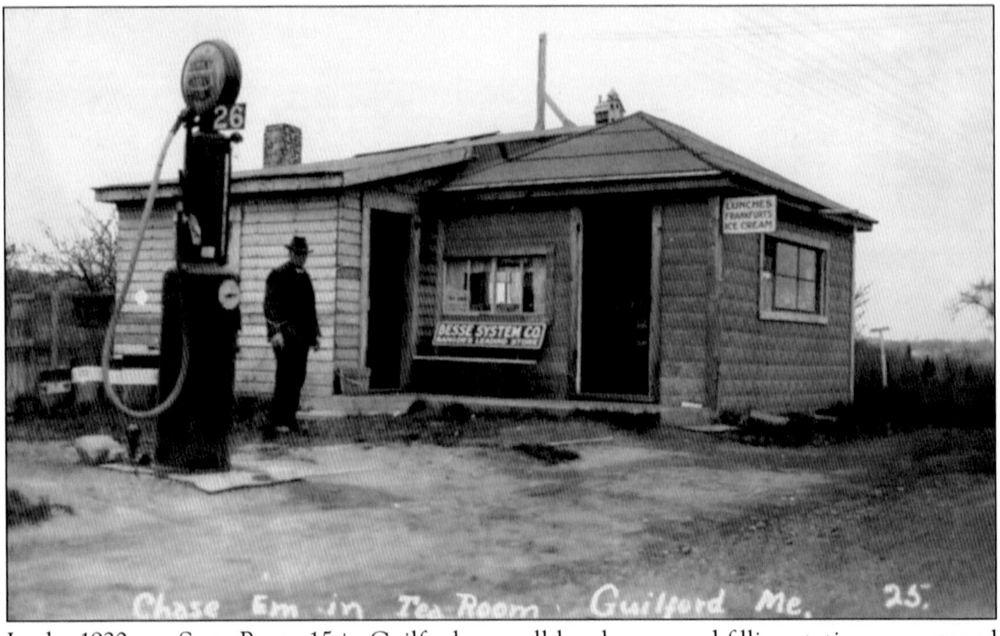

In the 1920s on State Route 15 in Guilford, a small lunchroom and filling station was opened for business. Known as the Chase-Em-In Tea Room, it was located at the top of the hill about two miles east of the village. Later it was rebuilt and became the Hill Top House, and after that it was known as Hall's Restaurant.

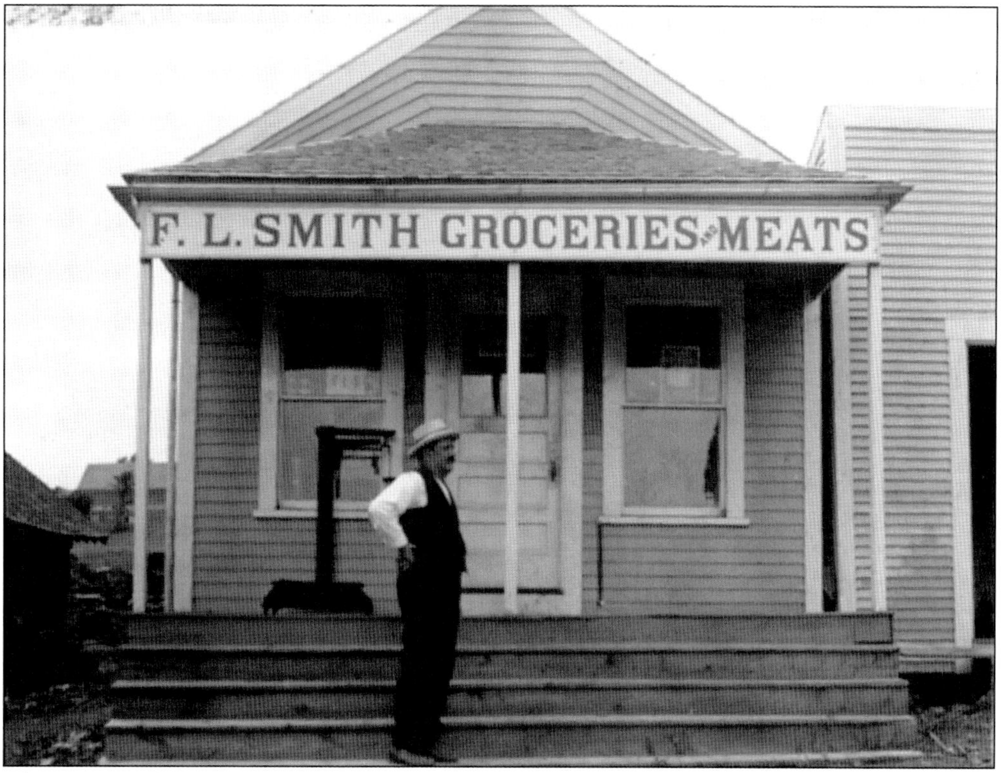

The F. L. Smith meat and grocery store was located on South Main Street in Guilford. Note the large set of scales in the front for weighing sacks of dry goods and grain.

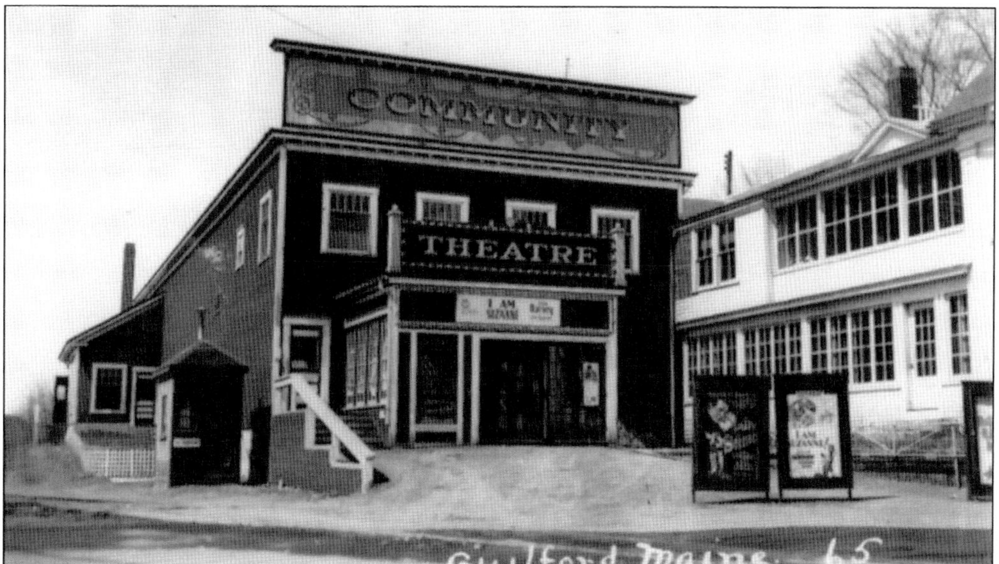

In 1932, Henry and Minnie Elliott opened the Guilford Community Theatre on North Main Street near the bridge and railroad tracks. The theater was run by their son Richard and his wife until it was sold to the Cronin family in the late 1940s. The small building on the left was used by the crossing guard for the railroad that crossed Main Street at this location.

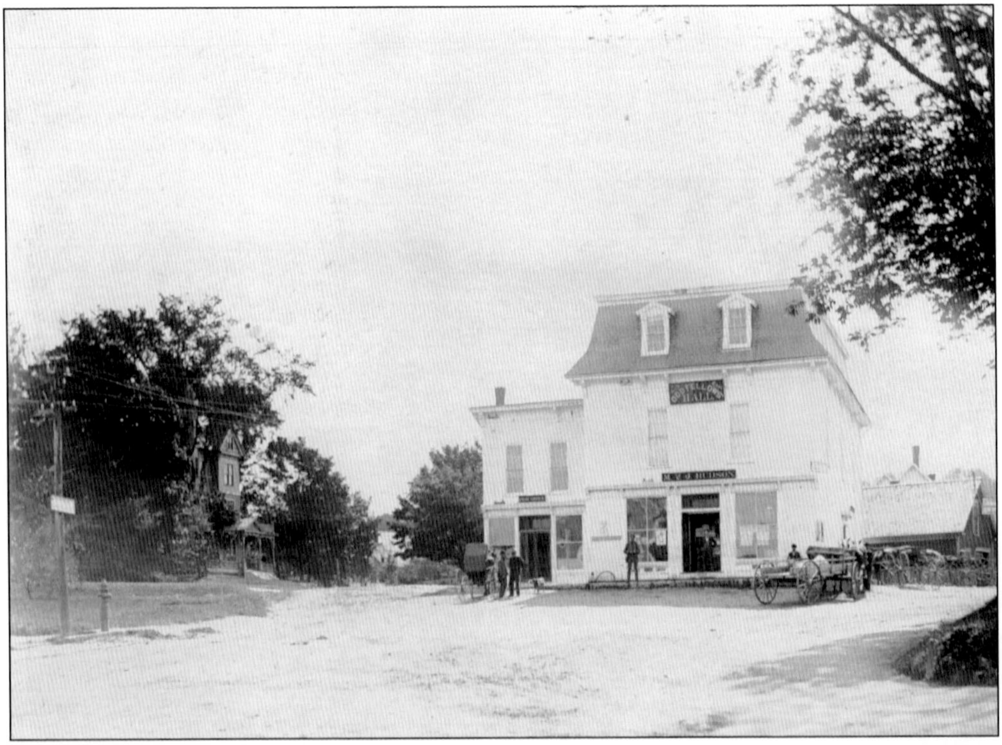

The general store of Micajah and James Hudson was located at the intersection of North Main Street and Hudson Avenue in the late 1800s. The Odd Fellows hall was located on the second floor, and the U.S. post office occupied the wing on the left. Another wing was later added to the right side.

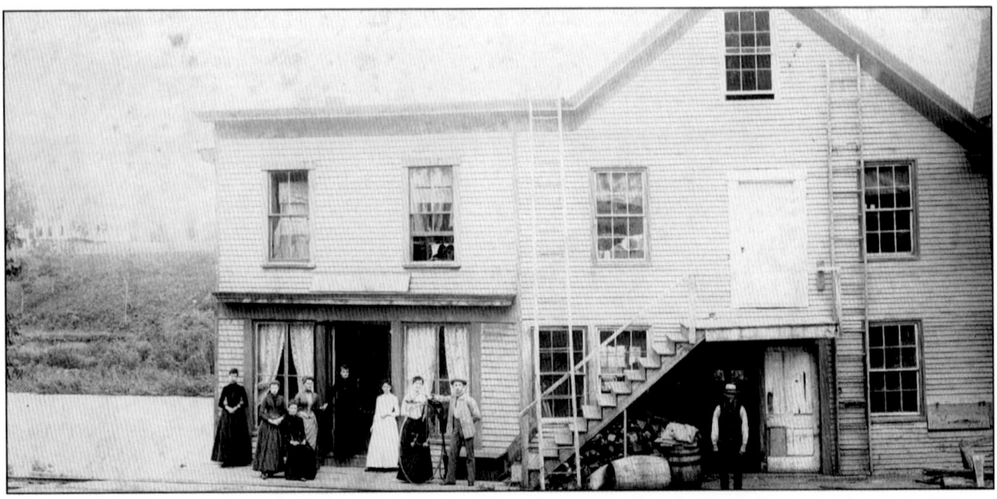

Also in the late 1800s, Erastus Hussey owned and operated a feed and grain store on Water Street. Pictured here, from left to right, are Mary Edes, Maud Hussey, Bertha Starbird, Jean Chandler, Polly Murphy, Lucie Livermore, Jean Hussey, Sumner Bennett (with high wheeler bicycle), and Erastus.

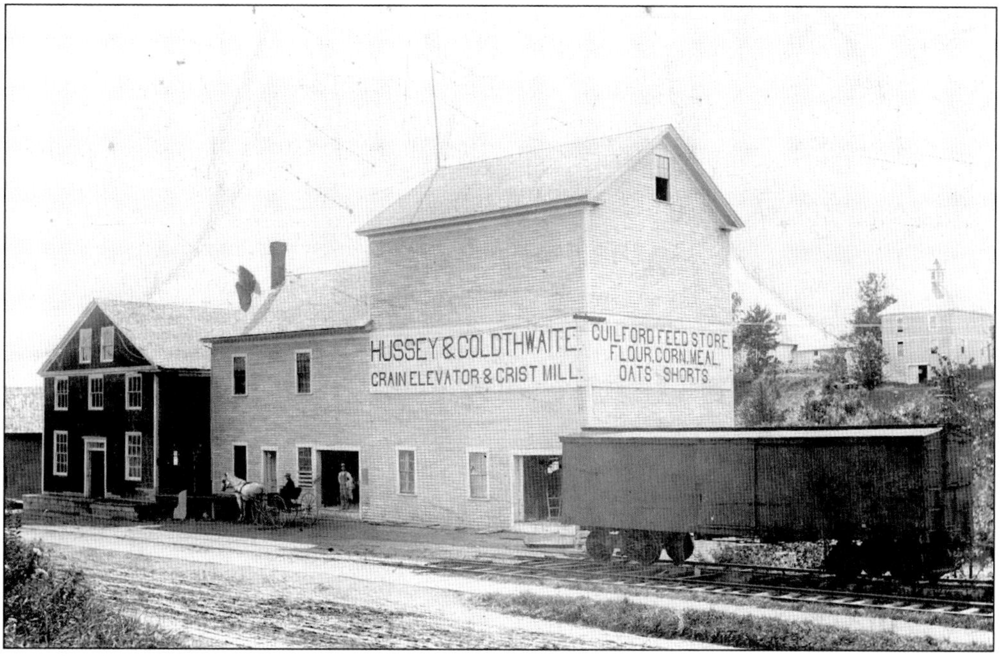

Another business located on Water Street somewhere near where the war memorial is now located was the Hussey and Goldthwaite gristmill and grain elevator. The railroad tracks ran between the road and the businesses in this area, and some had their own sidings where boxcars could be left to be loaded or unloaded. This business was later owned by Frank Palmer.

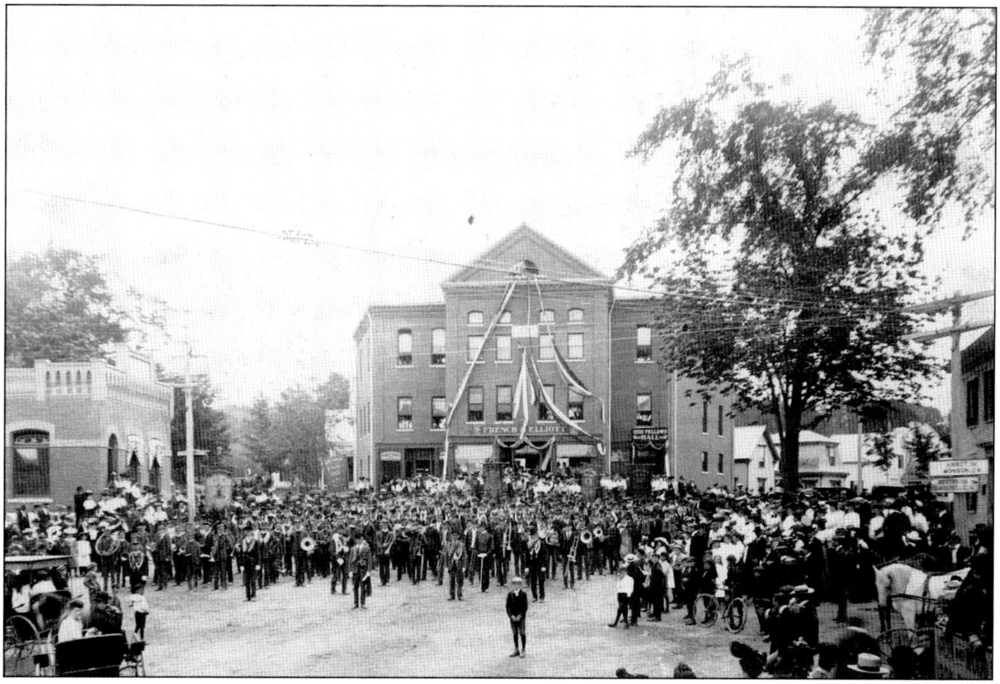

After the Hudson store and Odd Fellows hall burned in 1902, a large brick building was built on the same footprint. When finished in 1904, a huge dedication ceremony took place in Bank Square that was attended by hundreds of people.

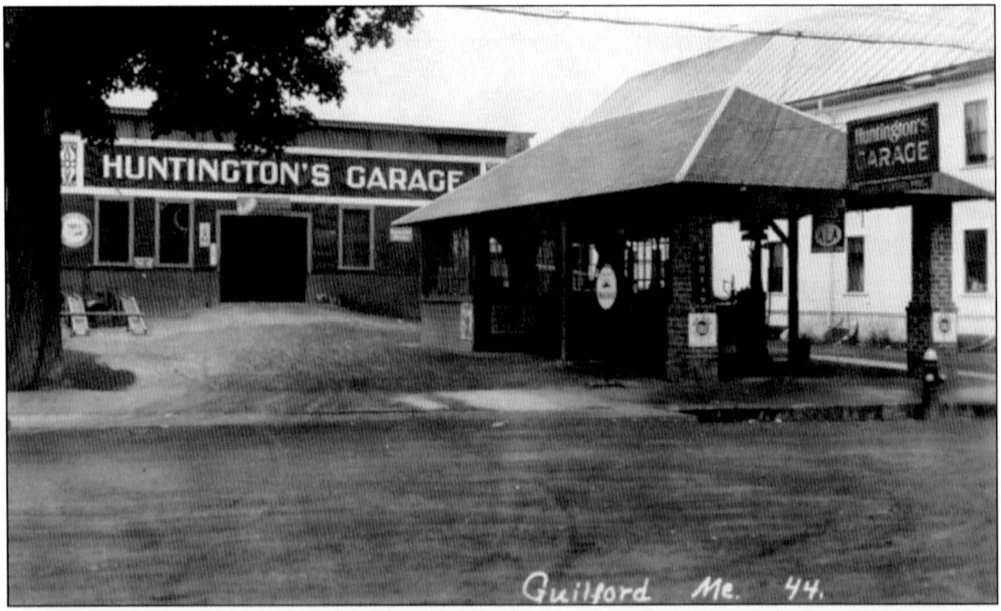

In 1919, Huntington's Garage opened on the south side of Elm Street in Guilford. This was in the lot adjoining the current Robinson Mobil Mart. Considered state of the art for its time, the gas pumps were covered to protect patrons during bad weather. The garage also had the first radio in town, which at the time was referred to as a "wireless telephone."

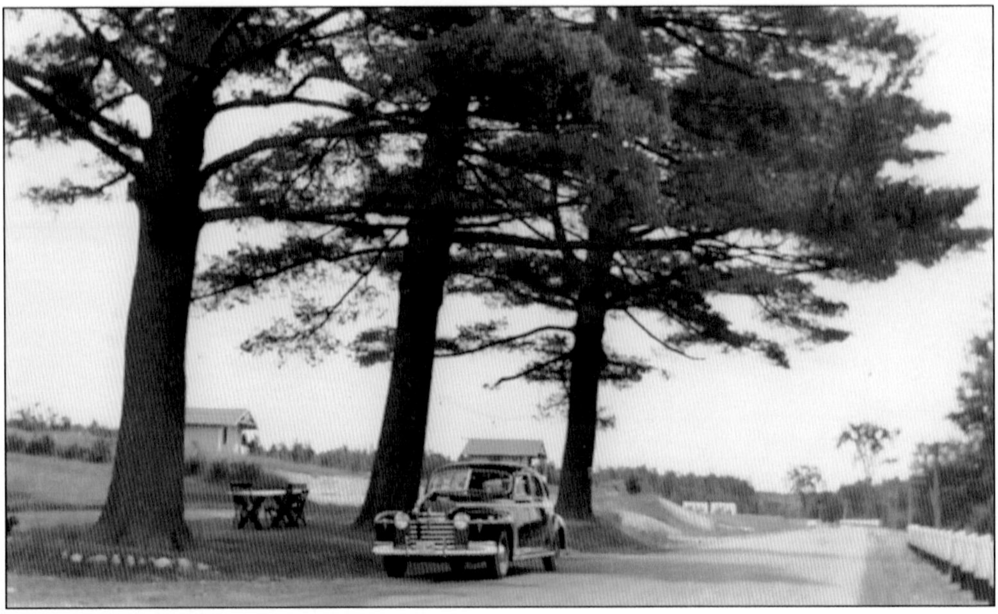

In 1941, Pooles Cabins were located on State Route 15 just past Lows bridge heading east. The Covered Bridge Motel currently occupies this site. The large billboards located far down on the left side of the road were once an integral part of the North American landscape.

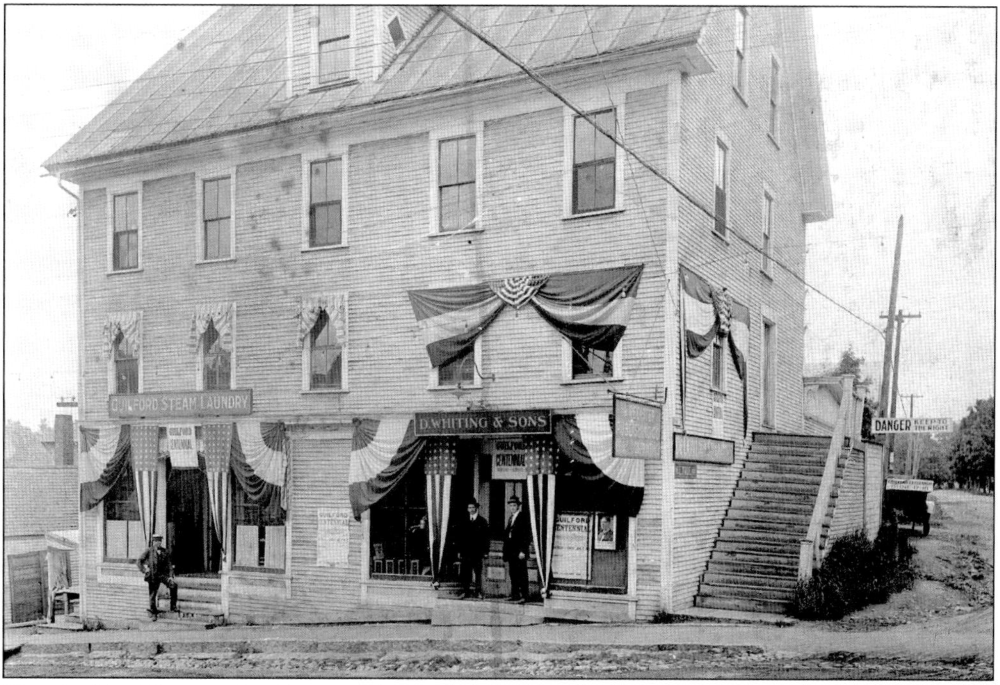

The Guilford Register Building was located at the corner of Oak Street and South Main Street and is shown here in 1916. The *Guilford Register* newspaper was published on the second and third floors while the Guilford Steam Laundry and D. H. Whiting and Sons occupied the first floor.

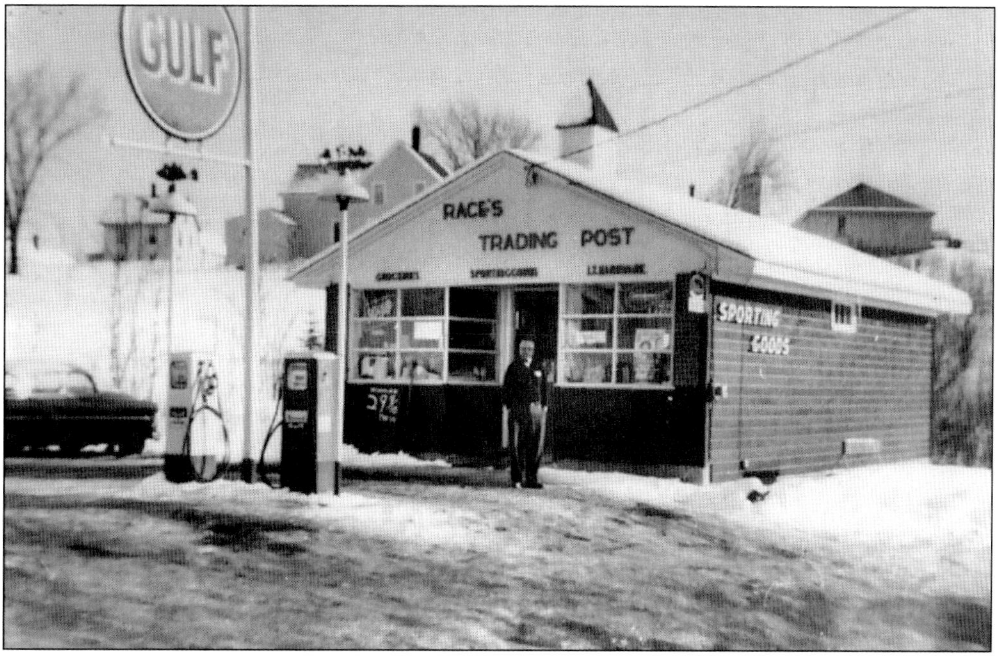

In 1956, George Race Sr. and his wife, Marion, opened a sporting goods store on Pleasant Avenue in Sangerville. He is seen here standing in front of the store in the early 1960s. In 1964, the store was sold to Lloyd and Gloria Hall, and it is now owned by the A. E. Robinson Company of Dover-Foxcroft. (Courtesy of Pam Kimball.)

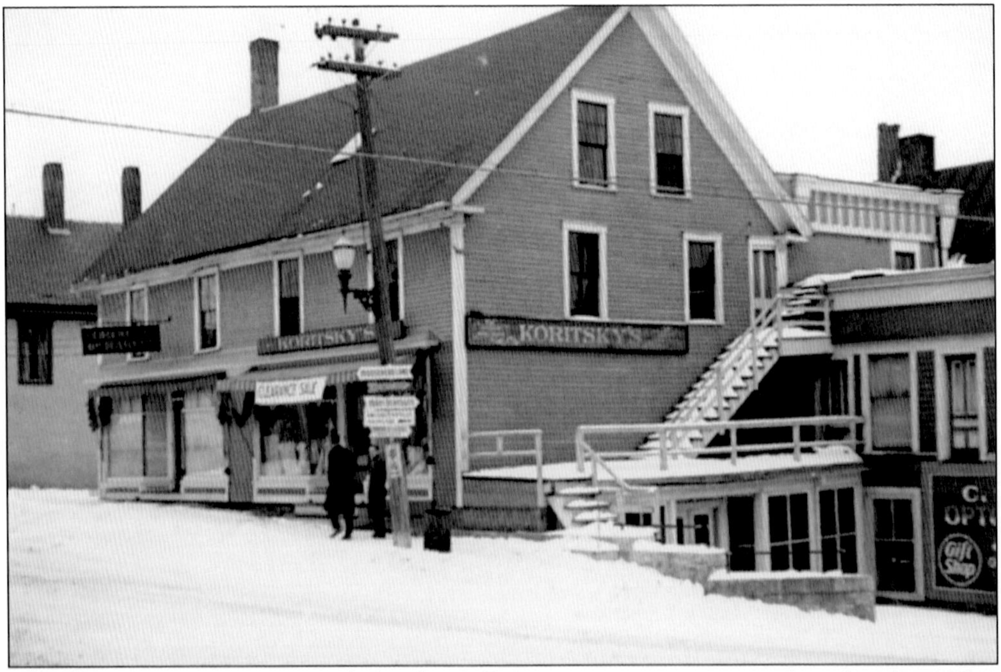

Koritsky's department store and Crockett's Bakery were two nice retail outlets located at the corner of South Main and Elm Streets in 1959. They were in business at this location from the 1930s until a disastrous fire in February 1969 completely destroyed them and two other businesses.

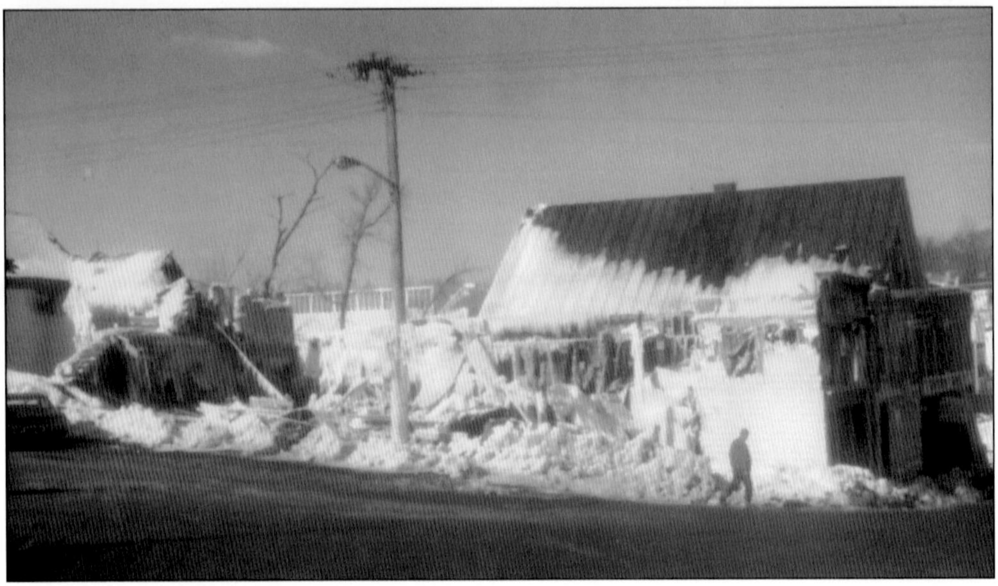

Four

Schools

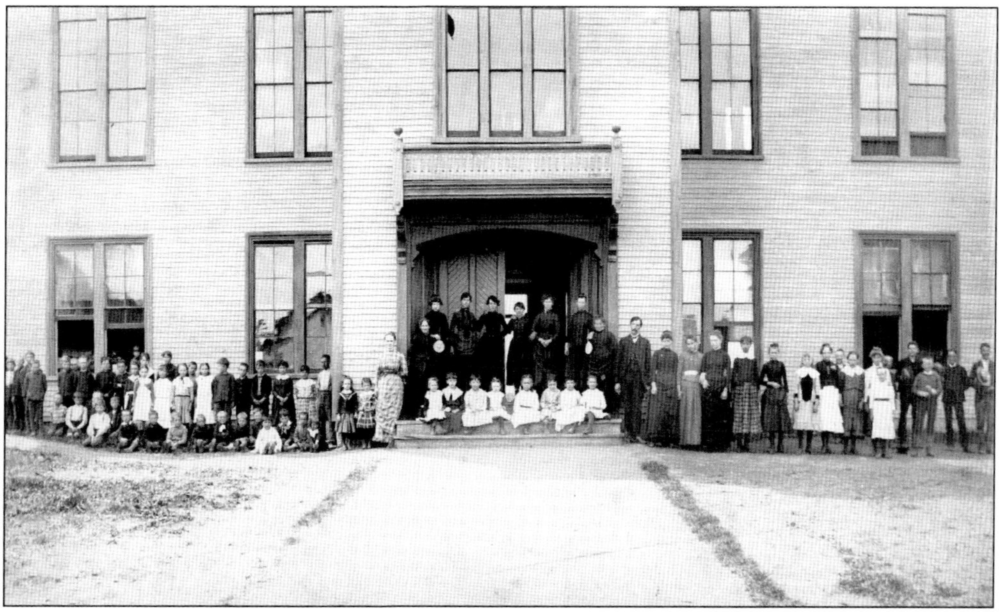

On June 20, 1887, Guilford's entire student body and teachers posed in front of the town hall where most of them attended classes. Two of the teachers were G. B. Hescock of Monson and Fronia Chandler of Abbot. There were 37 students absent from the photograph. Guilford had as many as six, one- and two-room schools in the late 1800s, including one in town, one near the top of Applebee Hill, one at North Guilford, one at Guilford center, one across from Low's bridge, and the Brown School on Sebec Shores Road. There may have been others. The schools at Low's bridge and Guilford center still exist today as private homes.

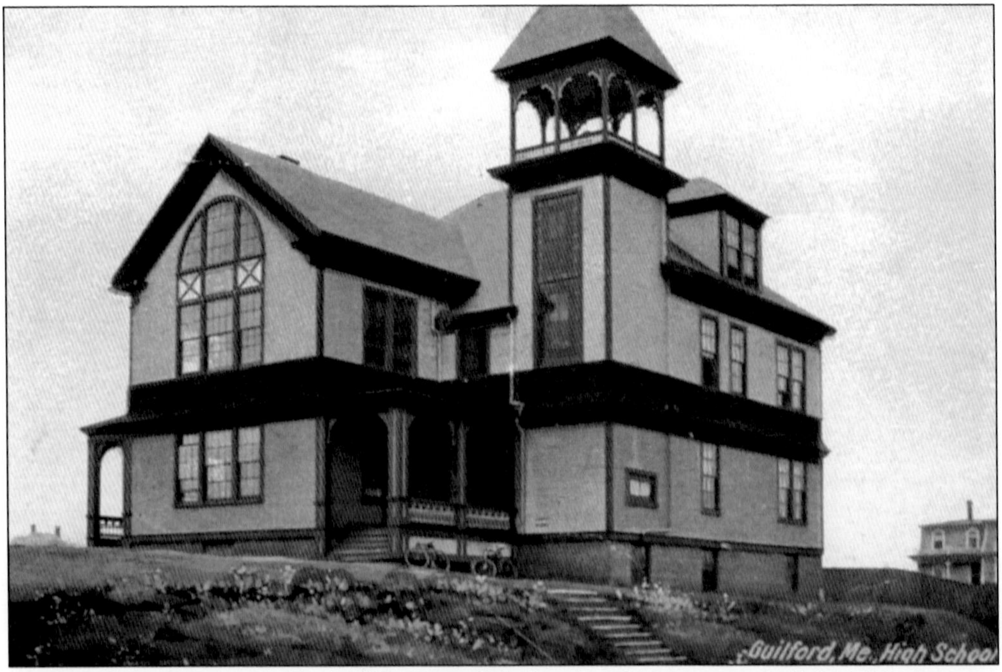

In 1880, all students in Guilford village attended school in the new town hall. In 1892, the town appropriated $15,000 and built a new high school, shown here, while the lower grades continued to be taught in the town hall. Shown above is the school in 1906.

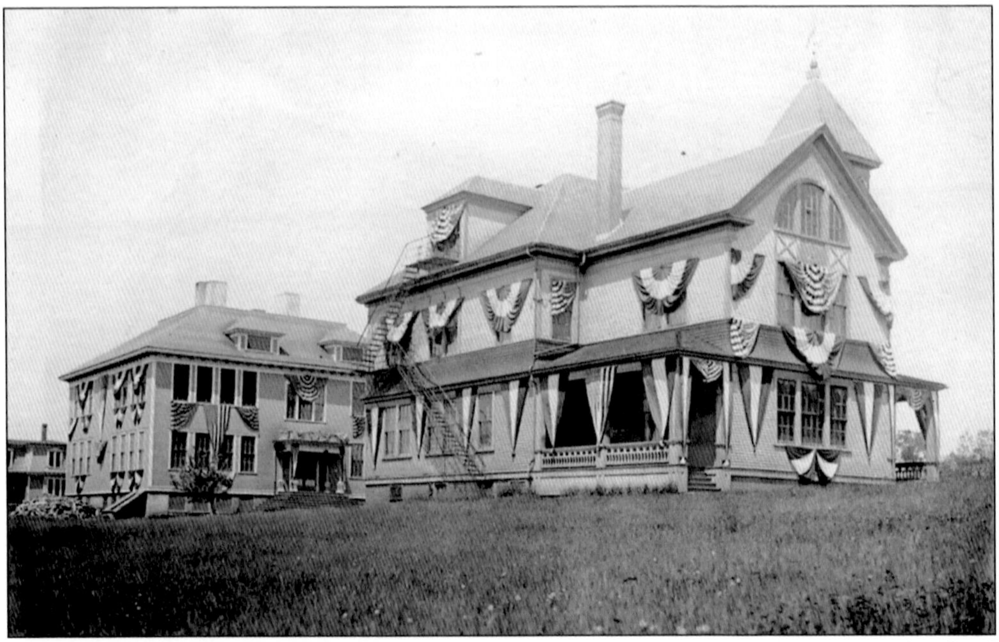

At the time of the centennial in 1916, Guilford had recently built a state-of-the-art grade school to go with its high school. Shown here, it is decked out for the grand festivities.

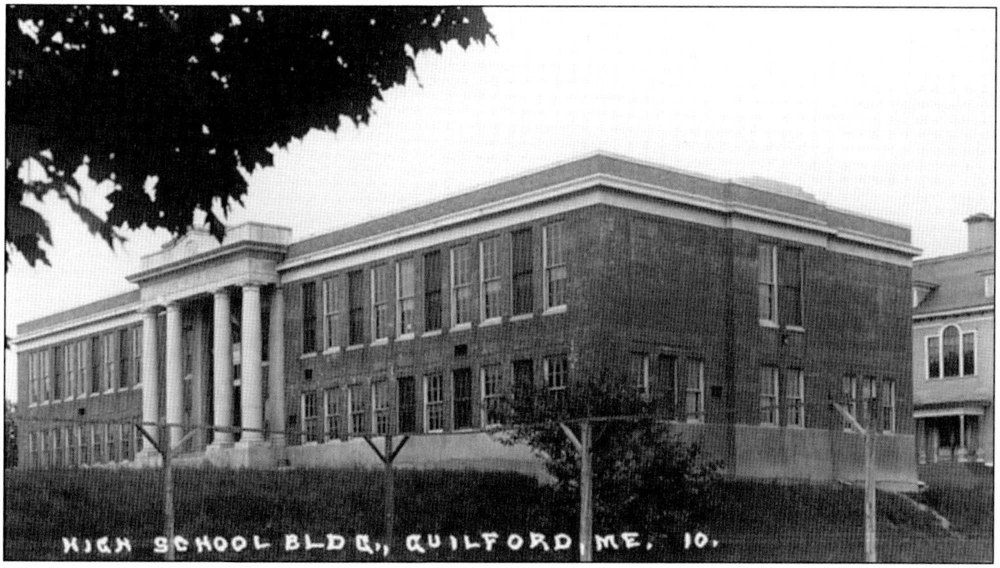

The devastating fire that leveled the high school in 1925 failed to dampen the spirits of the citizens of Guilford, and within one year, a new, ultra-modern high school rose from the ashes at a cost of $90,000. The school boasted a highly impressive entrance, exterior tennis courts, and a beautiful gymnasium and assembly hall with a well-appointed stage for putting on plays and so forth. When the school consolidation with the surrounding towns came in 1949, it became the foundation for Piscataquis Community High School. At that time, a new gymnasium was added to the building and the old one was converted to classroom space. When the new high school was built, the old building was used as a middle school until it was razed in 1997.

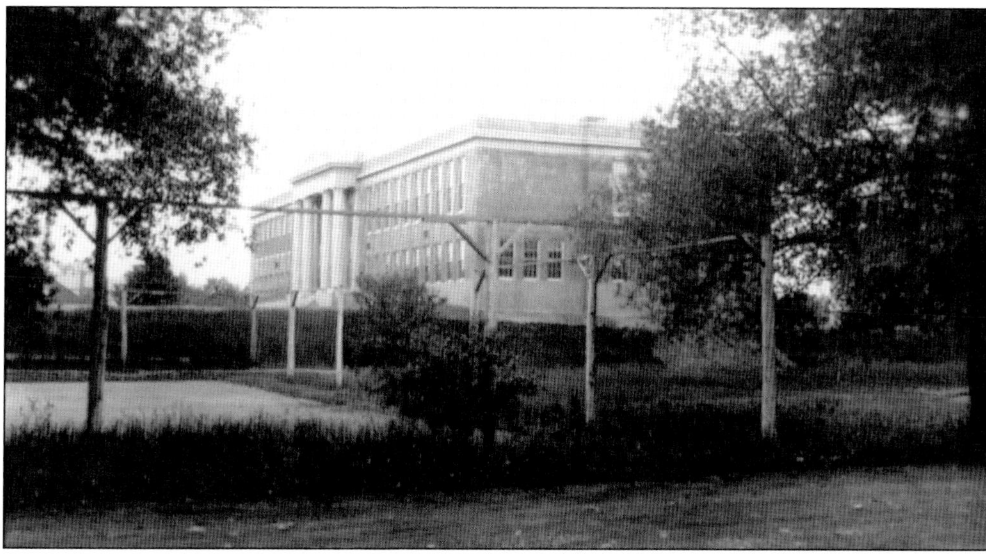

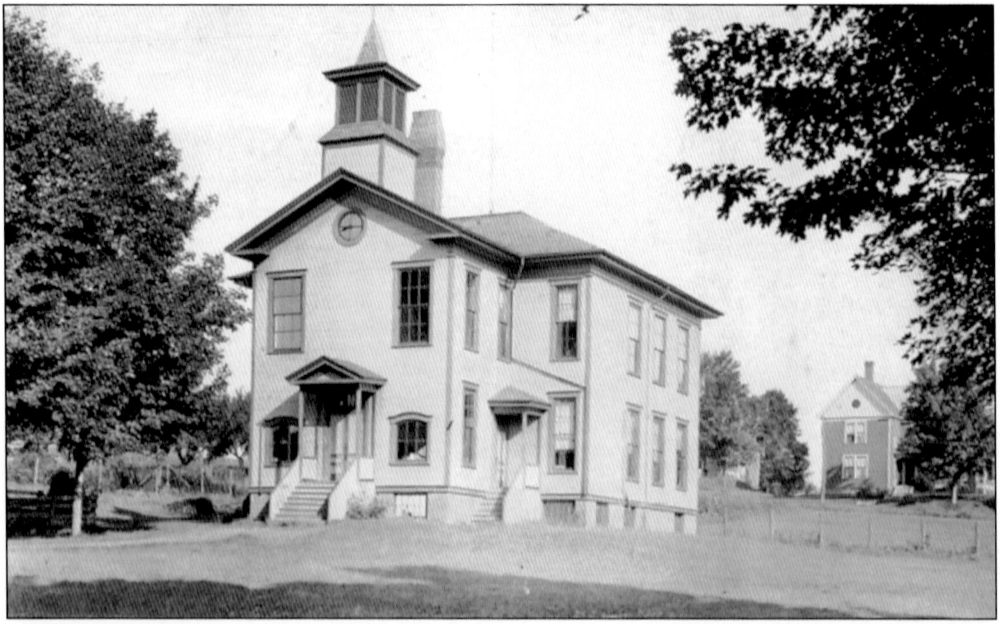

In 1890, the residents of Sangerville built a new high school on a large lot in town. This was quite a large school for a small town and was well appointed. The grade school students continued to attend the schoolhouse at the top of the hill on High Street until sometime in the 1920s, when the high school was enlarged to include the grade school and the two-room schoolhouse was sold and used as a private home. (Courtesy of Sangerville Historical Society.)

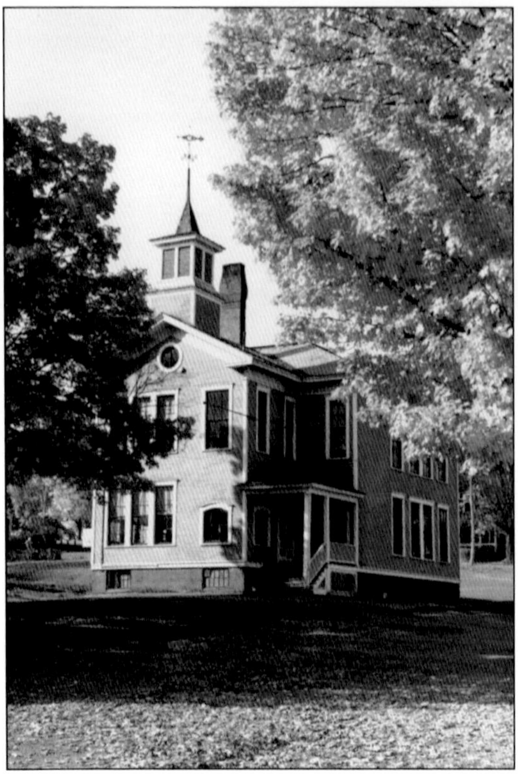

Sangerville's newly enlarged school contained both the high school and the grade school. The main entrance was moved from the front to the side of the building, and the space saved became the fourth-grade room. This was the only grade in a room by itself. (Courtesy of Sangerville Historical Society.)

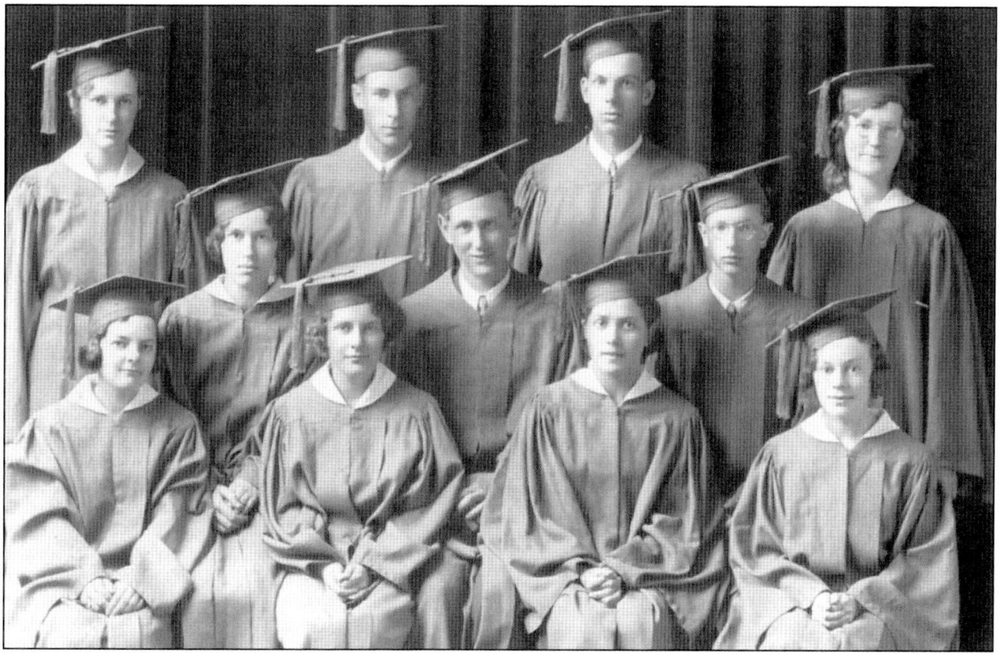

In 1932, Sangerville graduated 11 proud students. Shown here, from left to right, are (first row) Madeline Merrow, Bernice Pooler, Glenna Bragdon, and Marion Diffin; (second row) Hermia Campbell, Ralph Flanders, and Arthur Cleaves; (third row) Wilma Dexter, Ernest Mitchell, Donald Church, and Barbara Flanders. (Courtesy of Sangerville Historical Society.)

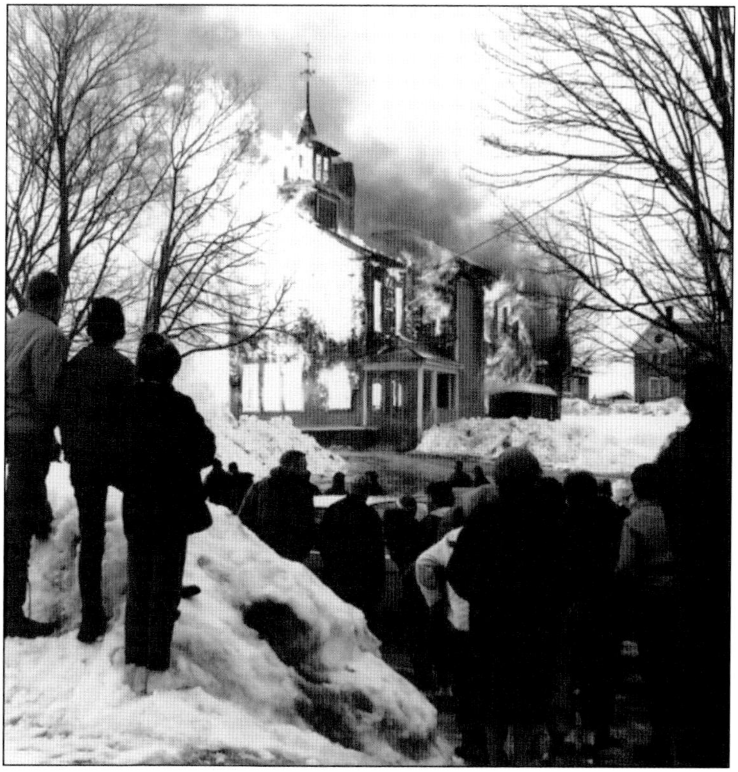

In 1969, the proud, old building in which hundreds of youngsters had been taught burned down. The suspected cause was arson by a juvenile. (Courtesy of Sangerville Historical Society.)

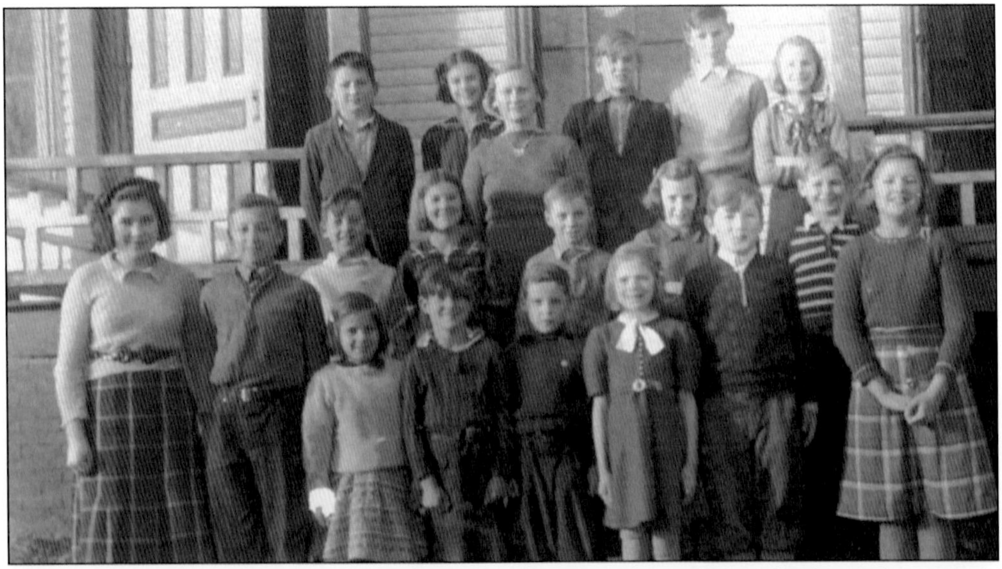

Up until the 1940s, the one-room schoolhouse with one teacher continued to be used in parts of Sangerville. Students at the East Sangerville School in 1938, from left to right, were (first row) Gladys Emerson, Merrill Burgess, Jeanette Richardson, Russell Moulton, David Lorrey, Arlene Knowlton, John Emerson, and Nora Emerson; (second row) Reynold Burgess, Dorothy Moulton, Harold Leland, Virginia Lorrey, and Frank Knowlton; (third row) Delmont Leland, Evelyn Moulton, teacher Marjorie Wilbur, Lester Moulton Jr., Russell Adams, and Louine Knowlton. (Courtesy of Sangerville Historical Society.)

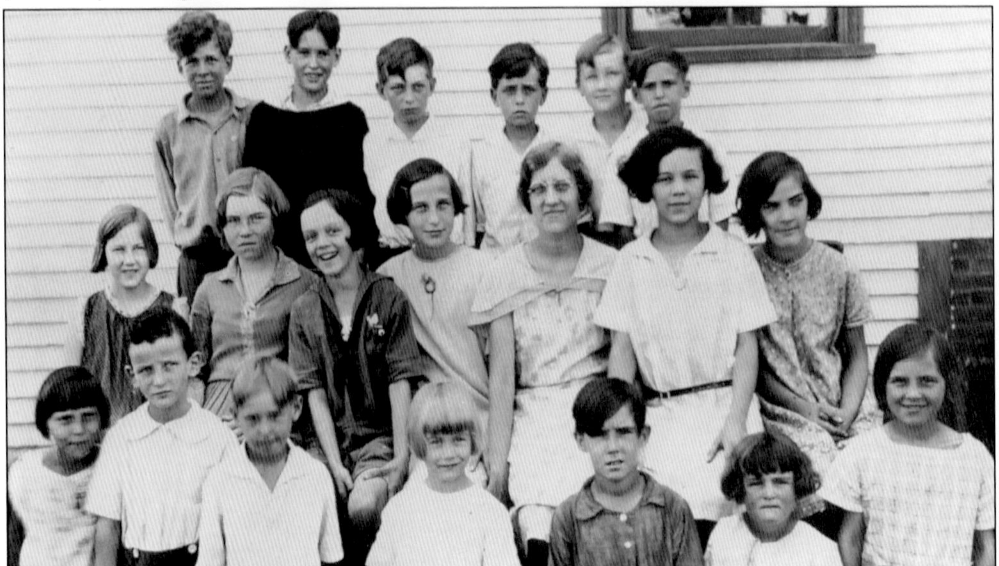

Pupils at the Sangerville Gilman's Corner School in 1930, from left to right, were (first row) Verona Reardon, Keith Parkman, Berl Reardon, Louise Grant, Carl Garland, Gertrude Moulton, and Opal Flewelling; (second row) Rebecca Grant, Glenys Flewelling, Muriel Starbird, Barbara Parkman, teacher Irene Bartlett, Ardelia Starbird, and Ruth Garland; (third row) Howard Flewelling, Paul Reardon, Lewis Gilman, Walter Gilman, Clarence Grant, and Dana Reardon. (Courtesy of Sangerville Historical Society.)

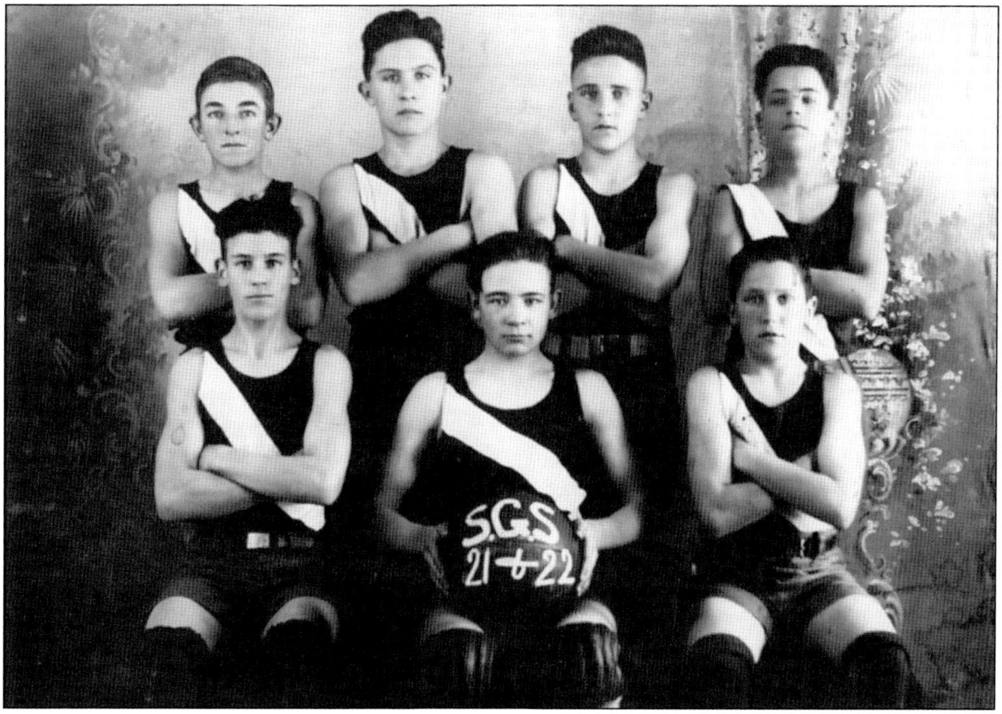

Because of the cold weather in Maine, basketball was the big sport in high schools, and almost every school had its own team. The Sangerville Grammar School team of 1922, from left to right, was (first row) Earl Humphrey, Orman Gray, and Orville Edes; (second row) George Pullyard, Ogden Carr, Milton Edes, and Gilbert Oulette. (Courtesy of Sangerville Historical Society.)

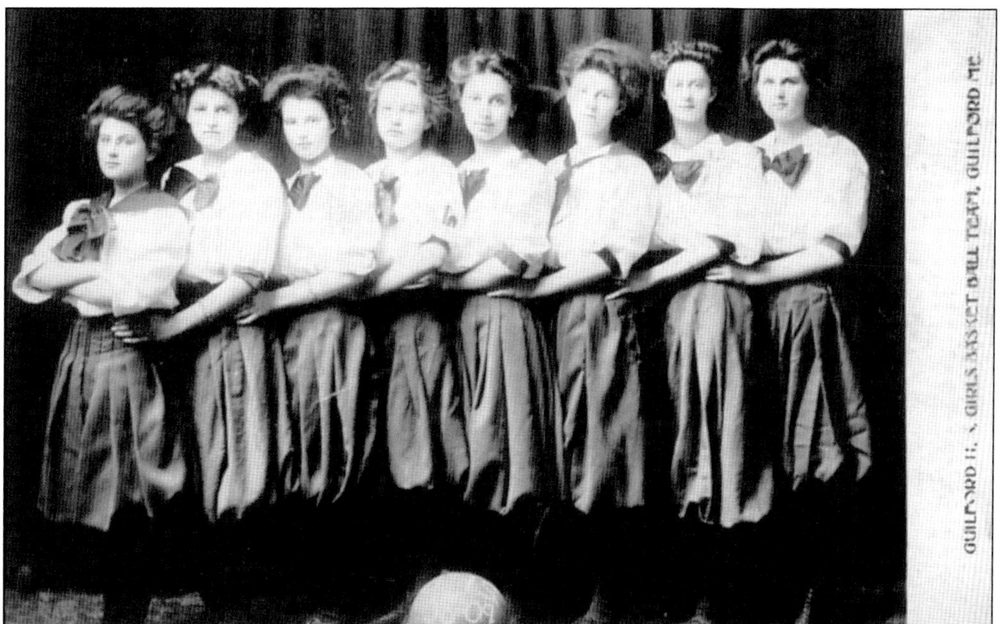

Pictured in 1909, the Guilford High School girls' basketball team included Nellie Davis, Avis Clark, Doris Merriot, Florence Appleyard, Helen Straw, Olive Harrington, and Vivian Cole.

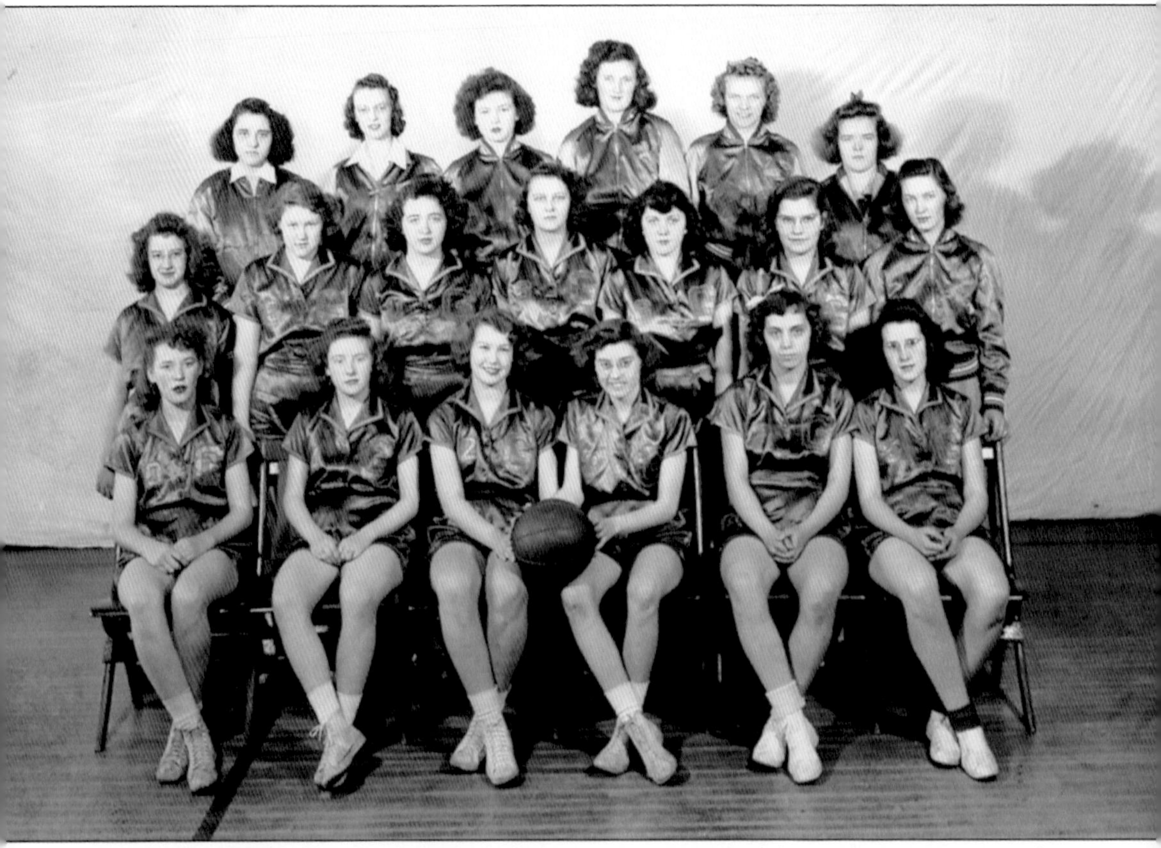

The Guilford High School girls' basketball team in 1943 was a little larger than in 1909. Members, from left to right, were (first row) Joan Lewis, Yvonne Michaud, Evelyn Andrews, Barbara Bickford, Joyce Prescott, and Beverly Crafts; (second row) Aylmer Crafts, Doris Cunningham, Alice Willey, Dorothy Lewis, Phyllis Brown, Harriett Mitchell, and coach Betty Meader; (third row) assistant manager Maxine Nesbit, manager Carolyn Crockett, Pauline Andrews, Irene Miner, Peggy Whiting, and Frances Cross.

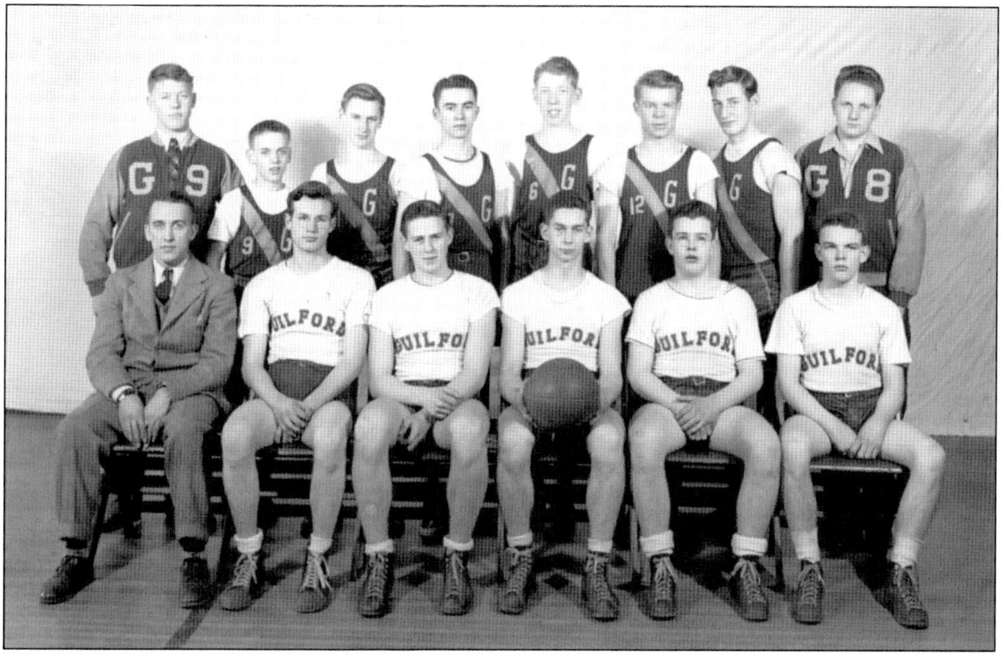

The 1943 Guilford High School boys' basketball team won the Piscataquis County championship. Pictured from left to right are (first row) coach Phil Clark, Mac Herring, Fred Blake, captain Tom Blake, Ruel Cross, and Hugo Cross; (second row) manager Donald Morin, Austin Dean, Dan Currie, Lawrence Jordan, John Leathers, Pete Gilman, Jimmy Brown, and Arthur Scales.

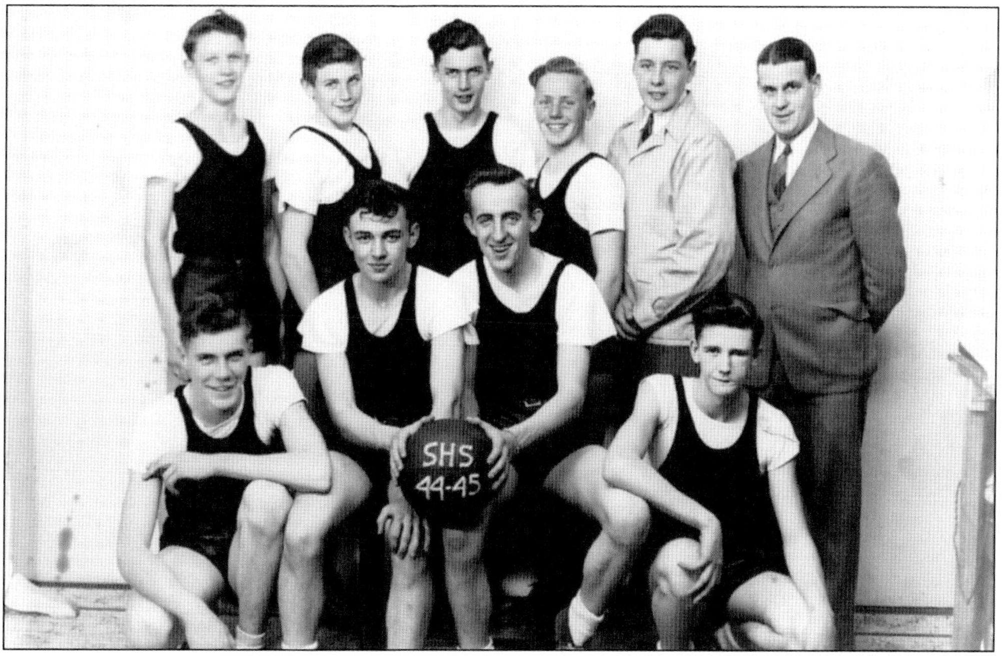

This is the 1943–1944 Sangerville High School basketball team. Pictured from left to right are (first row) Jack Crain, Robert Ronco, Earl Humphrey Jr., and Harlan Kimball; (second row) Ivan Higgins, Hollis Larrabee, unidentified, Donnie Hamilton, manager Herbert Crafts, and coach Earl Humphrey Sr. (Courtesy of Max Rollins.)

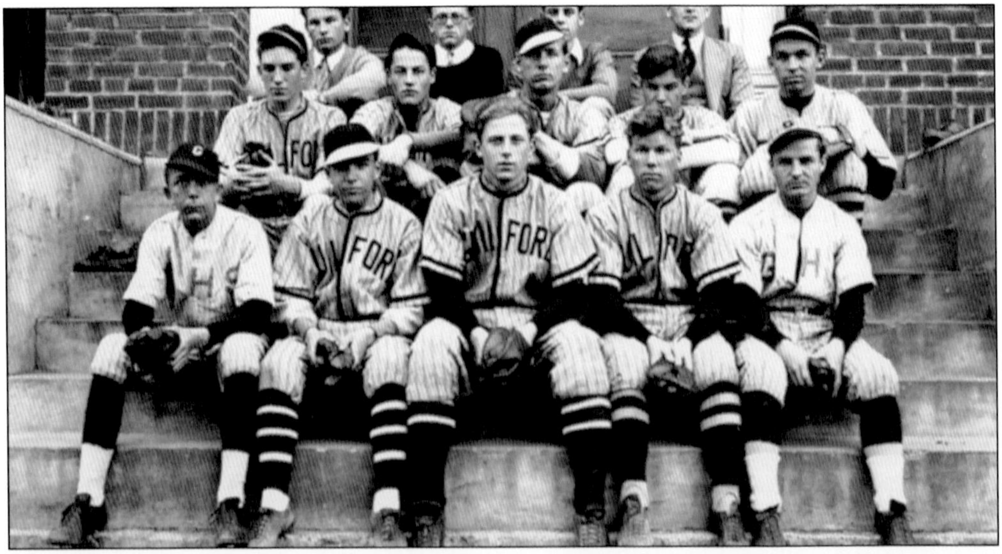

The 1932 Guilford High School baseball team included, from left to right, (first row) Frank Orff, Herbert Galusha, Orman Fortier, Maynard Ridley, and Merwin Bickford; (second row) Harry Houston, Halton Nesbit, Bert Page, Jack McEachern, and Carl McKusick; (third row) Lawrence Skillins, Paul Labree, John Masterman, and coach ? Hebert.

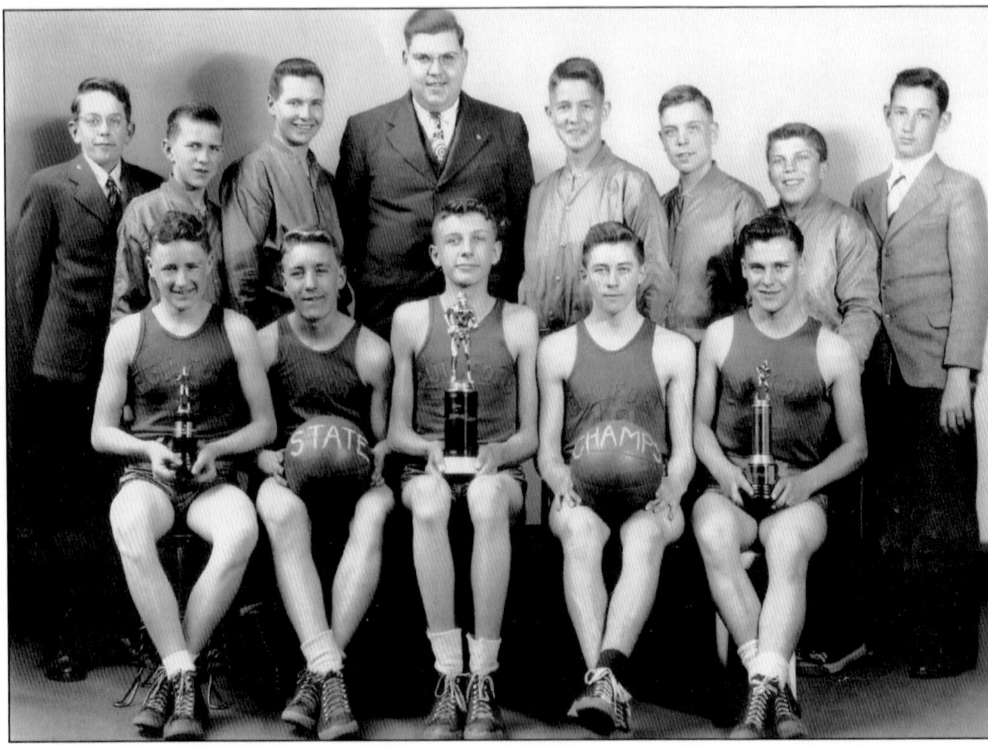

In 1948, the Guilford Grammar School boys' basketball team won the state championship. Pictured from left to right are (first row) Richard Cole, Mark Lovell, Donald Weston, Rodney Willey, and Clair Trafton; (second row) Duane Huff, Thomas Smart, Arnold Buzzell, coach Tim Mayo, Bernard Huff, Wayne Huff, Roger Morin, and manager Richard Skinner.

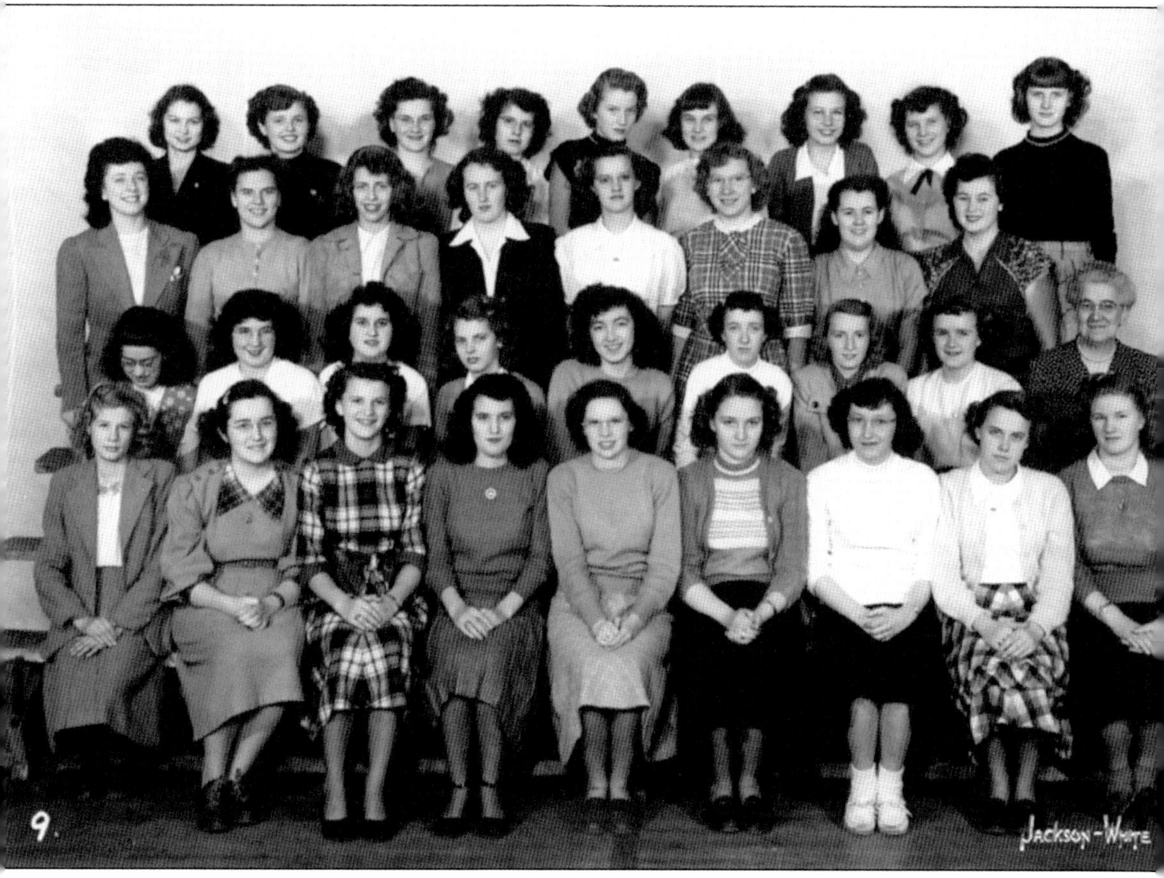

Here is the 1948 Guilford High School Glee Club. Pictured from left to right are (first row) Betty Beaver, Florence Kimball, Helen Morin, Jeannette Raymond, Mary Buzzell, Barbara Morse, Arlene Gilman, Elizabeth Knowles, and Bernice Bridge; (second row) Louise Ellis, Marilyn Leavitt, Mary Jane Leavitt, Ramona Ricker, Berle Getchell, Rita Foley, Evelyn Simmons, Norma Cole, and music teacher Florence Homer; (third row) Phyllis Libby, Anna Wyman, Freda Bishop, Jean Welts, Marilyn Harrington, Lillian Todd, Rita Garland, and Joyce Clark; (fourth row) Dorothy Hall, Wilma Hanscom, Kathryn Wilson, Marjorie Ladd, Barbara Bennett, Marion Foss, Janice Bridges, Carolyn Bridge, and Marilyn Bearce.

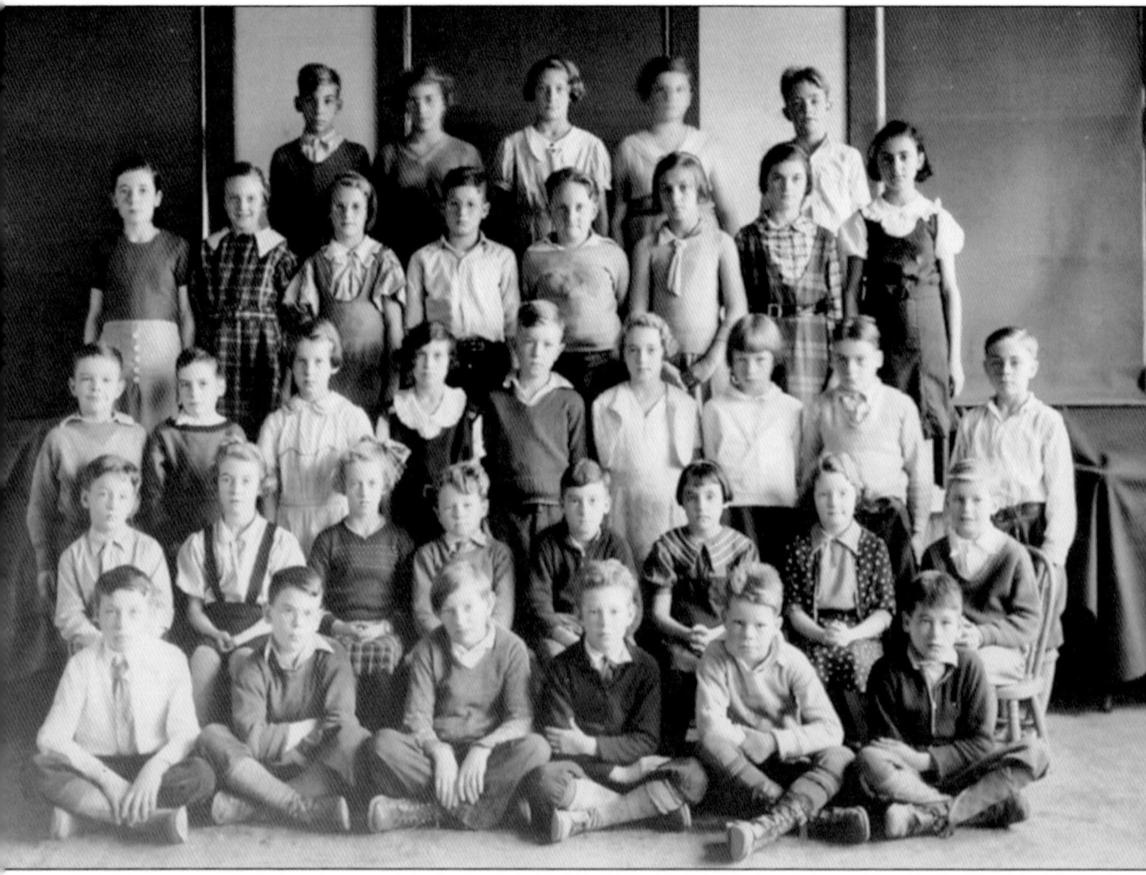

Guilford's 1936–1937 fourth-grade class consisted of 36 students, and the teacher was Agnes Hilton. Pictured from left to right are (first row) Lawrence Horton, Roy Fairbrother, Philip Stymiest, Robert Ames, Melvin Gilman, and Harrison Dean; (second row) Albert Dean, Lorraine Lewis, Elaine Dunton, George Rollins, David Dean, Maxine Nesbit, Yvonne Michaud, and Robert Bigger; (third row) Ruel Cross, Carroll Trafton, Eloise LaBree, unidentified, Derwood Perkins, Alice Willey, Martha Horton, Douglas Ellis, and Merle Michaud; (fourth row) Lillian Stymiest, Barbara Fox, Ethyl Priest, Malcolm Herring, Arthur Scales, Joyce Prescott, Maxine Doucette, and Joyce Woodbury; (fifth row) Harold Currier, Alice Priest, Louise Brawn, Thelma Sanborn, and Nelson Cunningham.

Five

LOOKING AROUND THE TOWNS

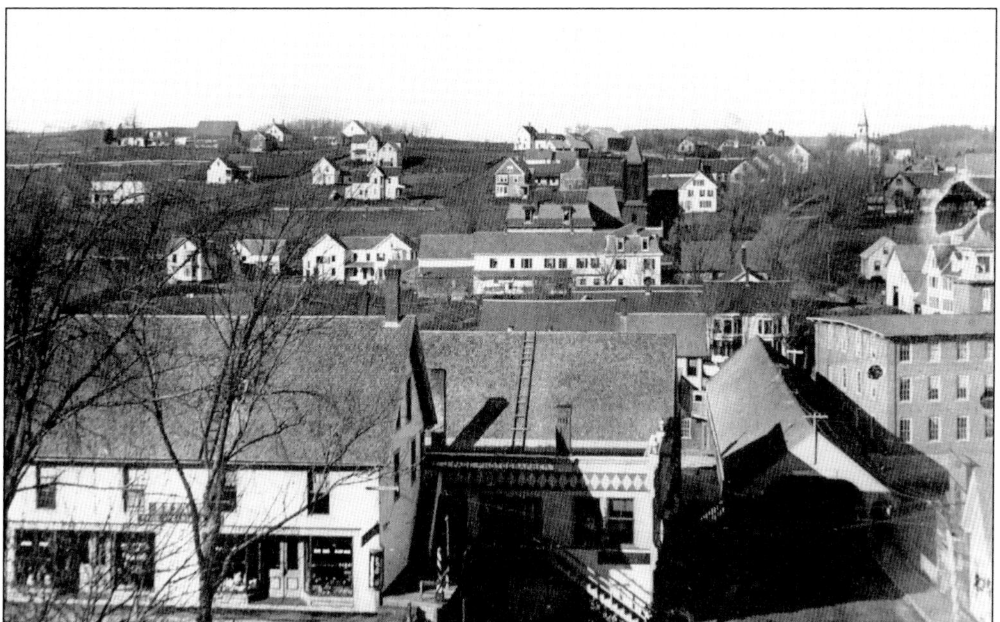

This picture of downtown Guilford was taken from the top window of the Masonic hall. At the top right, the Guilford Free Meeting House, built in 1834 by the Methodists and Universalists, can be seen. It is the current site of the First Pentecostal church. In the center is Otis Martin's former home, which was last used as the Red Maple Inn and is currently under renovation. Just above the peak of the covered bridge is a house that was once the home of M. L. Hussey and later the Elliott family. The roof of the town hall is just above the Martin house, and beyond that is the Universalist church.

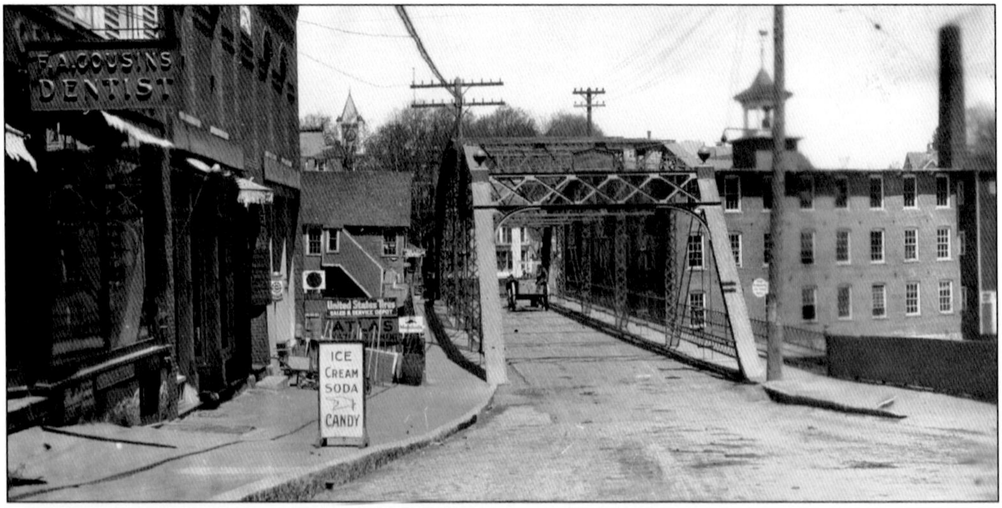

Looking down South Main Street to the bridge in 1925, one can see the Dr. F. A. Cousins dental office and Genthner's drugstore to the left and then the Scales block. Inside the bridge at the far end, a wagon has apparently broken down and the horses have been taken away.

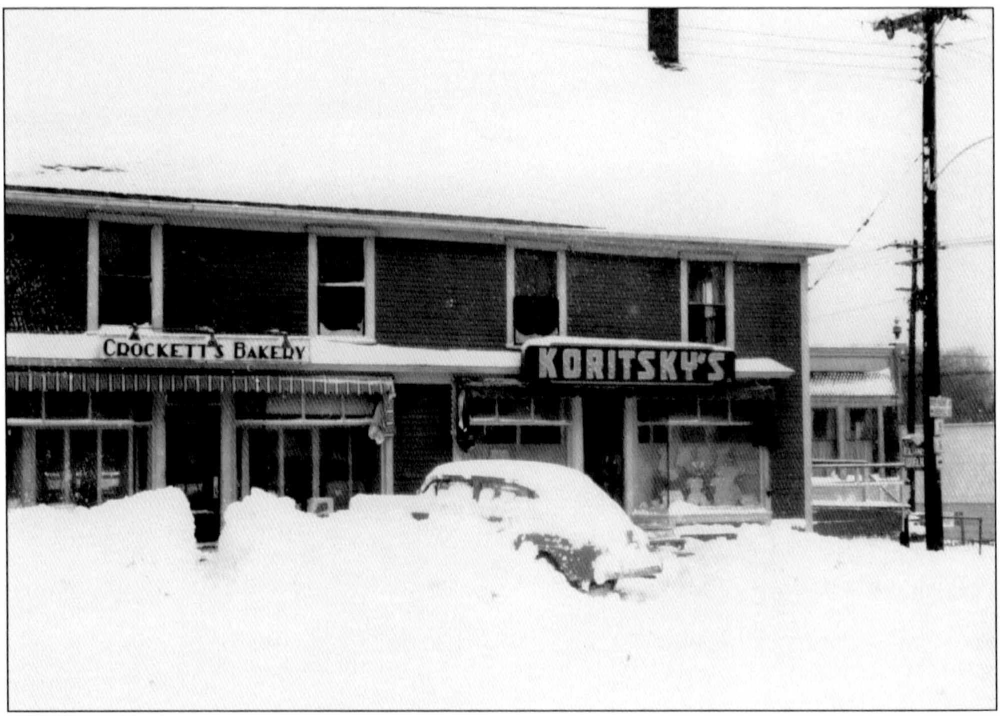

In this photograph of Guilford from 1959, Crockett's Bakery and Koritsky's department store seem to have more snow than they really need.

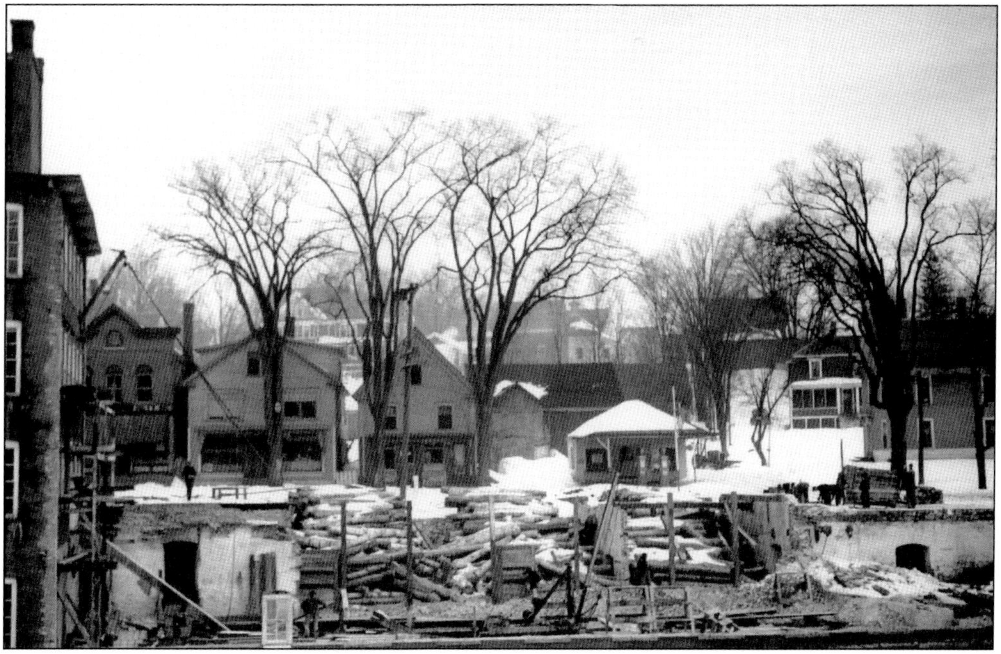

From the south side of the river looking north in the 1940s, one can see the end of Draper's Mill and yard prior to building a new plant two miles east of town. Across the street is the T and K store, Dan Poole's Bakery, Mom's Restaurant, and Eddie Bennett's filling station and taxi stand.

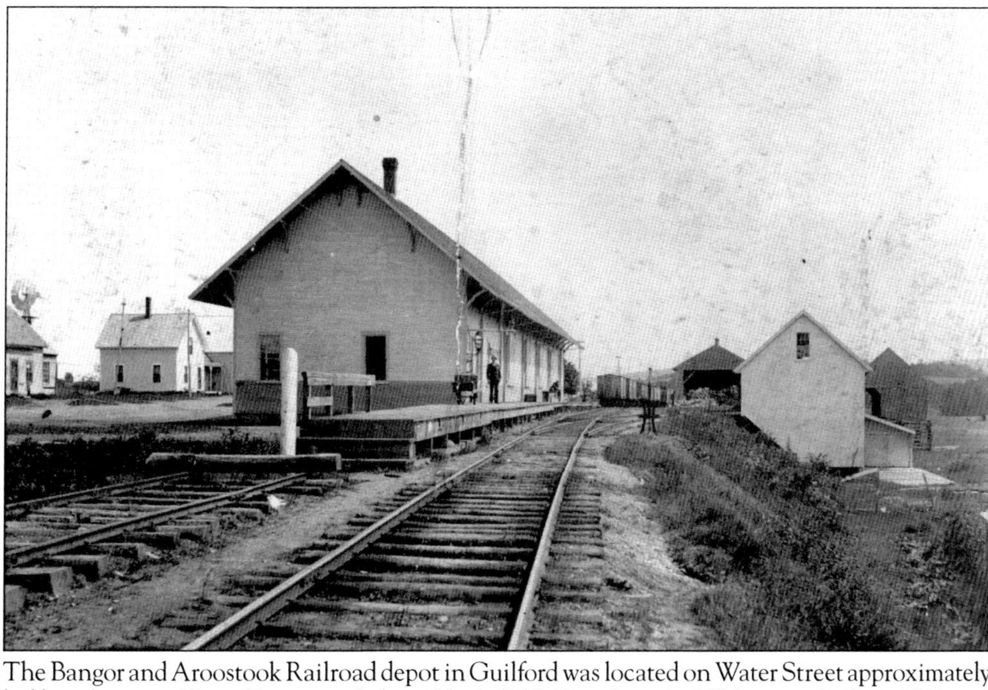

The Bangor and Aroostook Railroad depot in Guilford was located on Water Street approximately halfway between Tony Corner and the athletic field. Seen here in 1896, it was built in 1871 and razed in the fall of 1983.

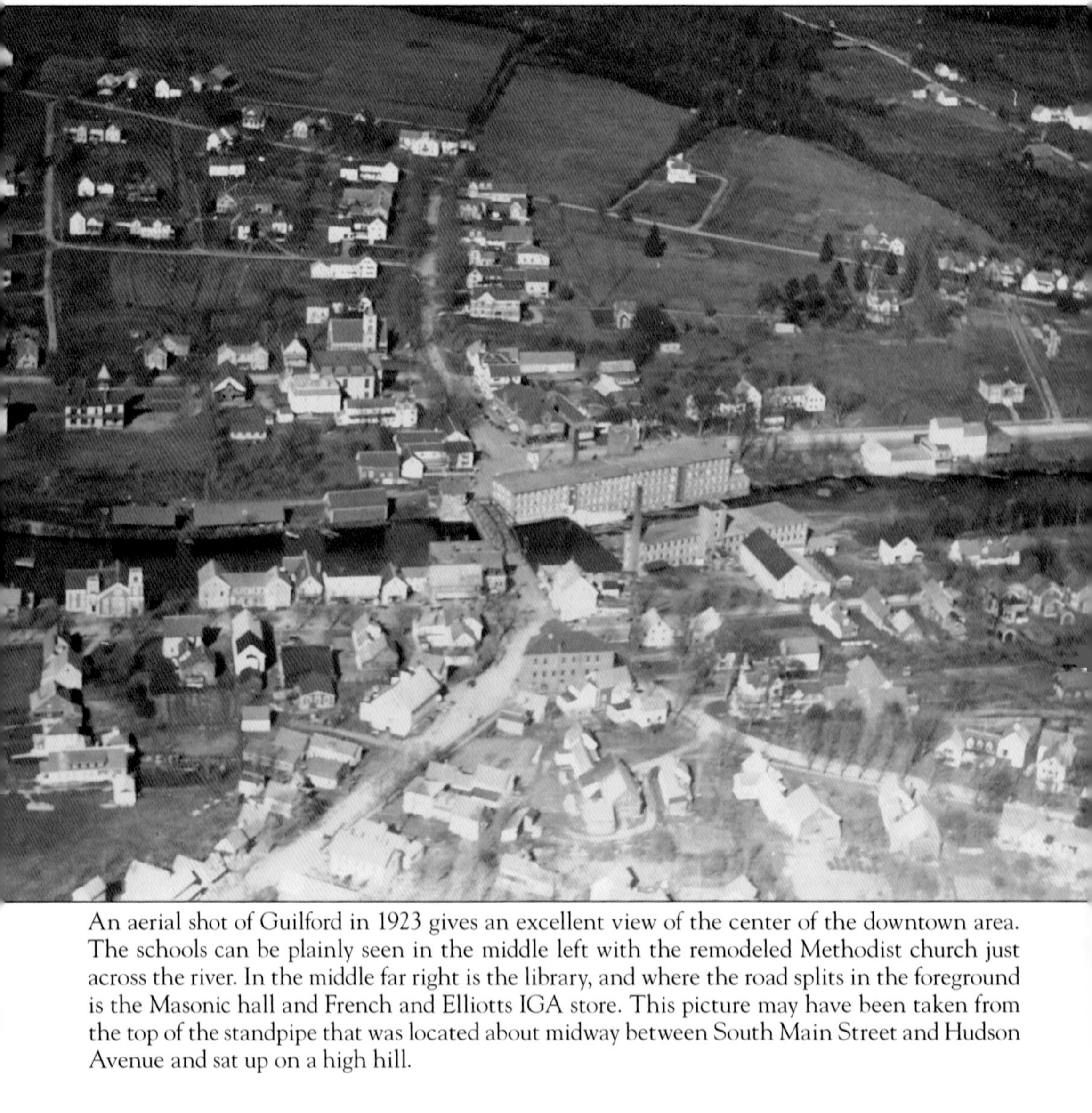

An aerial shot of Guilford in 1923 gives an excellent view of the center of the downtown area. The schools can be plainly seen in the middle left with the remodeled Methodist church just across the river. In the middle far right is the library, and where the road splits in the foreground is the Masonic hall and French and Elliotts IGA store. This picture may have been taken from the top of the standpipe that was located about midway between South Main Street and Hudson Avenue and sat up on a high hill.

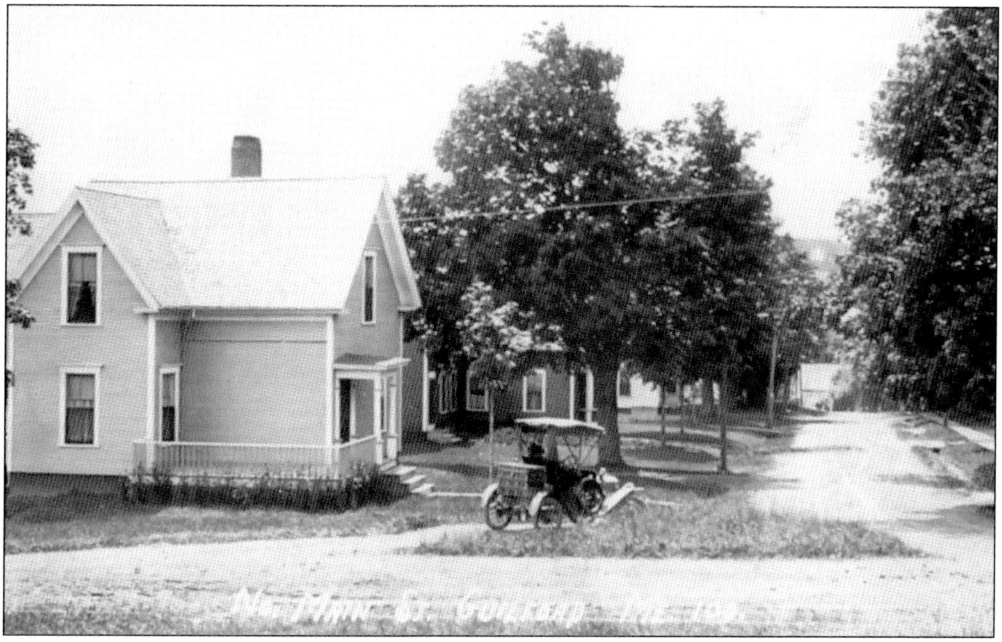

The corner of High and North Main Streets in Guilford looks much different today, although the house on the corner is still standing and was occupied by the Simmons family for many years. The driver headed down the hill seems more interested in the photographer than where he is going.

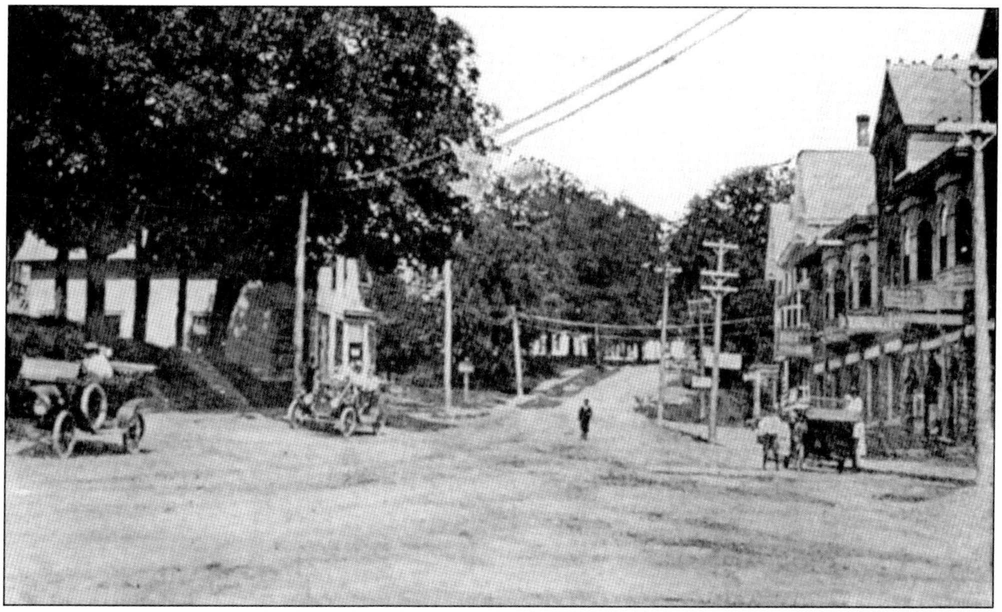

In 1915, traffic in Guilford was not a problem, even on North Main Street, and it was usually safe to walk down the middle of the road if one chose to do so. Parking spaces were plentiful, so no one had to ride around looking for a spot.

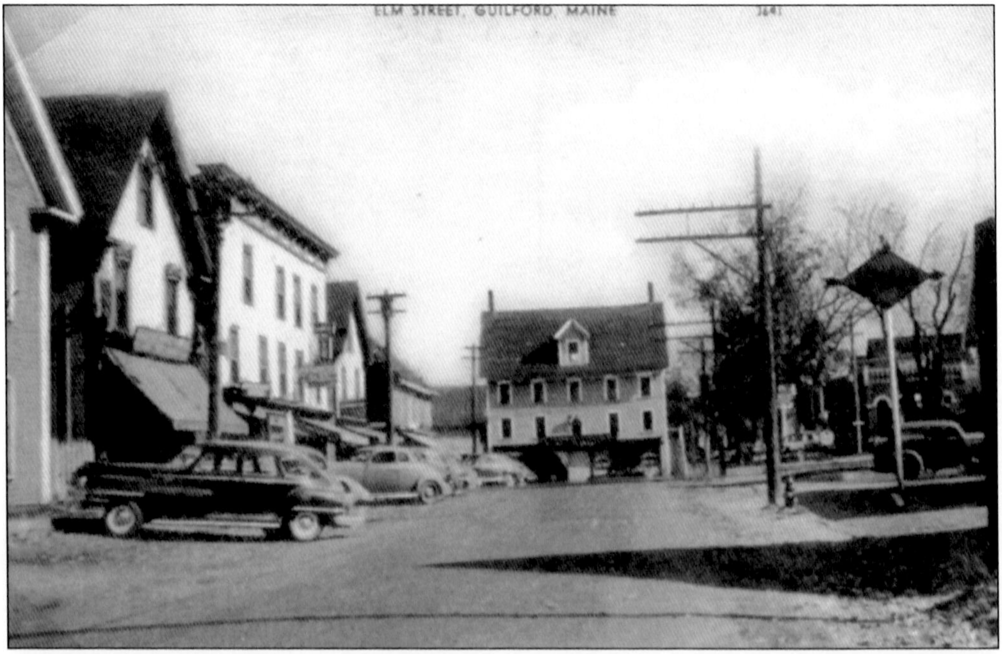

Looking east on Elm Street in the early 1940s, to the left one could see the Guilford Variety Store with the awning, the A&P store, the Gold Nugget Restaurant, and the First National store. Across Main Street was the Guilford Register building and the Guilford Trust Company.

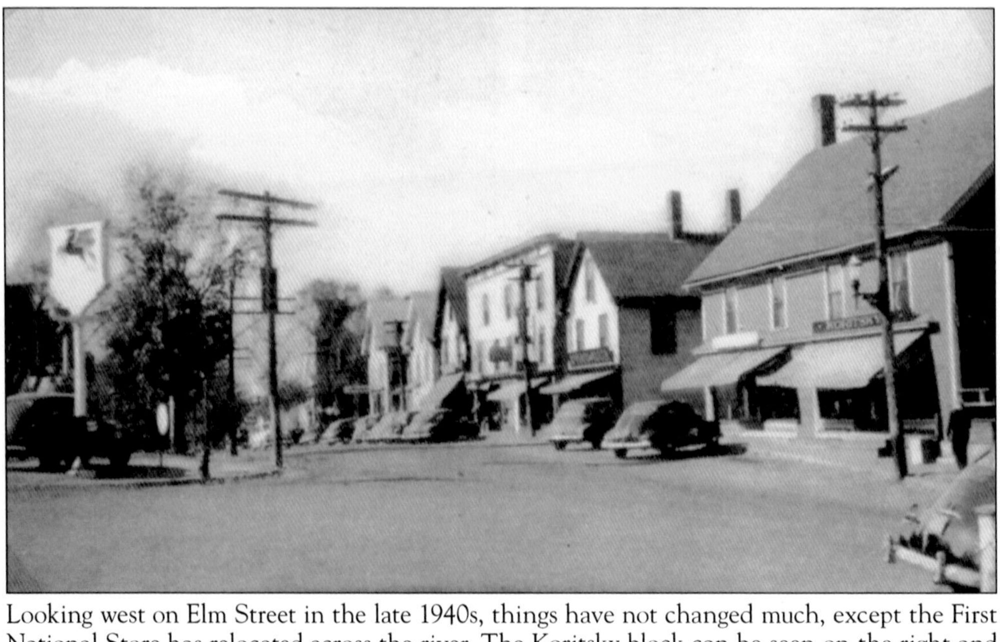

Looking west on Elm Street in the late 1940s, things have not changed much, except the First National Store has relocated across the river. The Koritsky block can be seen on the right and the Socony station to the left.

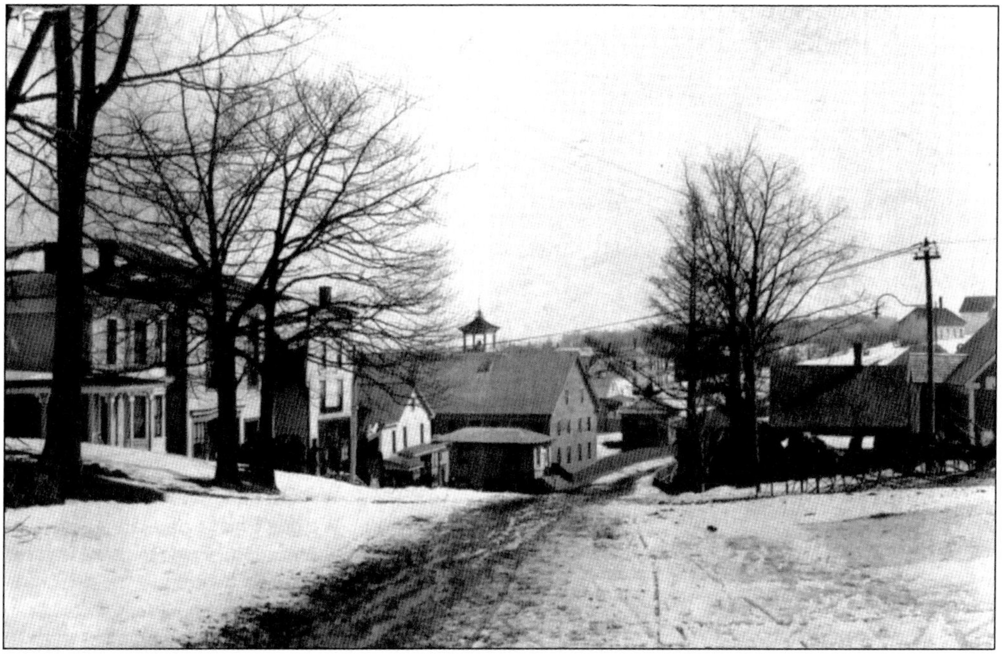

In 1905, one could look down Hotel Hill onto the robust little community of Sangerville. On the left is a stately home followed by the movie theater (now the Masonic hall), the Stott store (now the Legion hall), Sanders store, and the Carleton Mill complex. On the right are the livery stables for the hotel, and at the top of the hill is the village schoolhouse. Quite a few people are lined up at the entrance to the theater. (Author's collection.)

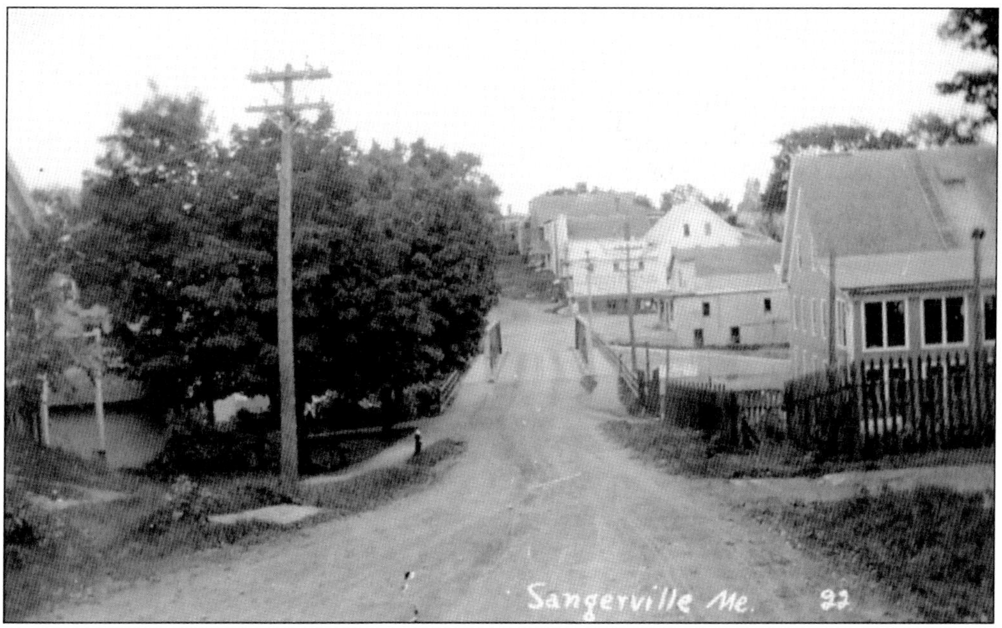

In this summertime view from the east side of town the steel bridge and the IGA store can be seen. The part of the mill complex on the west bank of the river seen in the previous shot is gone. This photograph was probably taken in the early 1930s. (Courtesy of Sangerville Historical Society.)

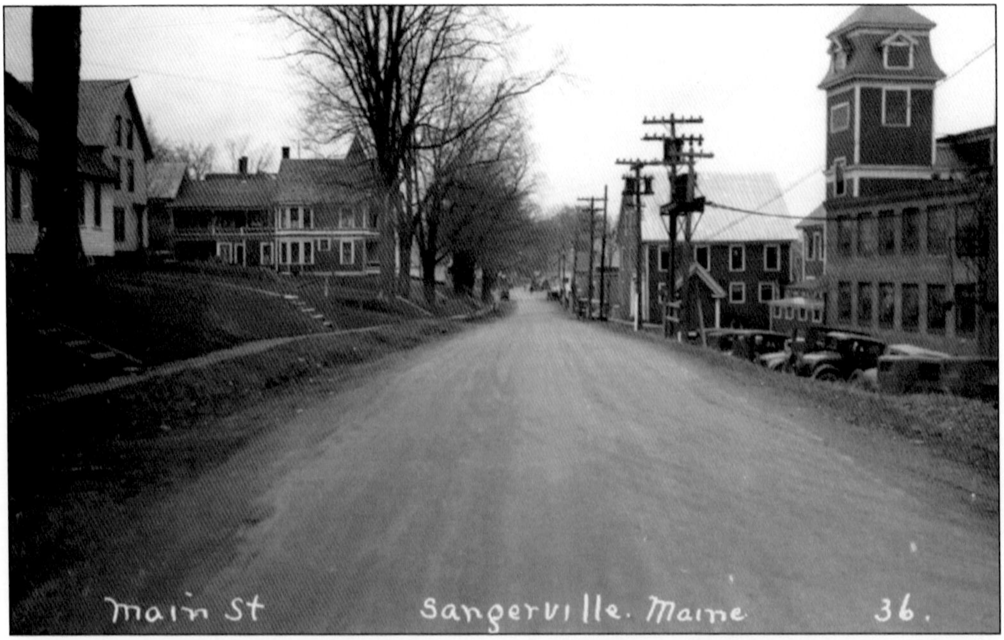

In 1930, South Main Street in Sangerville was a model of well-ordered neatness. The sidewalks and the road were kept in good repair, as were the steps and driveways leading to the different homes. Alden Sanders's large, three-story home with the turret was one of the nicest homes in town and boasted a large loft on the third floor. The Sangerville Woolen Company mill was always kept neat and tidy and in good repair. (Author's collection.)

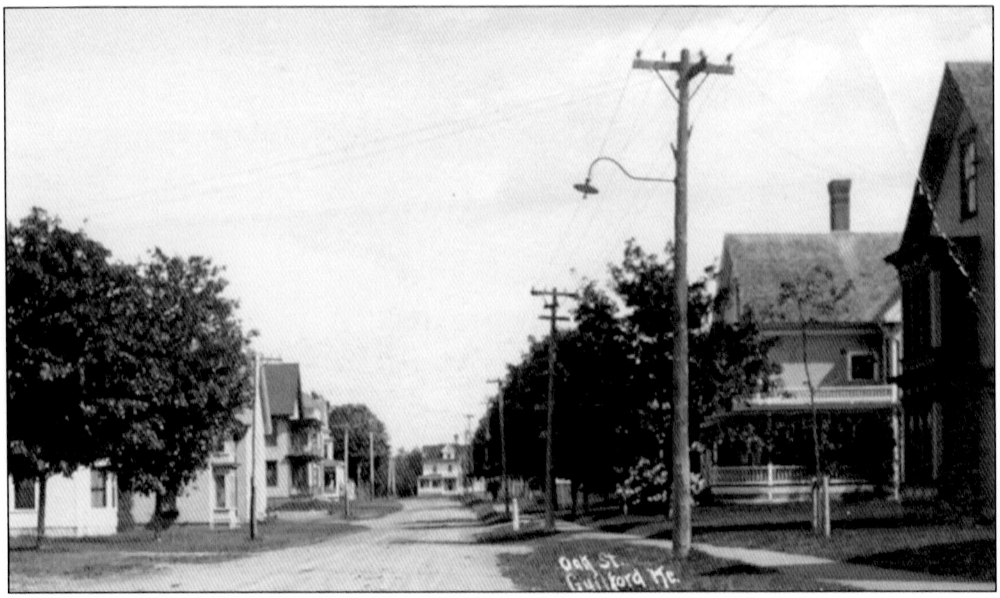

In the first half of the 20th century, Oak Street in Guilford contained most of the homes of the well-to-do. In 1921, the mansion at the end of the street was purchased by Louise Chase of Dover-Foxcroft and converted into a fine hospital. The hospital stayed in business for roughly 20 years and then became the home and office of Dr. George Howard.

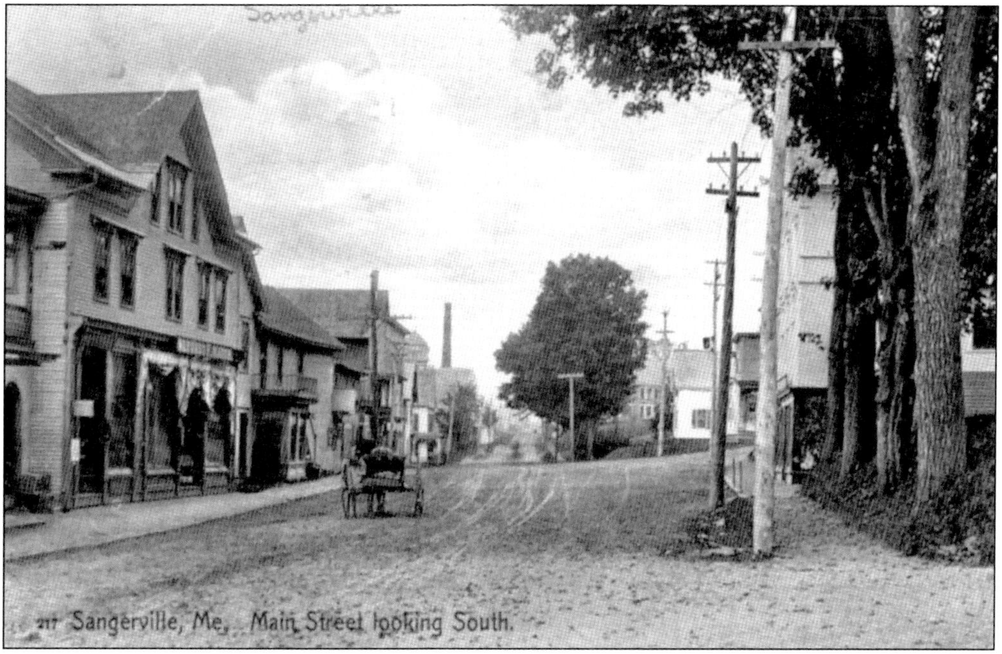

Here are two scenes of Main Street in Sangerville from 1904. The above photograph shows the intersection looking south from about 200 yards north. The first building on the left was a drugstore that is still standing. All else is gone, with the exception of the one house far down on the left and the house across from it on the right. The photograph below shows the intersection looking north from about 200 yards south. Everything shown in this photograph is now gone. (Courtesy of Sangerville Historical Society.)

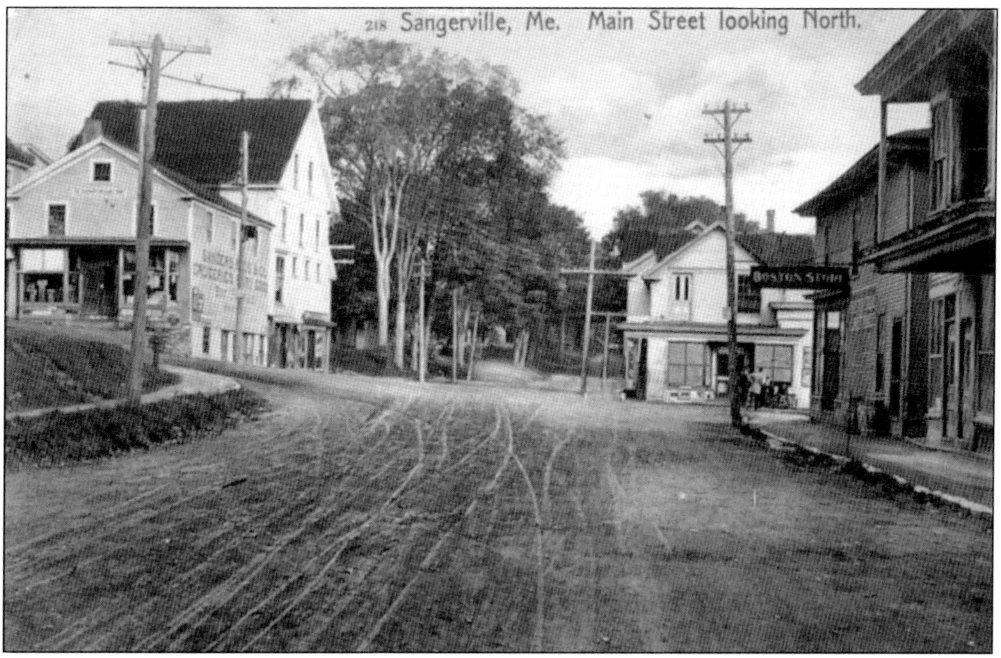

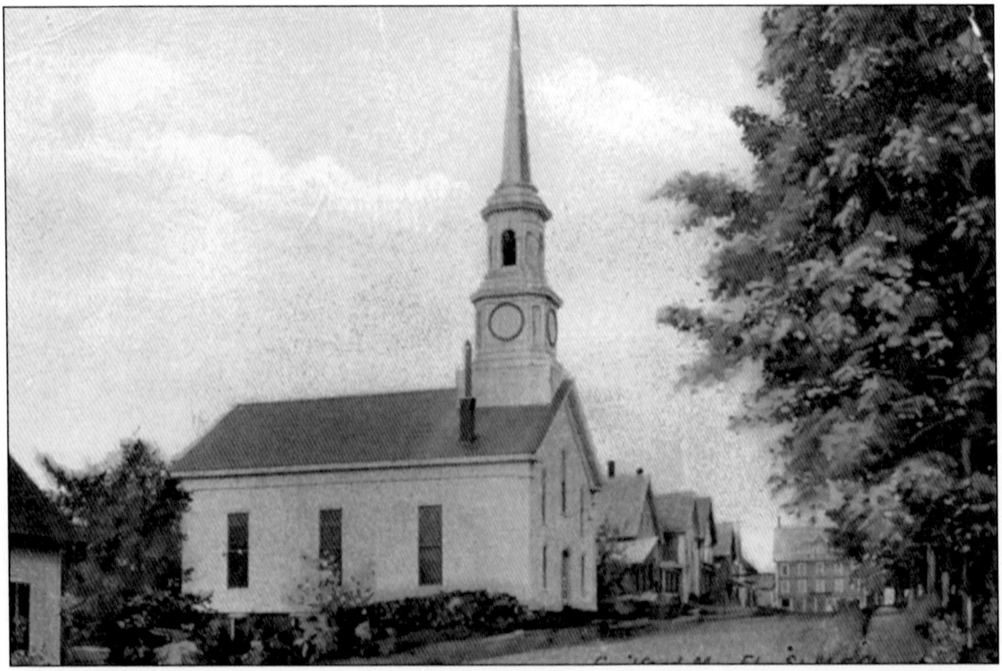

Here are two scenes of Elm Street in Guilford in the early 1900s. In the above photograph, looking east, is the Elm Street Methodist church on the left and the Guilford Register building at the far end, which is on the other side of Main Street. The photograph below was taken from Main Street looking west. The first building on the right burned in 1969 and, with the exception of the church, the others remain to this day and still house businesses.

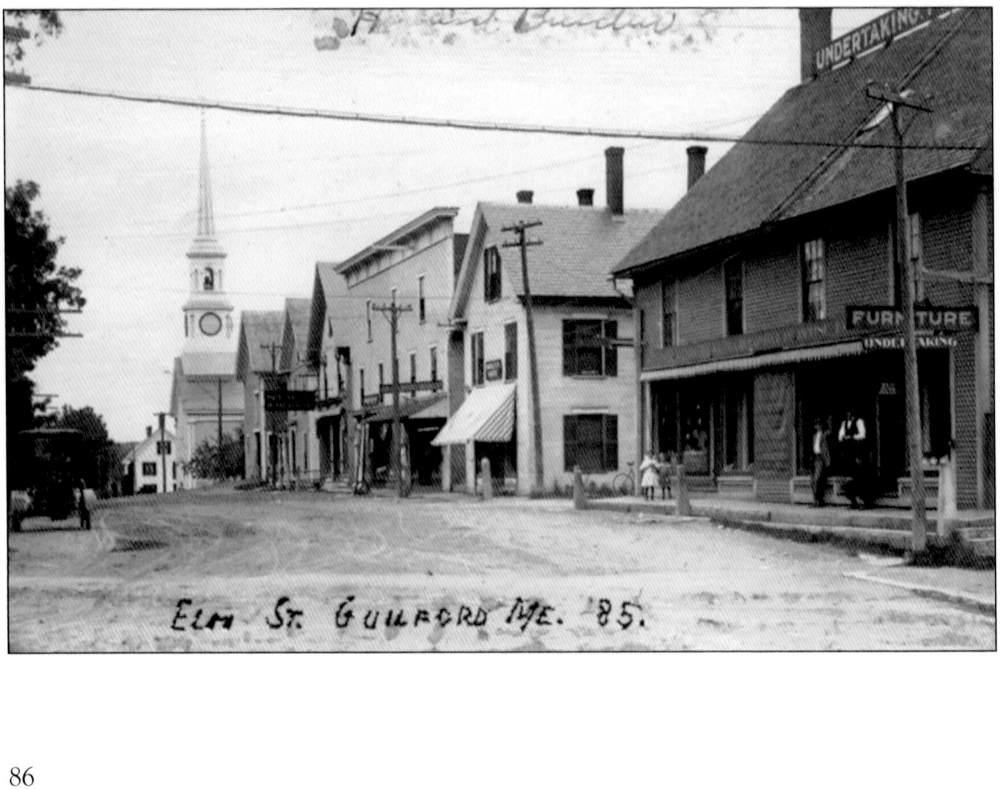

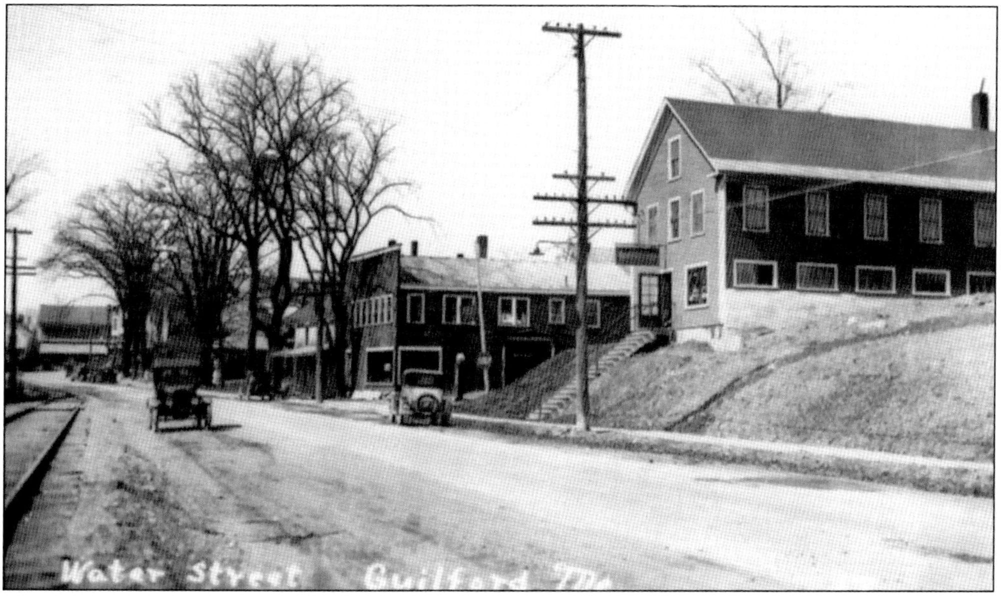

In Guilford, looking up Water Street toward town around 1930, one can see the railroad tracks on the left and Maurice Holbrook's Bowling Alleys and Pool Hall and Willis Bennett's Garage on the right. At the far end of the street stood Douglass store (with the awning). Looking the other way and a little farther down, one can see the Preble Farm during the 1936 flood. The Gray Gable Tea House, which was operated by Elsie Preble, was mostly destroyed. The house still exists, and the Guilford Hardware store currently occupies part of the site.

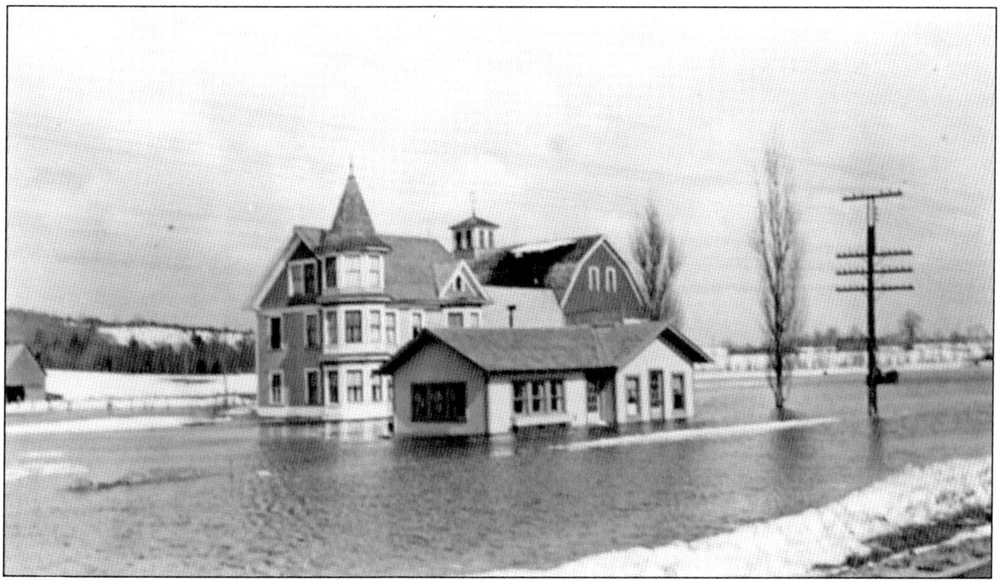

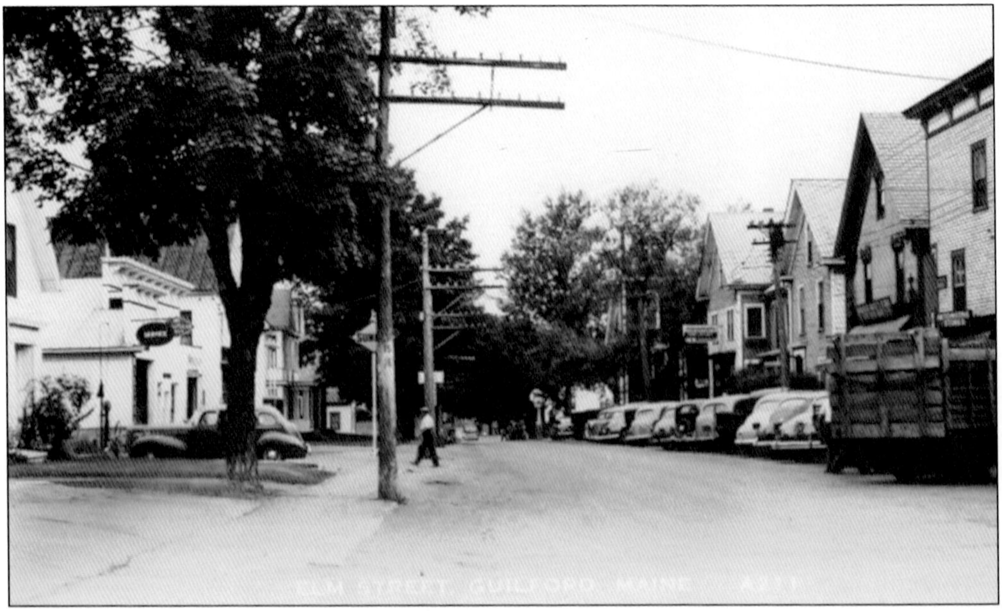

A few changes have taken place on Elm Street in the late 1940s. The former Huntington's Garage on the left is now a Sunoco station, and on the right an automotive store occupies the site of the former A&P store. Far down on the right a Tydol station can be seen.

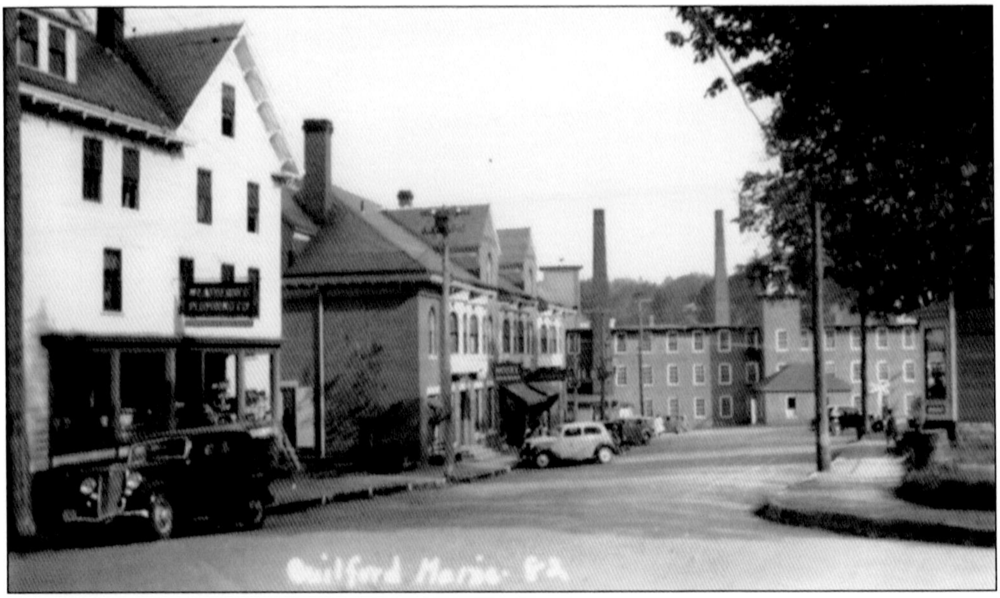

Looking south on North Main Street in Guilford in the late 1930s, one can see that Weatherbee's Plumbing and Heating occupies the ground floor of the former Turner House, with the upper floors being used as an annex to the Braeburn Hotel. On the ground floor of the Braeburn is Jackson's Clothing store, the Rexall drugstore, and the U.S. post office.

This photograph of Main Street in Sangerville, looking north through the town square, was taken in the early 1900s. Sander's store is on the left, and the Boston store is on the right. It is not known what was sold there. Beyond there is the building that later became the IGA store. (Courtesy of Sangerville Historical Society.)

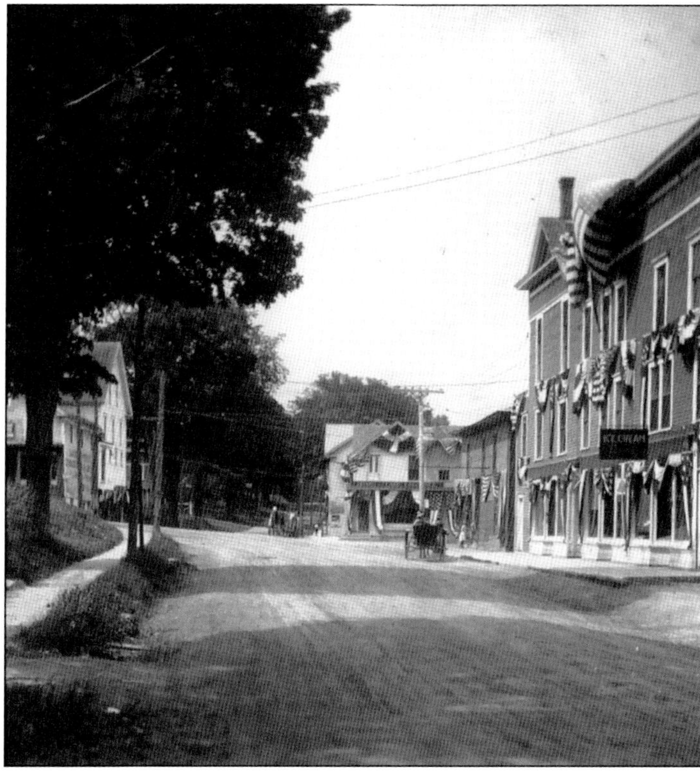

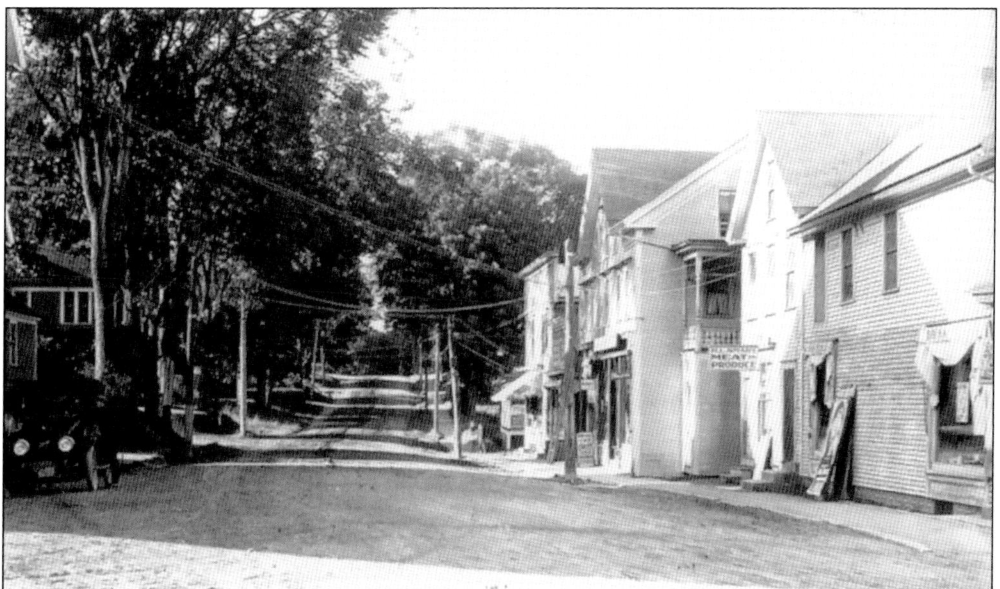

North Main Street in Sangerville was typical of small-town America in the early 1920s. The streets were still unpaved but well kept with neat sidewalks. On the east side of the street was W. A. Hill's grocery store, Bert Smart's meat market, the Sangerville drugstore, a barbershop, and Drake and Carr Groceries, which was later converted to a tenement house and then a restaurant that is now closed. (Author's collection.)

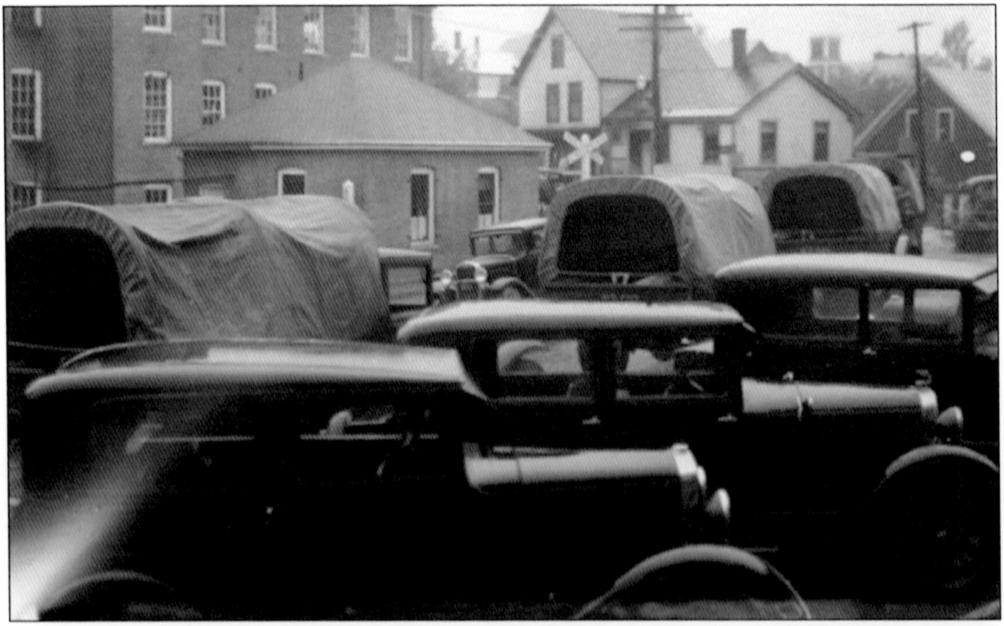

In September 1934, union organizers from out of town were attempting to sign up local members and were involved in picketing activities against the woolen mills. The county sheriff and the local constabulary, fearing that violence might break out, decided to call in the National Guard to maintain order. A convoy of trucks arrived from Pittsfield on September 17, and armed troops were deployed along the railroad tracks between the picketers and the mill. The local populace was somewhat amused but also highly resentful of the interference of outsiders in the town. In the end, only one worker joined in the so-called strike.

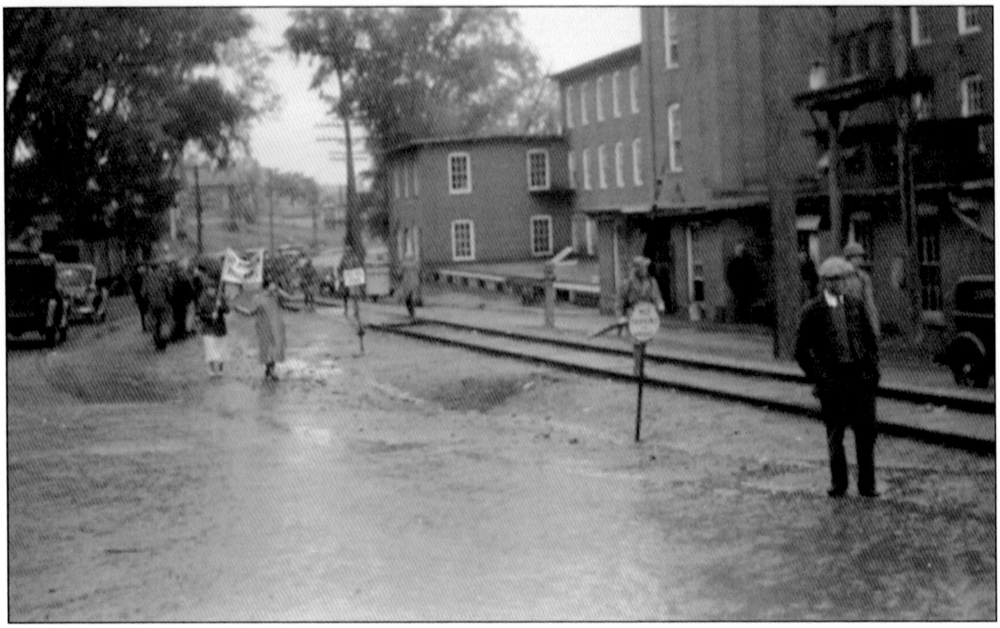

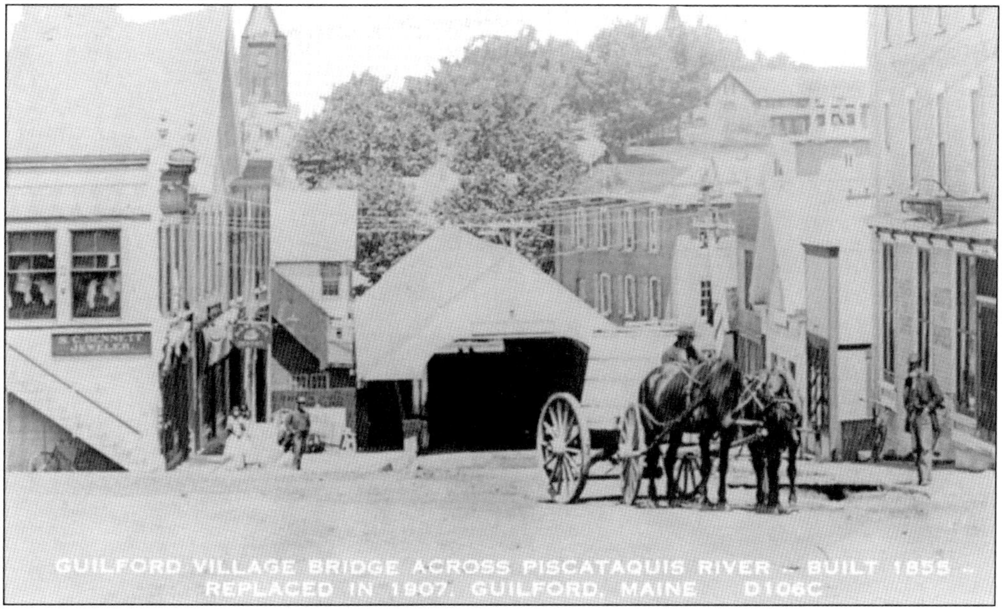

Even before the advent of the automobile, South Main Street in Guilford was usually a busy spot. Several pedestrians can be seen to the left in the late 1800s. In addition to the horse and wagon seen in the foreground, another one can be spotted inside the bridge.

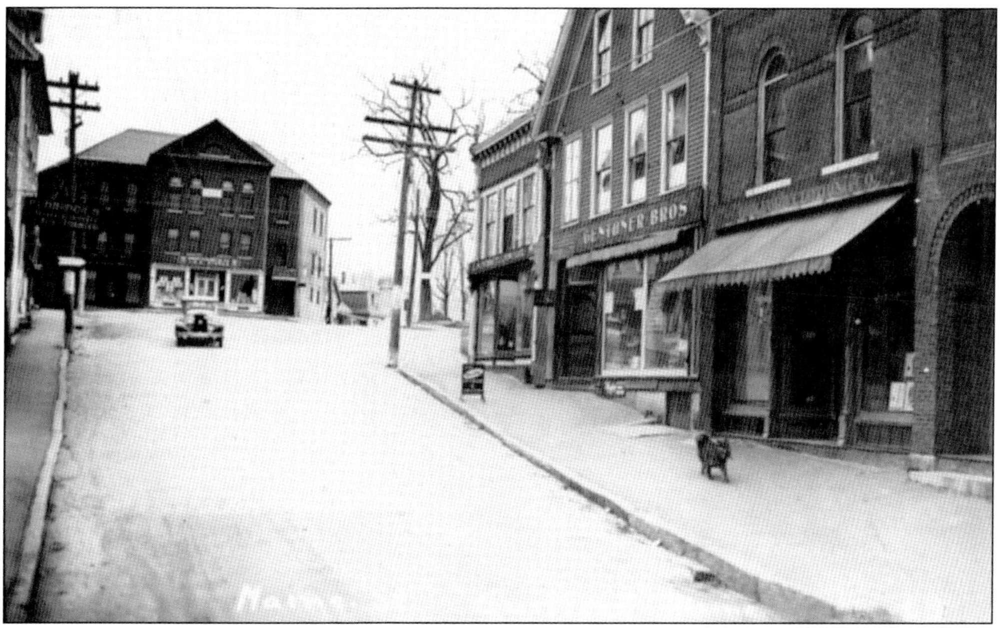

During World War II, not many automobiles were seen on the streets because of gasoline rationing and lack of tires and tubes. Also no new cars were being manufactured as all plants were being used for the war effort. Looking south up the hill in Guilford from the bridge, only one car can be seen.

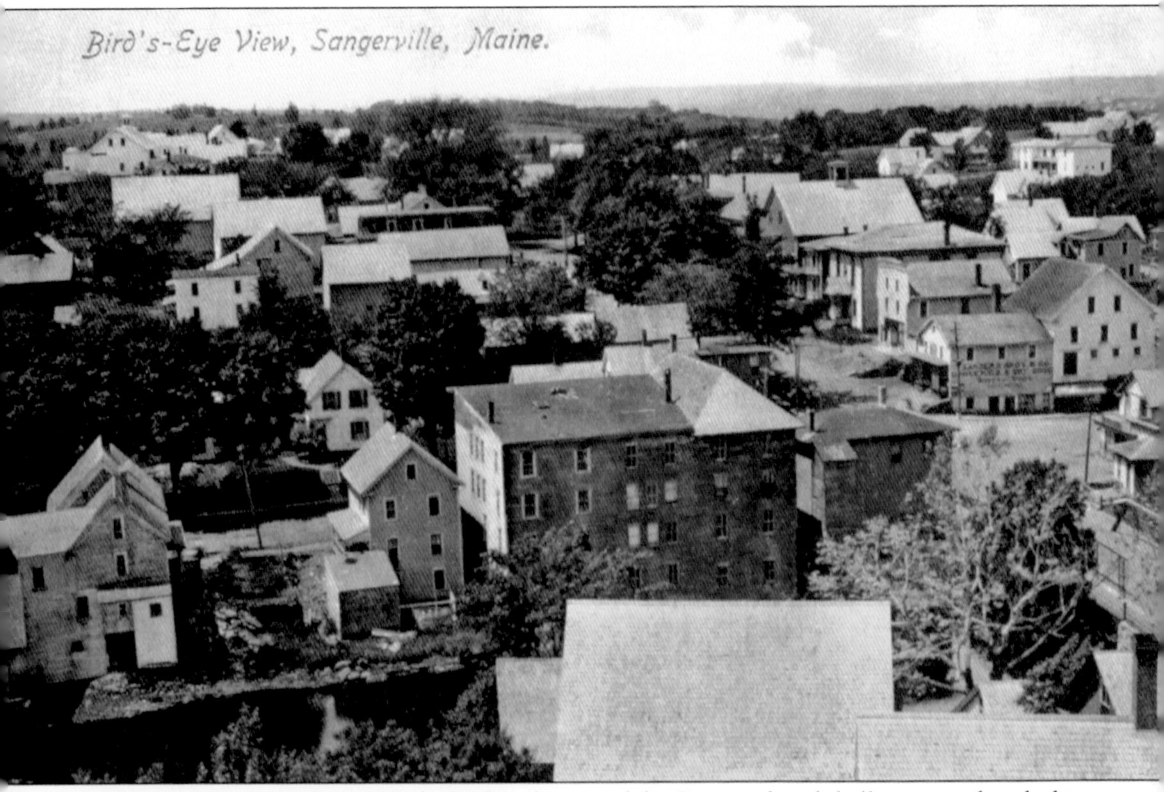

Around 1910, an intrepid soul climbed to the top of the Baptist church bell tower and took this bird's-eye view of Sangerville looking west. It provides an excellent view of the town square. The large building in the center foreground is the Carr building, and to the right of it is the Boston store. At some time in the 1930s, Howard Greene had a small grocery business in the store to the left, but it is unknown when he started there. The bridge to the right crosses Carleton Stream and is the start of Douty Hill Road. In the far right corner is the W. A. Hill store, later the IGA store. Across the street is Sanders store, and located up the hill is Stott's Dry Goods store followed by the movie theater. The mansard roof seen around the middle is the Sangerville Hotel. The vacant space in the foreground across the river is where Harold Buzzell built his garage and his grocery store. The backs of several buildings have jut-outs built on them. These were the bathroom facilities of the times that allowed waste to go directly into the river. Needless to say, swimming was not done downstream. (Courtesy of Sangerville Historical Society.)

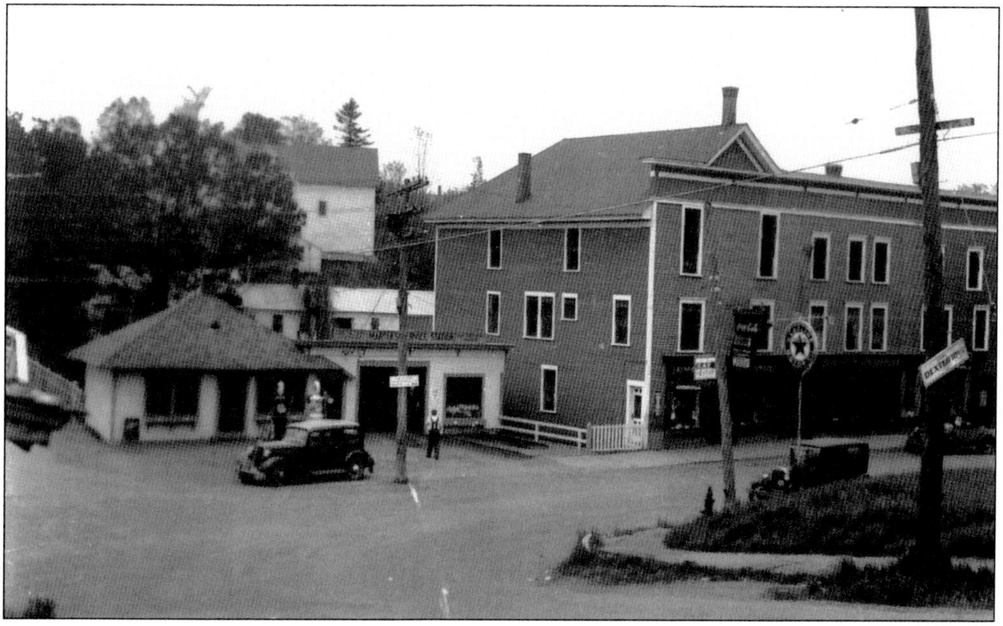

As one came down Hotel Hill in Sangerville in the 1930s, Morris Martin's garage and filling station came into view on the southeast corner of the block, located where the Boston store had previously been. Rather unique was the outdoor grease pit on the side of the lot. At the far end of the Carr building, Deckerhoff's Beer Saloon had replaced Les Seabury's candy store, and beyond that Harold Buzzell had opened a filling station and garage. (Author's collection.)

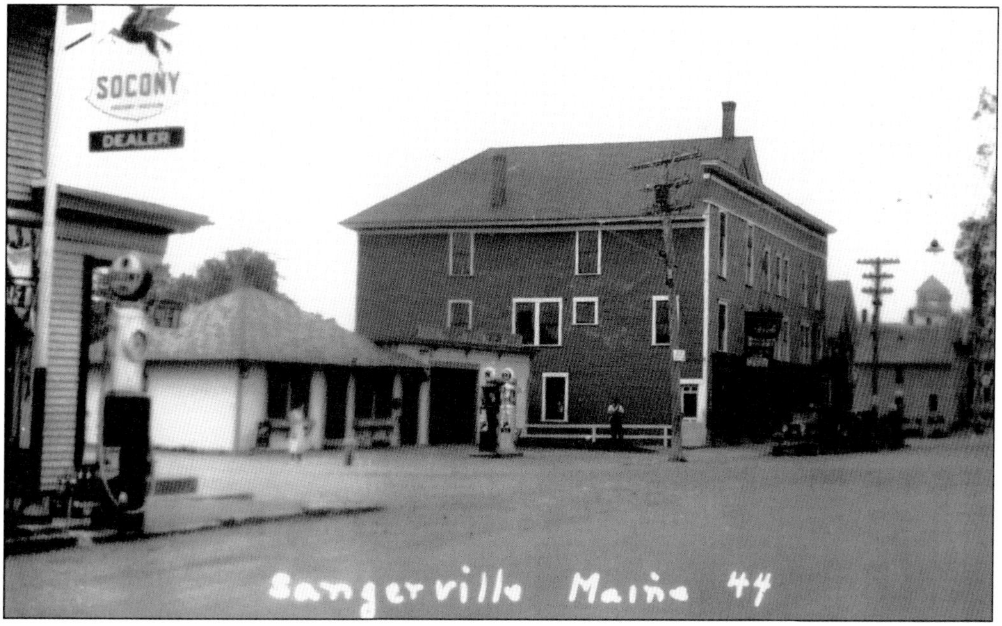

Taken around the same time as the above photograph, this one looks down South Main Street. To the extreme left is the IGA store, which also sold gas. Somewhat odd was the Texaco sign that was actually located across the street from Martin's filling station. It is unknown what type of store was housed in the building at the far end of the Carr block at this time, but it may have been a beer parlor. (Author's collection.)

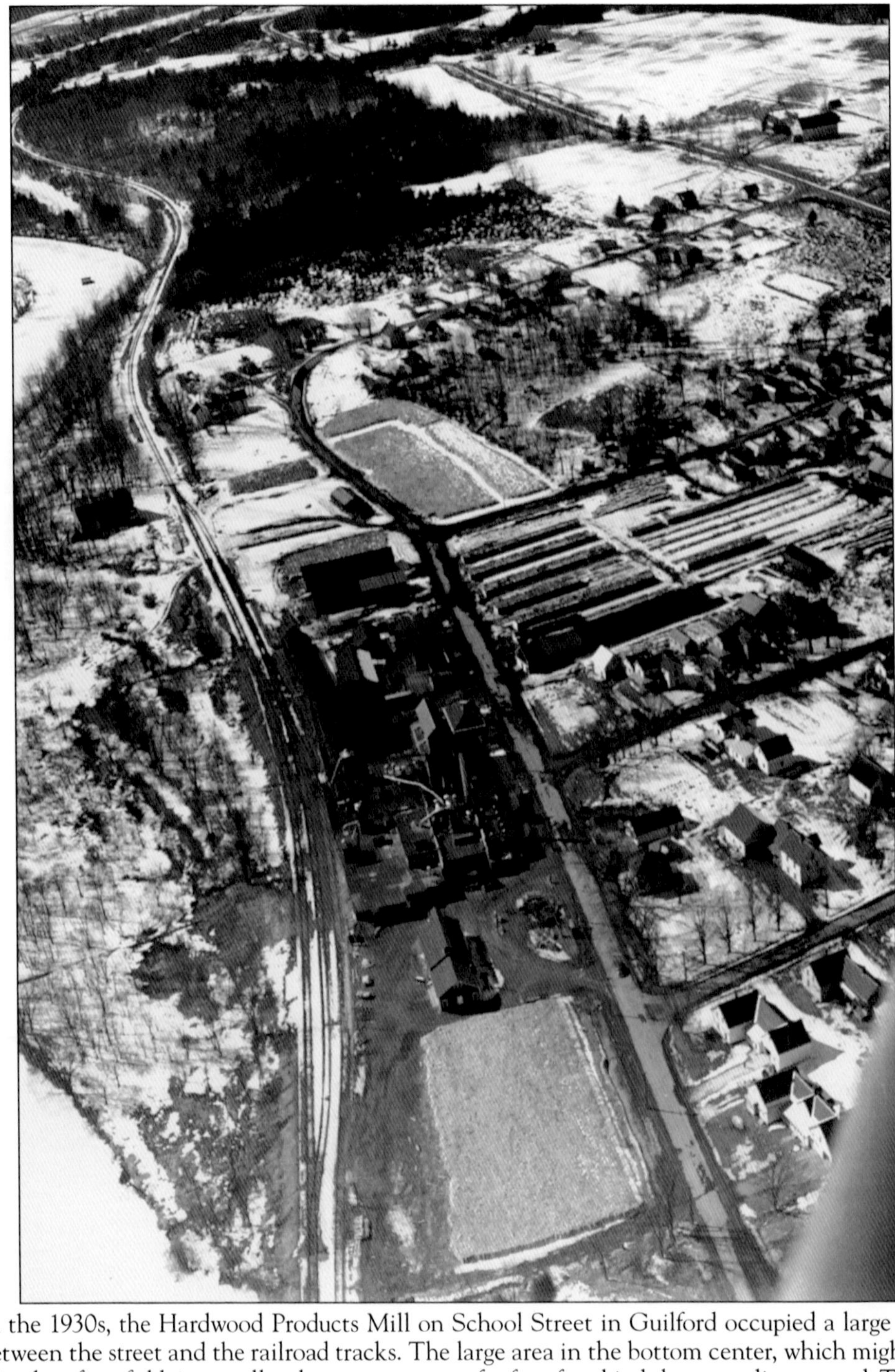

In the 1930s, the Hardwood Products Mill on School Street in Guilford occupied a large area between the street and the railroad tracks. The large area in the bottom center, which might be mistaken for a field, is actually a large storage area for four-foot birch logs standing on end. These logs were the raw material that actually fed the mill. Another area is in the center just above the mill. To the left is the Piscataquis River, and at the top right is High Street, or the "back Abbot Road." Directly across the street from the main part of the mill is Race's Market, which was operated by Alfred Race and his wife for many years.

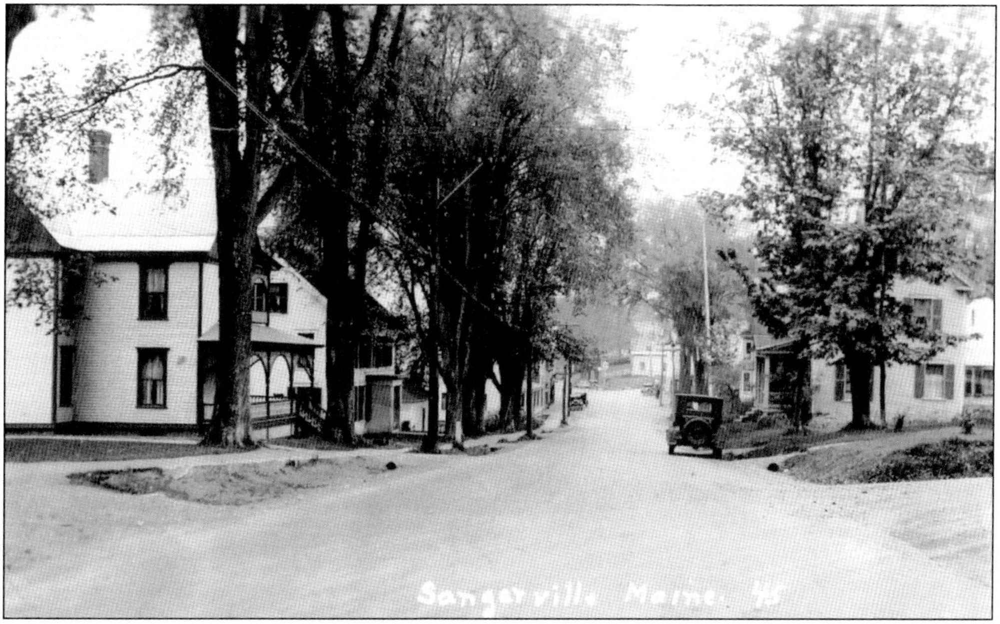

The homes on North Main Street in Sangerville were well kept with giant elm trees lining the sides of the road in the late 1920s. This photograph was taken from the crown of the hill at the intersection with Church Street and looks south to the center of town.

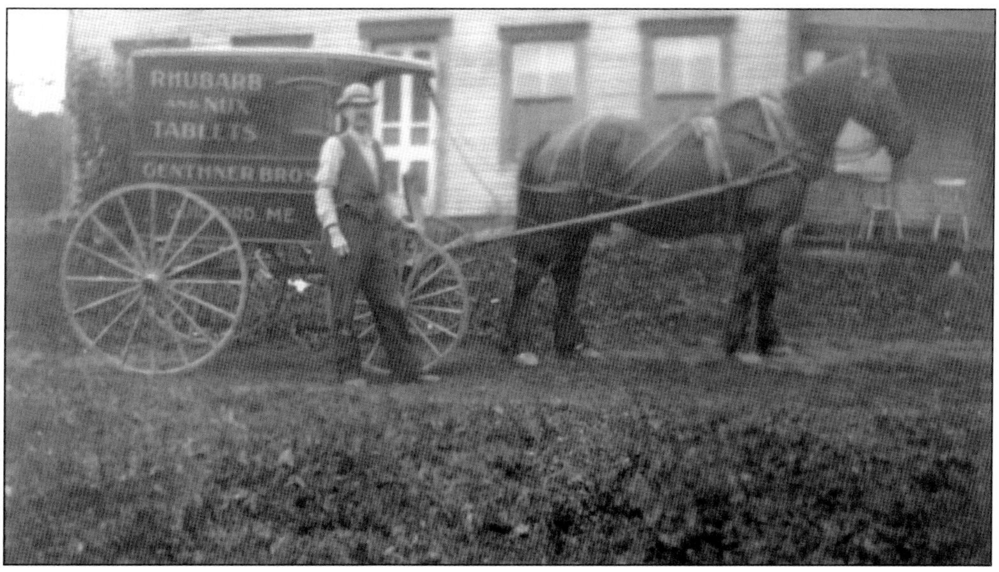

In the early years of the 20th century, peddlers drove their wagons around town selling almost anything. A typical example is George Rollins selling patent medicines for Genthner Brothers of Guilford, although the location where he is parked is not known.

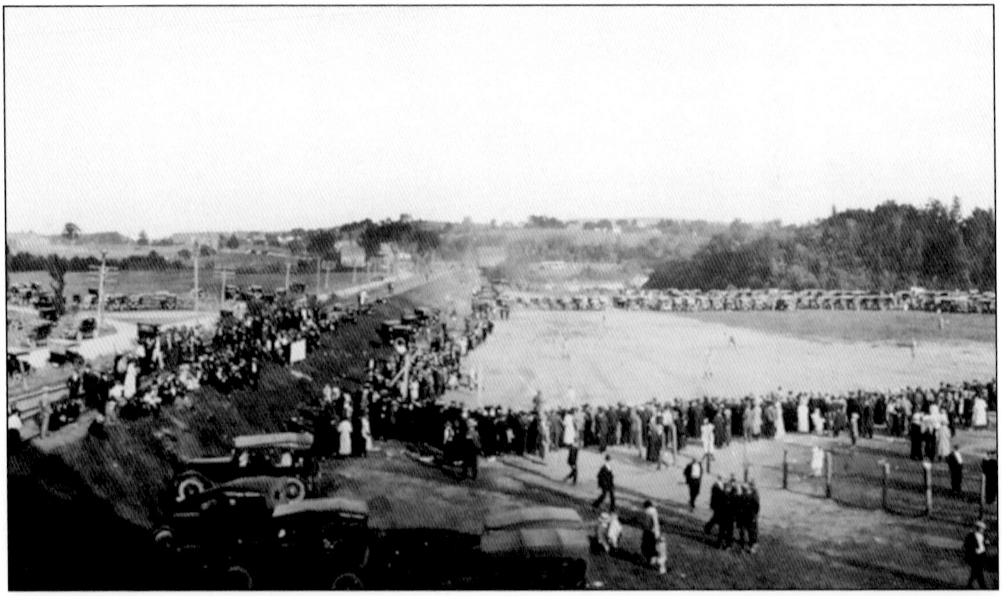

Around 1920, the Guilford Athletic Association was formed and a semiprofessional baseball team, called the Advertisers, was put together. A new playing field was developed at the end of River Street just off Water Street where the fairs were held, across from where the Guilford Hardware store now stands. After a few years, a beautiful grandstand was built (below) and, after that, bleachers were added down the third baseline. During one of the floods, large ice cakes destroyed the bleachers and seriously damaged the grandstand.

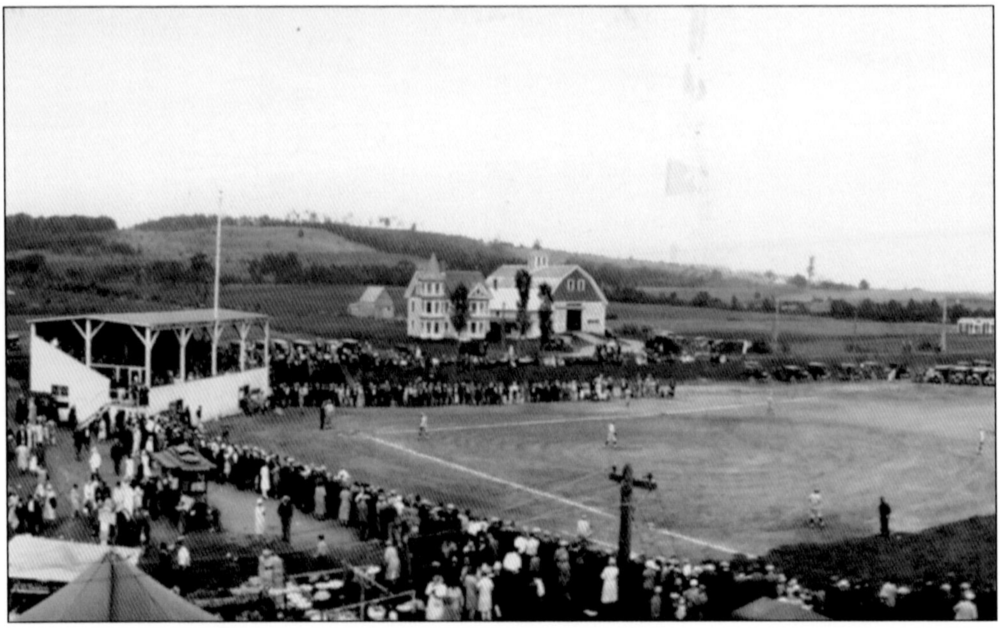

Six

Public Buildings and Notable Homes

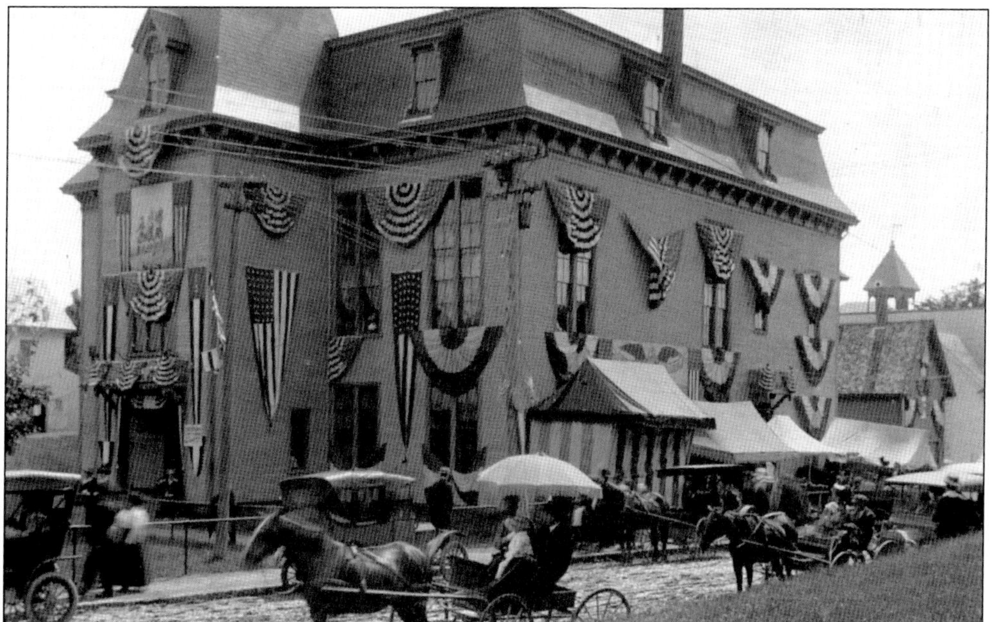

At the time of the Guilford centennial in 1916, a huge celebration was planned with almost all the public and commercial buildings in town properly decked out for the occasion. The expanded town hall and the fire station behind it were especially well done up and, as the big day arrived, the crowd started to gather early. Entrepreneurs had set up tent booths to hawk souvenirs, victuals, and drinks to the celebrants, and everyone was in a festive mood. Many speakers, including Henry Hudson and the Reverend George A. Martin, addressed the crowd, and the celebration was a highly successful affair with a good time being had by all.

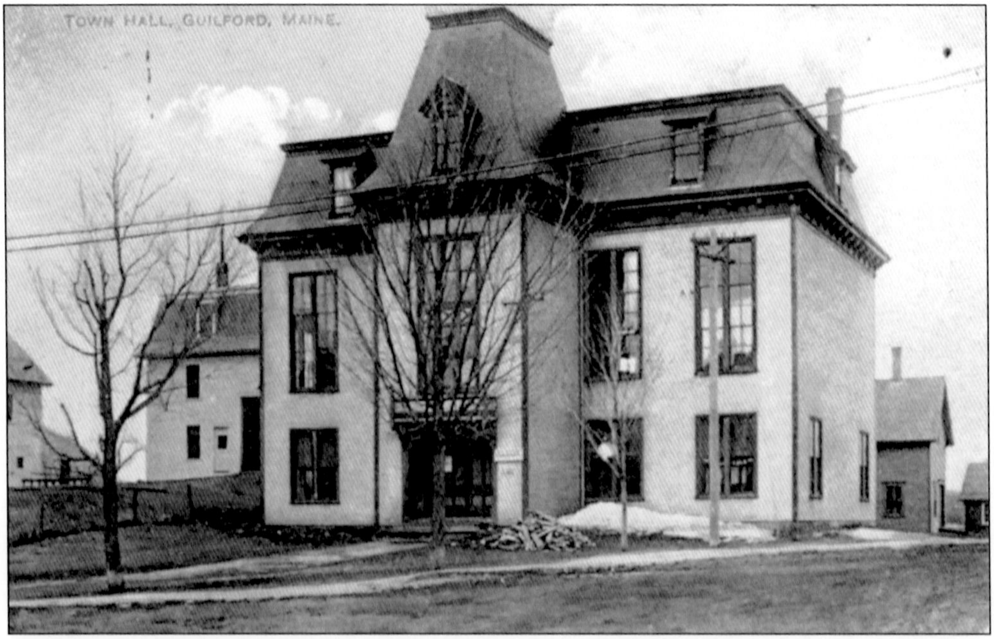

In 1880, Guilford built a new town hall at the corner of School and North Main Streets. It allowed for the seat of government to be moved there from Guilford center and all of the intown students to attend school there. The school at Tony Corner was closed. These two photographs show the hall as originally built and again after the addition was put on the rear. The hall also housed the first motion picture theaters in town.

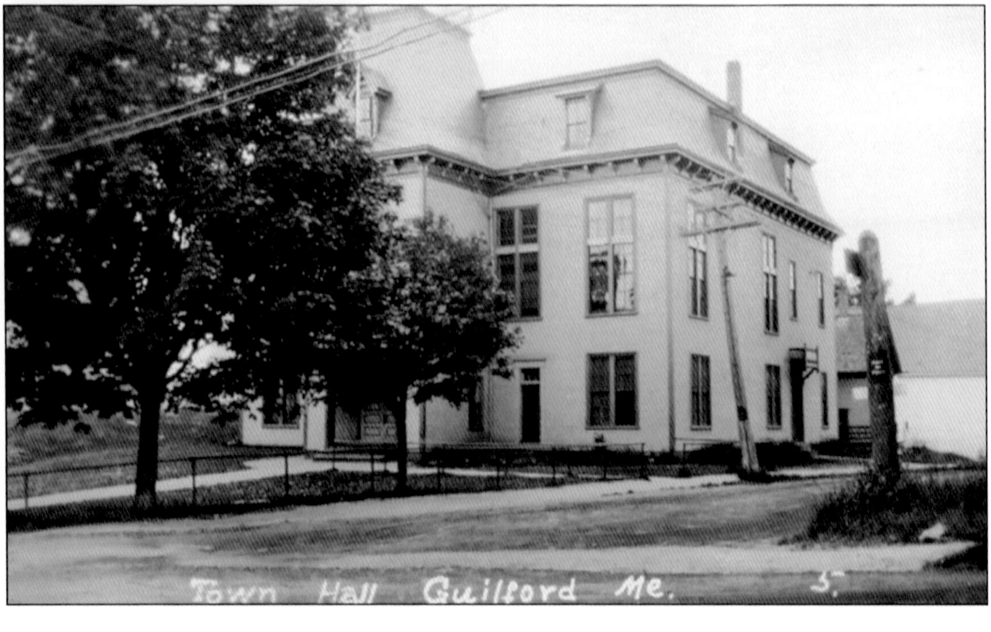

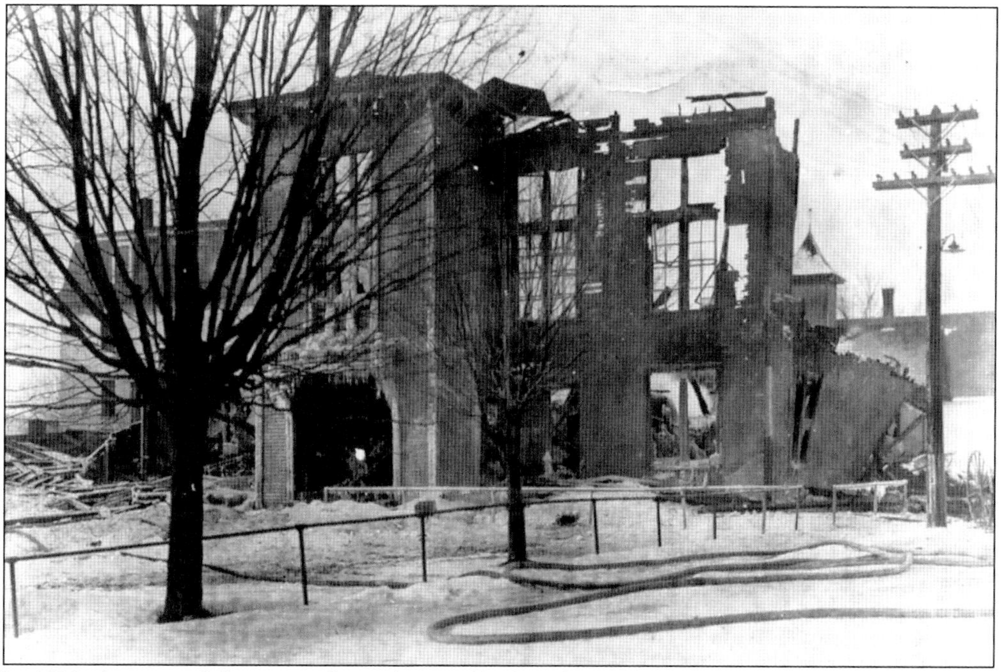

In 1928, the second disastrous fire to hit Guilford in three years completely destroyed the town hall and much equipment and records. It had only been three years since the high school had burned down. Unlike the high school, the town hall was not rebuilt.

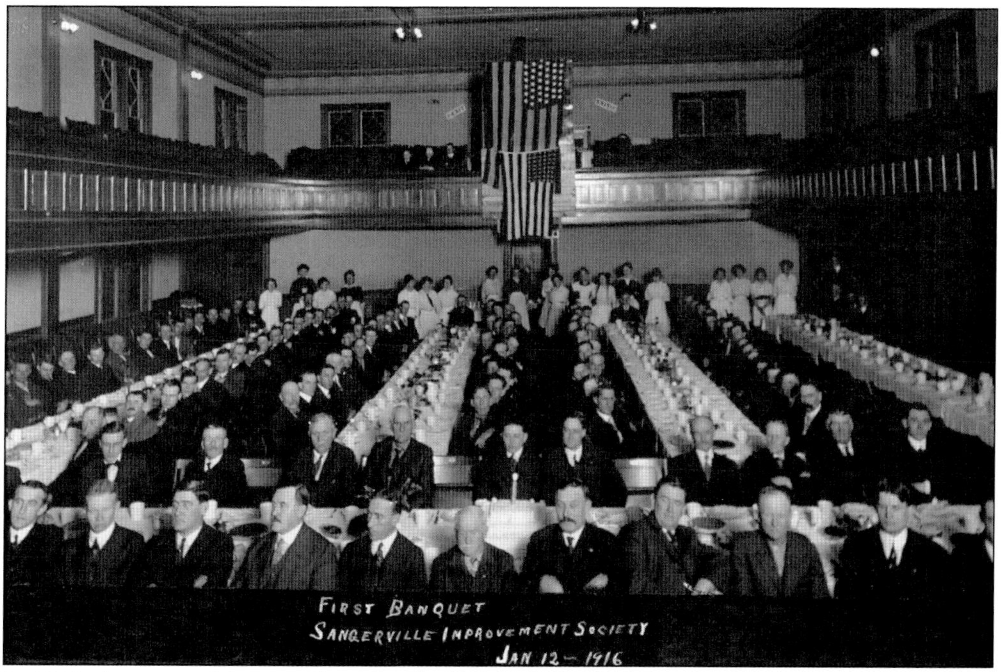

In 1902, the town of Sangerville erected a large town hall on North Main Street. The first floor contained the town office, the town library, and a stall for the town's horse-drawn hearse. The second floor contained a large hall, seen here, with a stage across the front for putting on plays and shows. It also served as the town basketball court. (Courtesy of Sangerville Historical Society.)

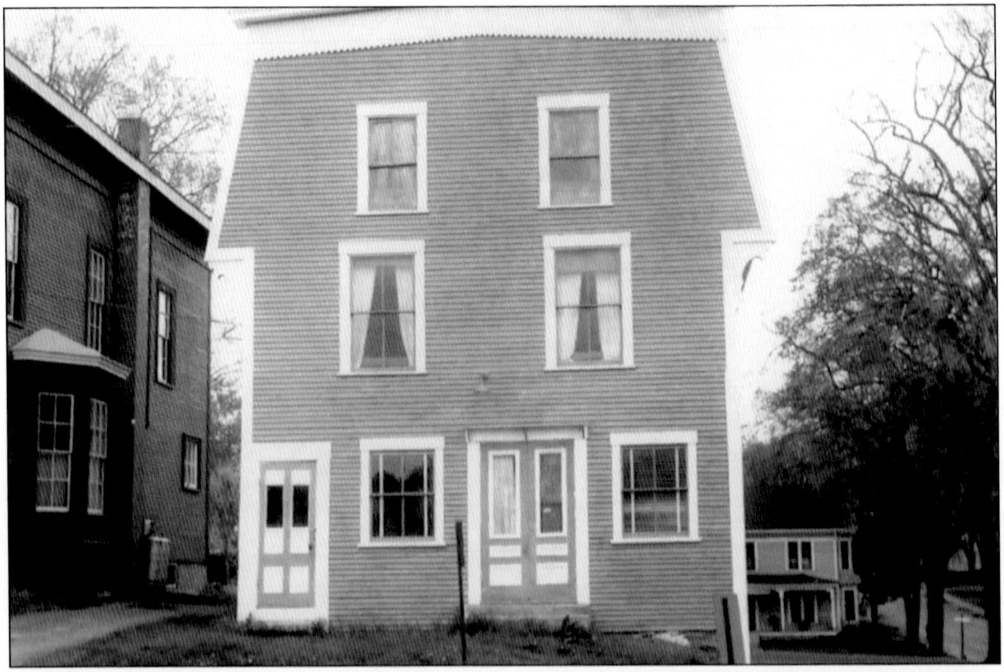

Used as a store for many years, this building was sold to the Sangerville American Legion post shortly after World War II. Located next to the Masonic hall on Hotel Hill, it has served as the legion post headquarters since they acquired it. (Courtesy of Sangerville Historical Society.)

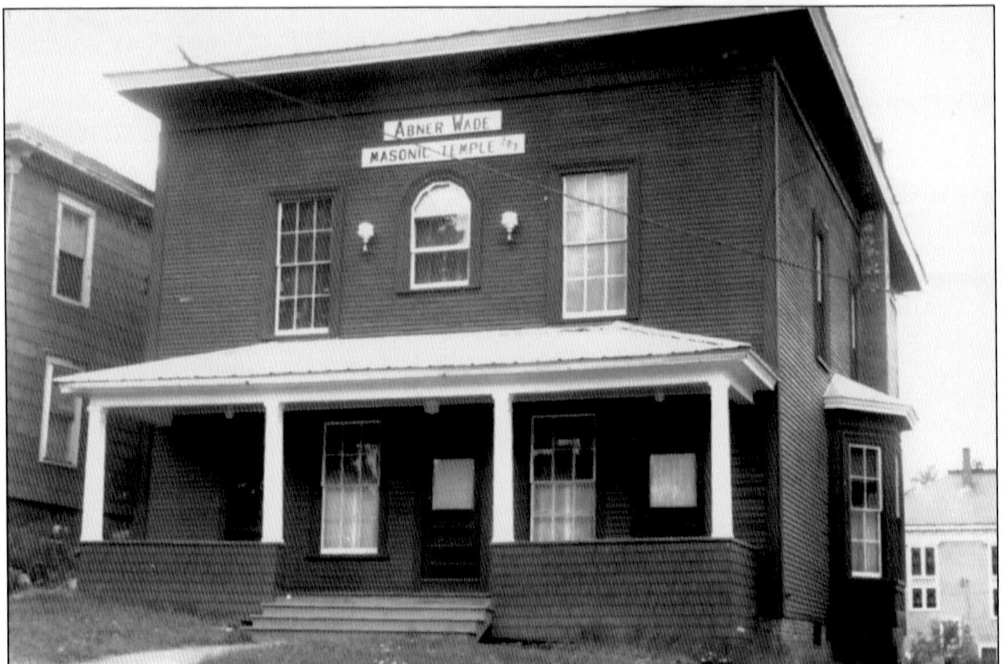

Next to the legion hall going up the hill stands the Abner Wade Masonic lodge. Originally erected as a motion picture theater, it is not known when it was acquired by the Masons. (Courtesy of Sangerville Historical Society.)

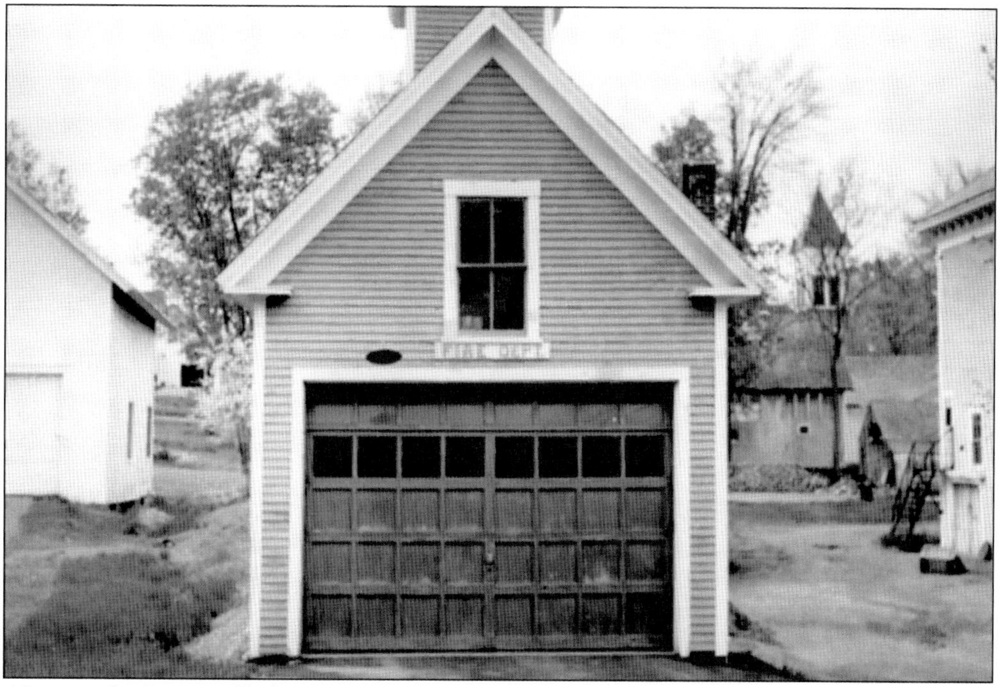

Above is the Sangerville fire station around 1940, and to the right is the back of the town hall. The set of double doors on the first floor of the hall is the entrance to where the town kept the horse-drawn hearse. (Courtesy of Lisa Fortier.)

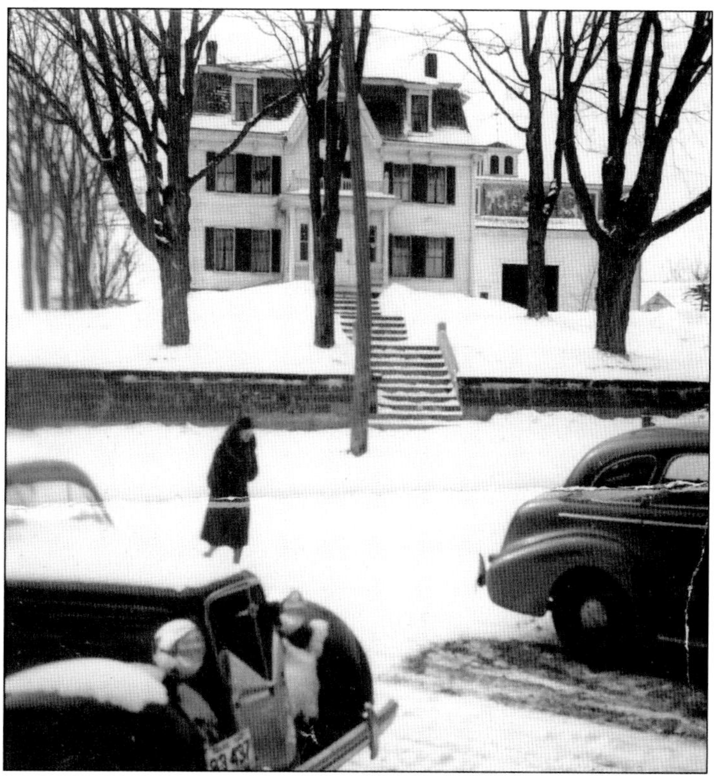

One of the first frame homes built in Guilford village was the Martin home, seen here in the 1930s. It has been used as a nursing home and later became the Red Maple Inn. It is currently being restored again for use as a restaurant. The fate of the barn on the right is unknown.

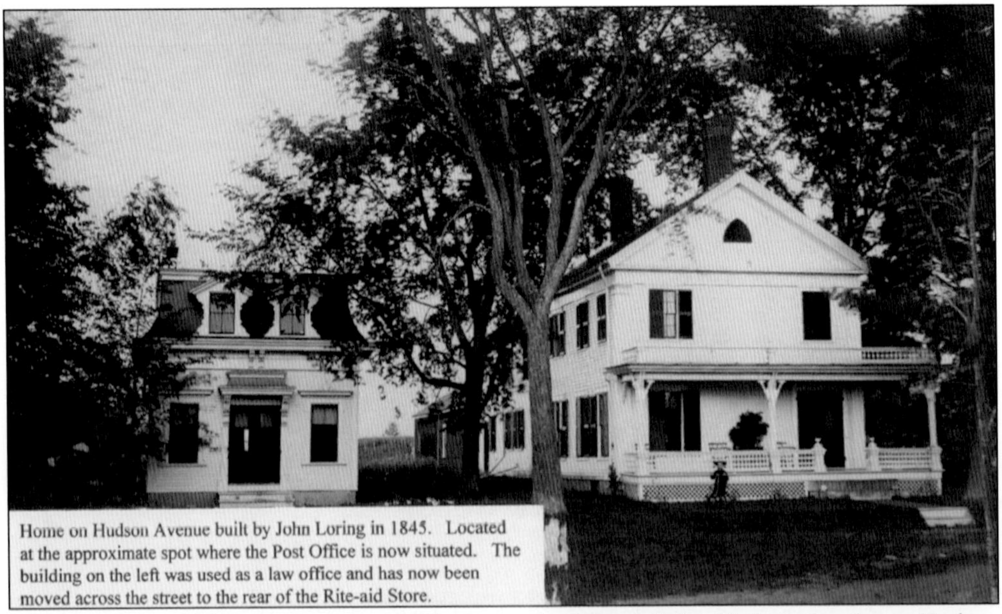

Home on Hudson Avenue built by John Loring in 1845. Located at the approximate spot where the Post Office is now situated. The building on the left was used as a law office and has now been moved across the street to the rear of the Rite-aid Store.

The grandest and largest home in Guilford was the home of the Hudson family on Hudson Avenue, which was built by John Loring in 1845. Originally a two-story, Georgian-style home, it was extensively remodeled around 1895 by Henry Hudson, who added another story, extended the carriage barns, and added a four-story turret, basically turning it into a Queen Anne–style home. This beautiful mansion fell to the wrecking ball in 1961 to make way for the new post office. To the left of the house is the Hudson's law office, which today has been moved across the street and was last used as an insurance office.

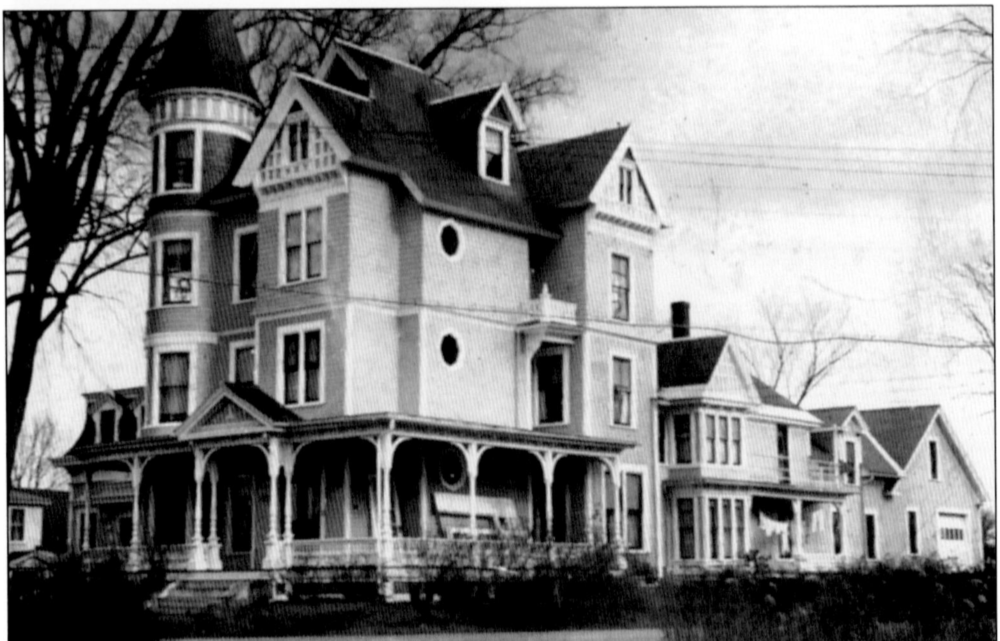

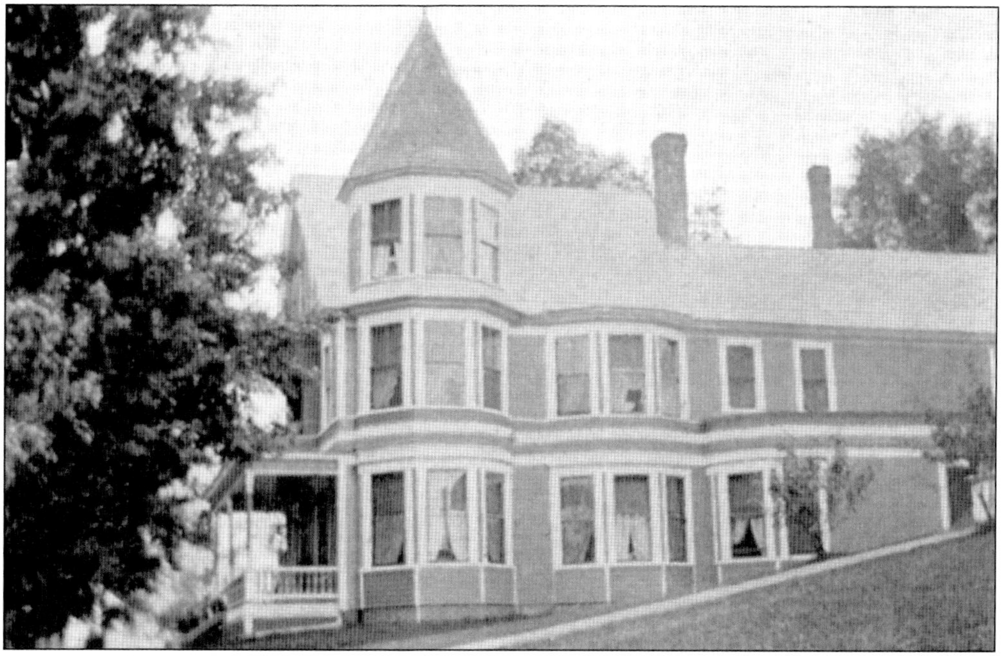

In Sangerville two large mansions were located beside each other on South Main Street. The first (above) was the home of Angus O. Campbell, who, with his brother and father, was heavily involved in the woolen industry in Sangerville. The home still stands today and is the home of Richard and Diana Bowley. The second (below) was built and owned by Alden Sanders, the owner of Sanders Brothers store. This was a large three-story house with porches on the front and one side. Last occupied by the family of William Church, it was razed in the 1960s. (Courtesy of Sangerville Historical Society.)

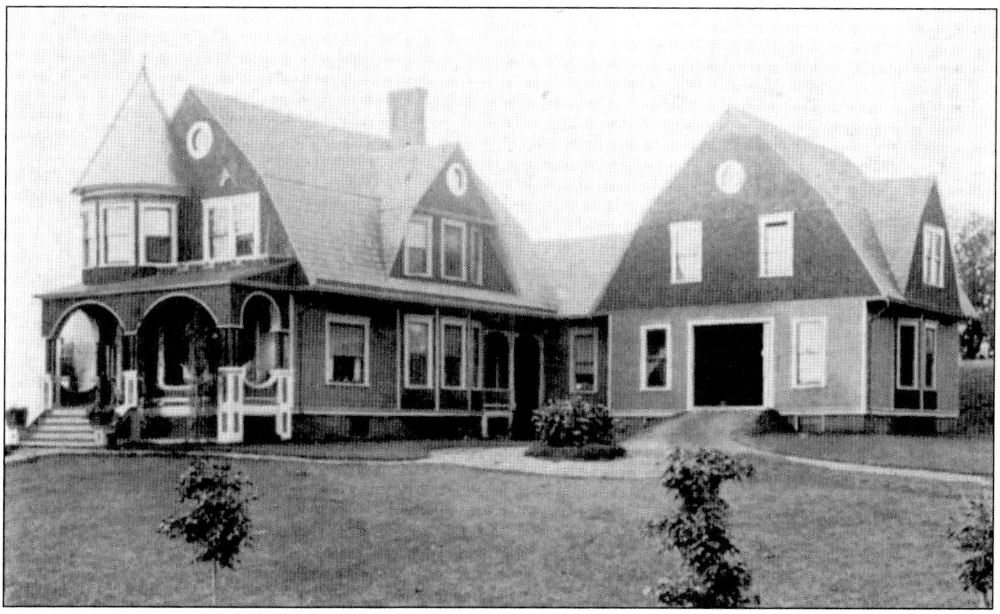

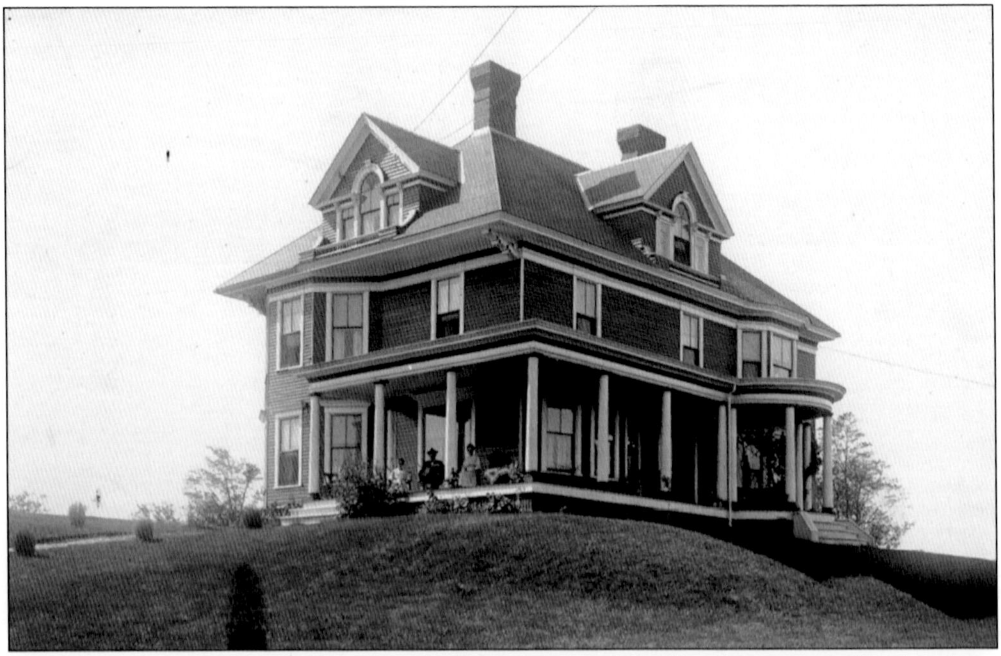

The home of Micajah J. Hudson around 1918 was located on Elm Street in Guilford and was purchased from the Genthner family. Over the years, it was owned by a Drake family and also a Cummings family, and it is currently the Guilford Bed and Breakfast.

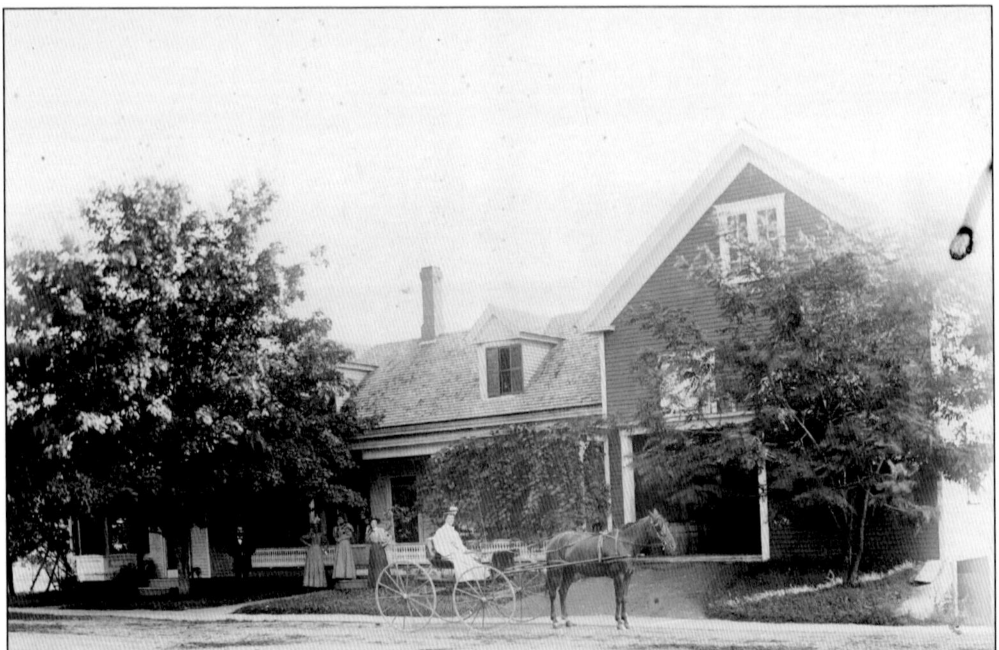

Prior to the purchase of the home pictured above, Hudson owned this home on Hudson Avenue. It was later owned by L. L. Colson. Built in 1872, it was razed in 1999 to make room for the Rite Aid pharmacy.

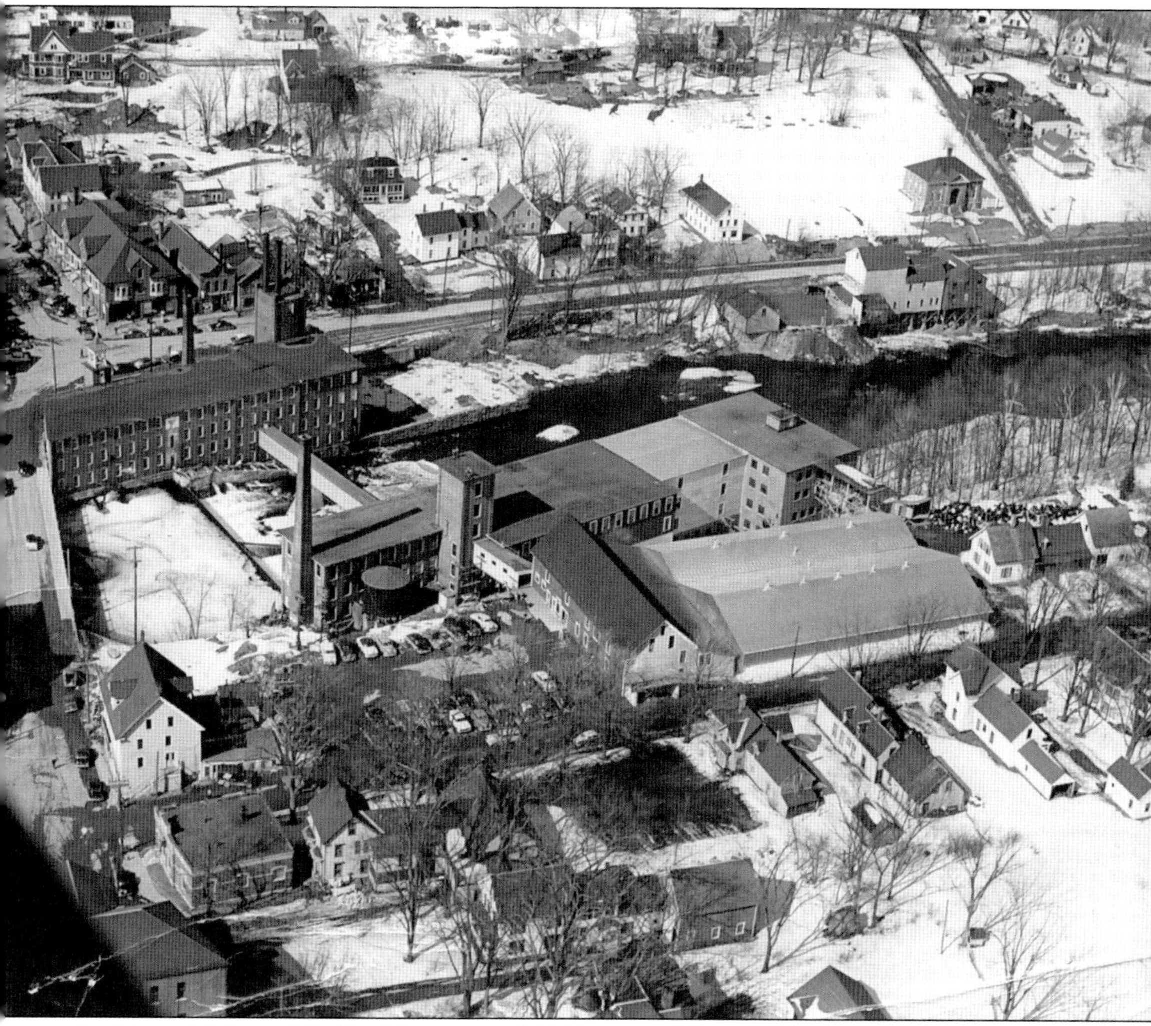

In this aerial shot of Guilford from around 1960, some of the notable homes on the north side of the river can be seen. At the far left and second from the top is the home of Dr. Charles Lightbody. At the center is the Straw house, which is now the Trebor Mansion Inn, and at the far right is the Stevens house.

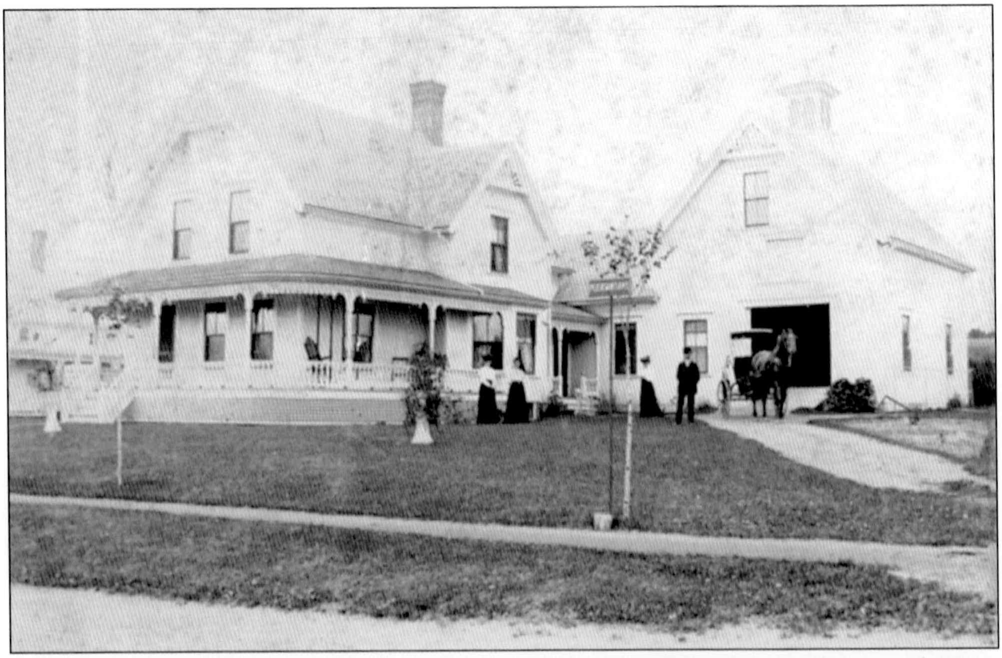

Another fine home in Sangerville was located on Pleasant Avenue and is still occupied. Many families have resided here over the years, including those of John Murray and Donald Osborne. The wrap-around porch shown in this picture is still attached to the home.

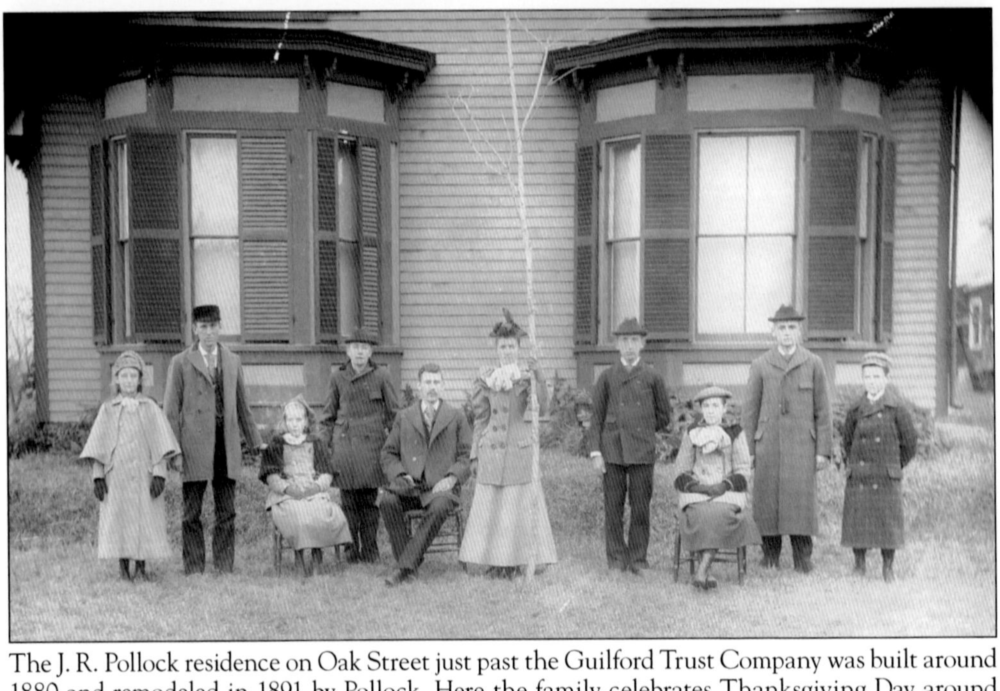

The J. R. Pollock residence on Oak Street just past the Guilford Trust Company was built around 1880 and remodeled in 1891 by Pollock. Here the family celebrates Thanksgiving Day around 1895. On the lawn, from left to right, are Florence Martin, Frank Martin, Laura Hudson, Cary Henderson, George Martin, Lettie Hudson, Carl Martin, Martha Hudson, James Hudson, and Leslie Hudson.

Seven

CHURCHES AND GRANGE HALLS

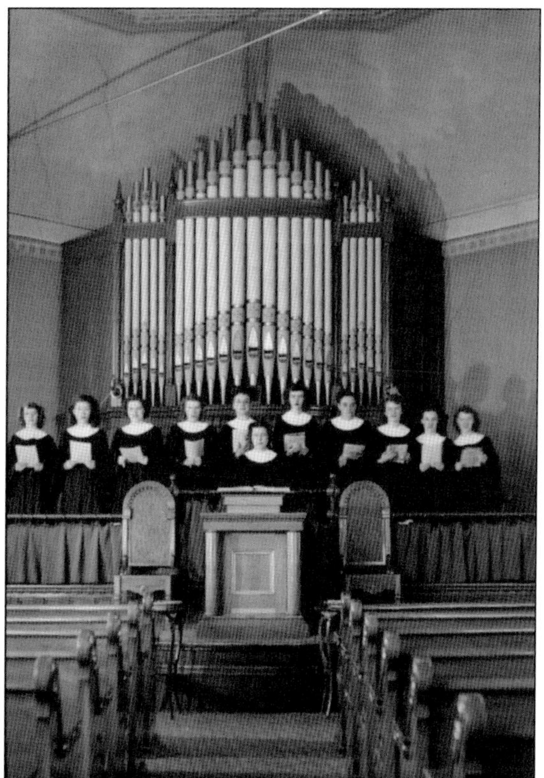

Church attendance was a big part of the lives of citizens of both Sangerville and Guilford and remains so to this day. Of the many functions carried out by the churches, having a choir to lead the congregation in the singing of hymns was considered to be one of the most important. Here the choir is in front of the beautiful pipe organ at the Universalist church in Sangerville around 1949. Members of the choir, from left to right, are Meredith Edes, Sylvia McCorrison, Diane Edes, Nadine Wilson, Marjorie Smart, Charlene Edes (standing at the pulpit), Joyce Steeves, Edith Steeves, Norma Higgins, Thelma Clements, and Lucille Higgins. (Courtesy of Sangerville Historical Society.)

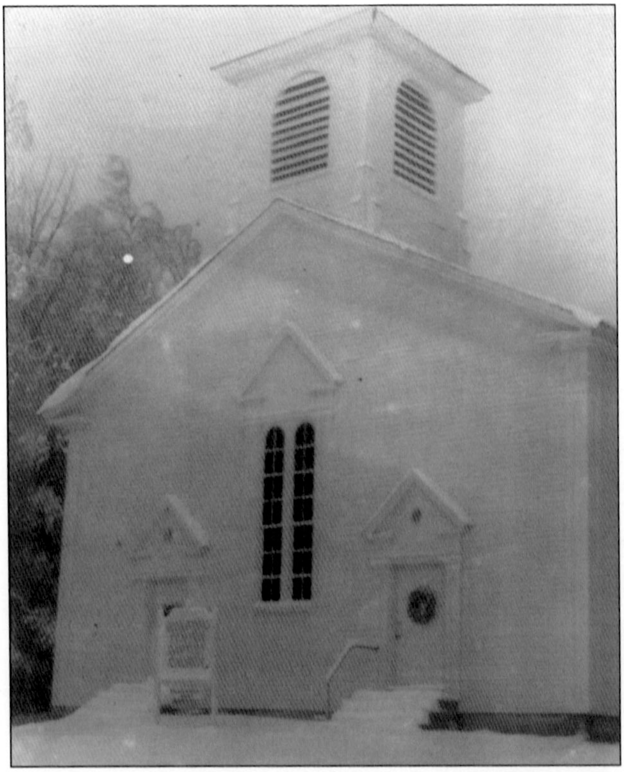

The first church of any consequence in Guilford was the Guilford Center Baptist church, built on Butter Street around 1831. The first minister was Thomas Macomber, and the church still holds Sunday services to the present day. The second church was the Free Meeting House on High Street in the village, but close-up pictures of that no longer remain.

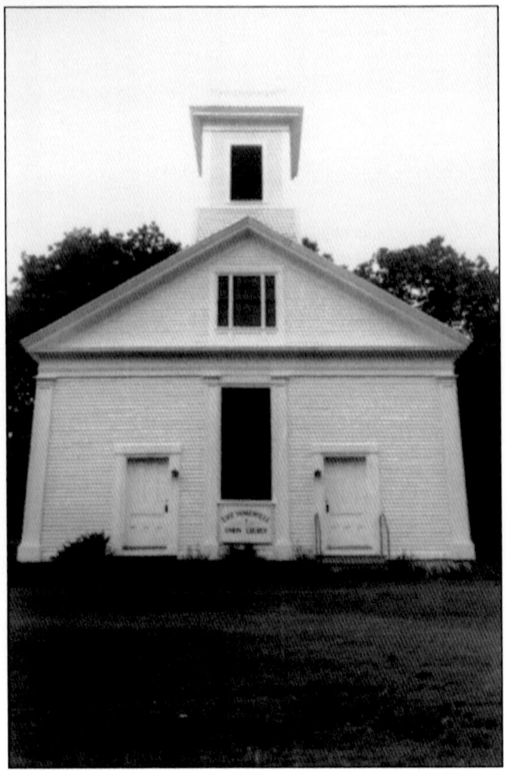

In 1843, the Union church was built in East Sangerville by Leonard Dearth at a cost of $700. In the late 1800s, it was used jointly by Union churchgoers and the East Sangerville Grange until the Grangers built their own building beside it. Services are still held here in the summertime. (Courtesy of Sangerville Historical Society.)

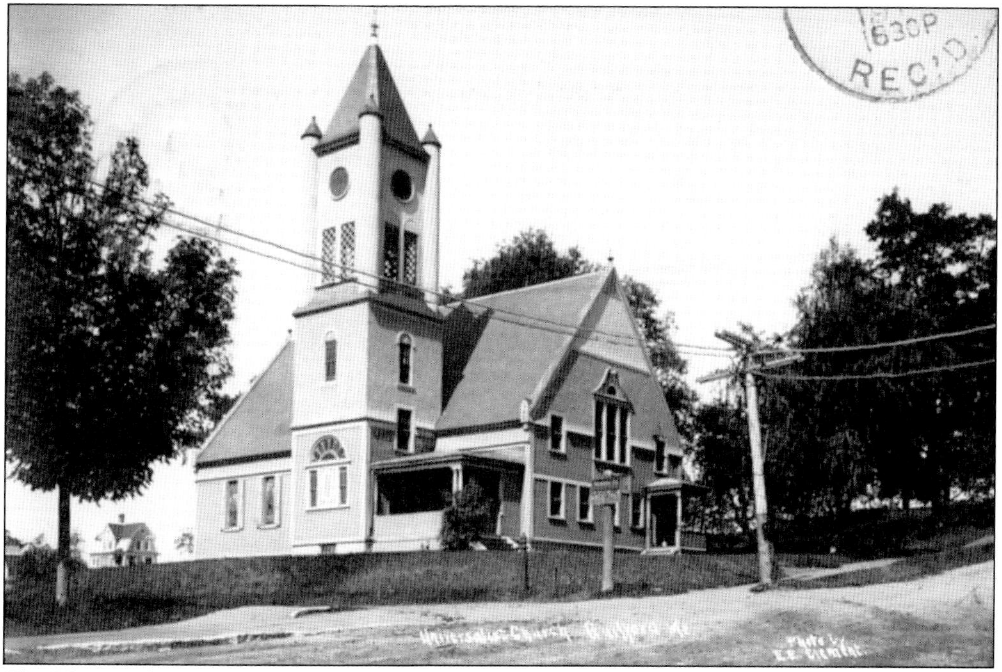

The Universalist church in Guilford was built in 1890 and dedicated in 1891. Located on the corner of North Main and School Streets and seen here in 1908, it has been remodeled many times and is now the United Methodist church.

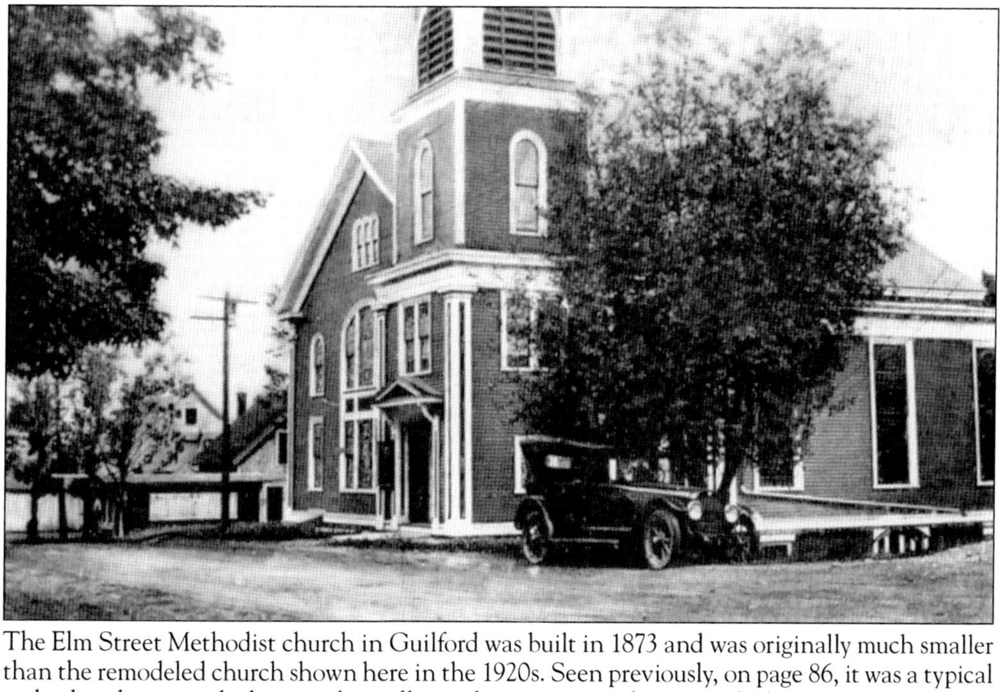

The Elm Street Methodist church in Guilford was built in 1873 and was originally much smaller than the remodeled church shown here in the 1920s. Seen previously, on page 86, it was a typical early church, painted white, with a tall steeple containing the town clock. In 1916 and 1917, it was extensively remodeled to the church shown here in the 1920s and no longer resembles the original church.

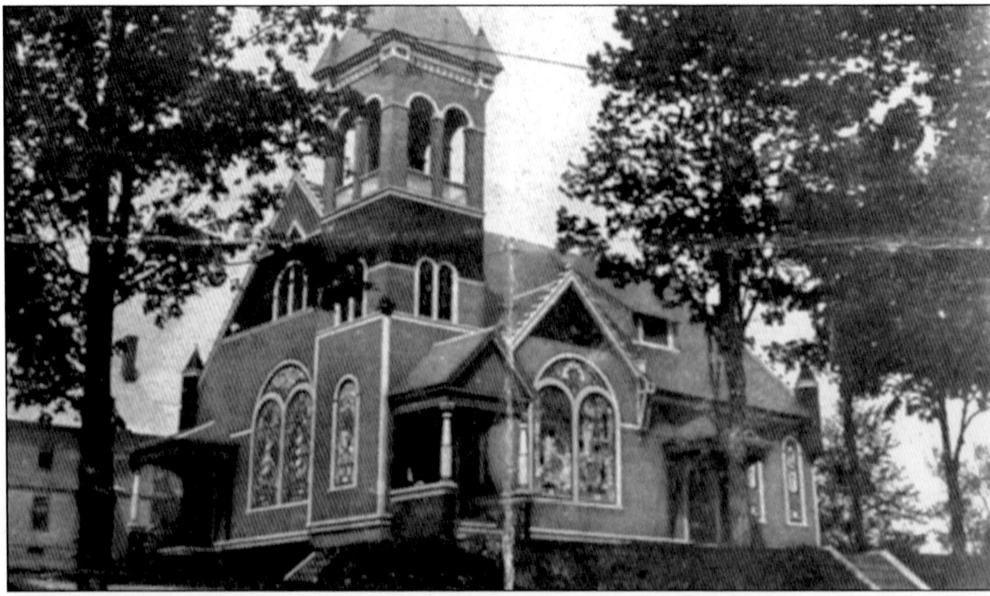

The First Universalist Church of Sangerville opened its doors in 1898 at the corner of Church and North Main Streets. In 1948, the parish united with the Methodists and became the United Church of Sangerville. This group later separated from the Universalists and, in 1981, built a new church on the former Oakes homestead on High Street, now Douty Hill Road. The land was donated by Lady Eunice Oakes. In 1985, the name was changed to Grace Bible Church, and the Grace Christian School was started for kindergarten through eighth grade in 1986. (Courtesy of Sangerville Historical Society.)

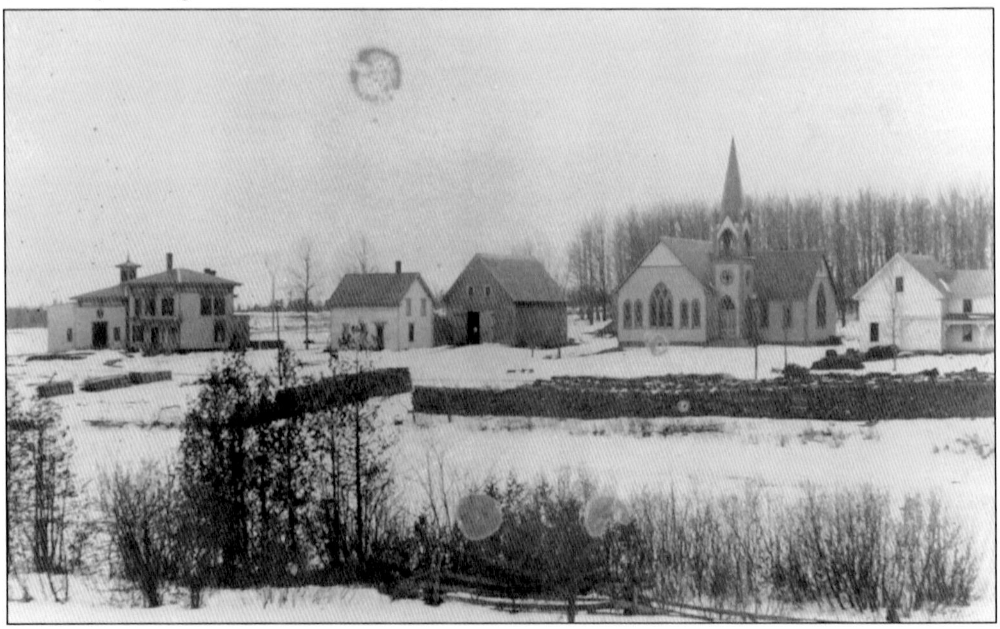

The Campbell Memorial Methodist Church was built in Sangerville in 1896 on South Main Street at the location currently occupied by the U.S. post office. It closed its doors, and the parishioners united with the Universalist Church around 1950. It was razed at some point thereafter. (Courtesy of Sangerville Historical Society.)

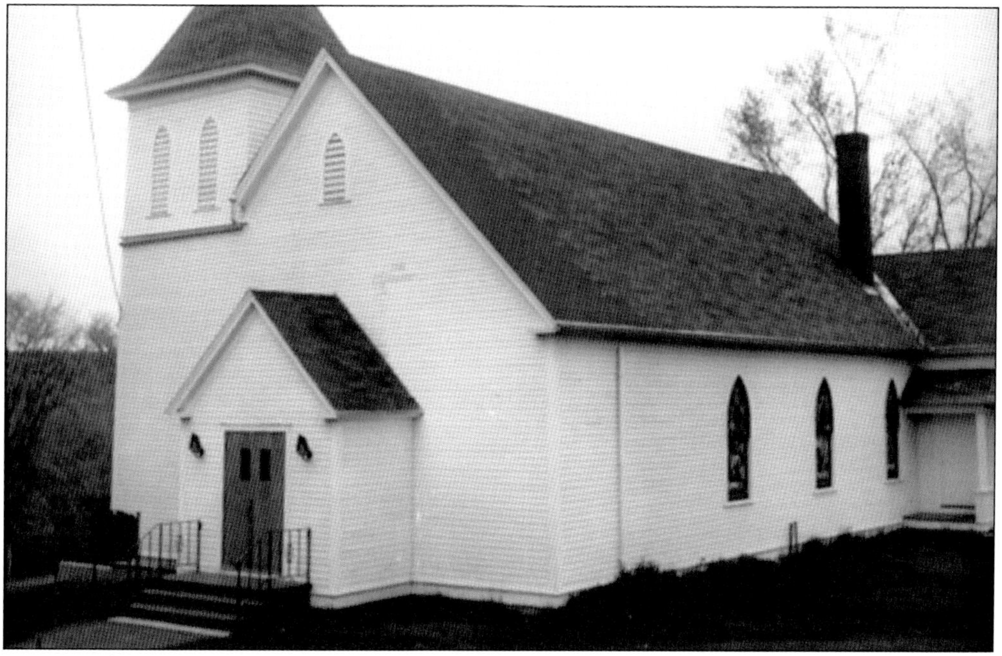

In 1898, the Catholic diocese purchased land on High Street in Sangerville for the location of a new church. The present Holy Family Church was built in 1918 on the land previously purchased, and starting in 1919, services were held here. Over the years, many renovations have taken place. (Courtesy of Sangerville Historical Society.)

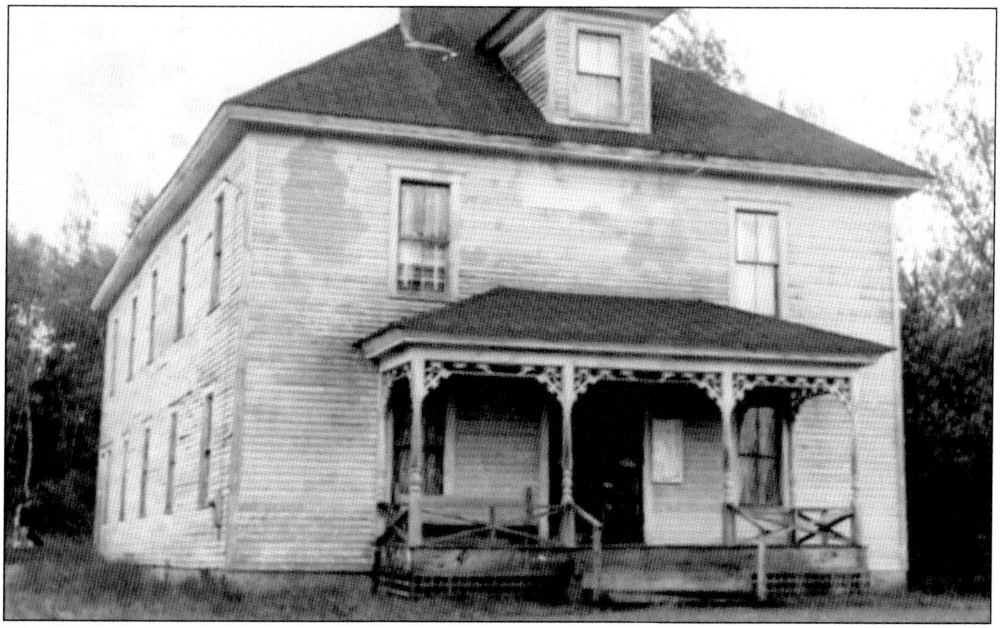

The East Sangerville Grange was organized in 1875, and meetings were held at various locations until 1895, when it moved to the East Sangerville church. The meetings were continued at the church until 1904, when the Grange built its own hall and moved into the unfinished building in October of that year. In 1902, it had a membership of 255. (Courtesy of Sangerville Historical Society.)

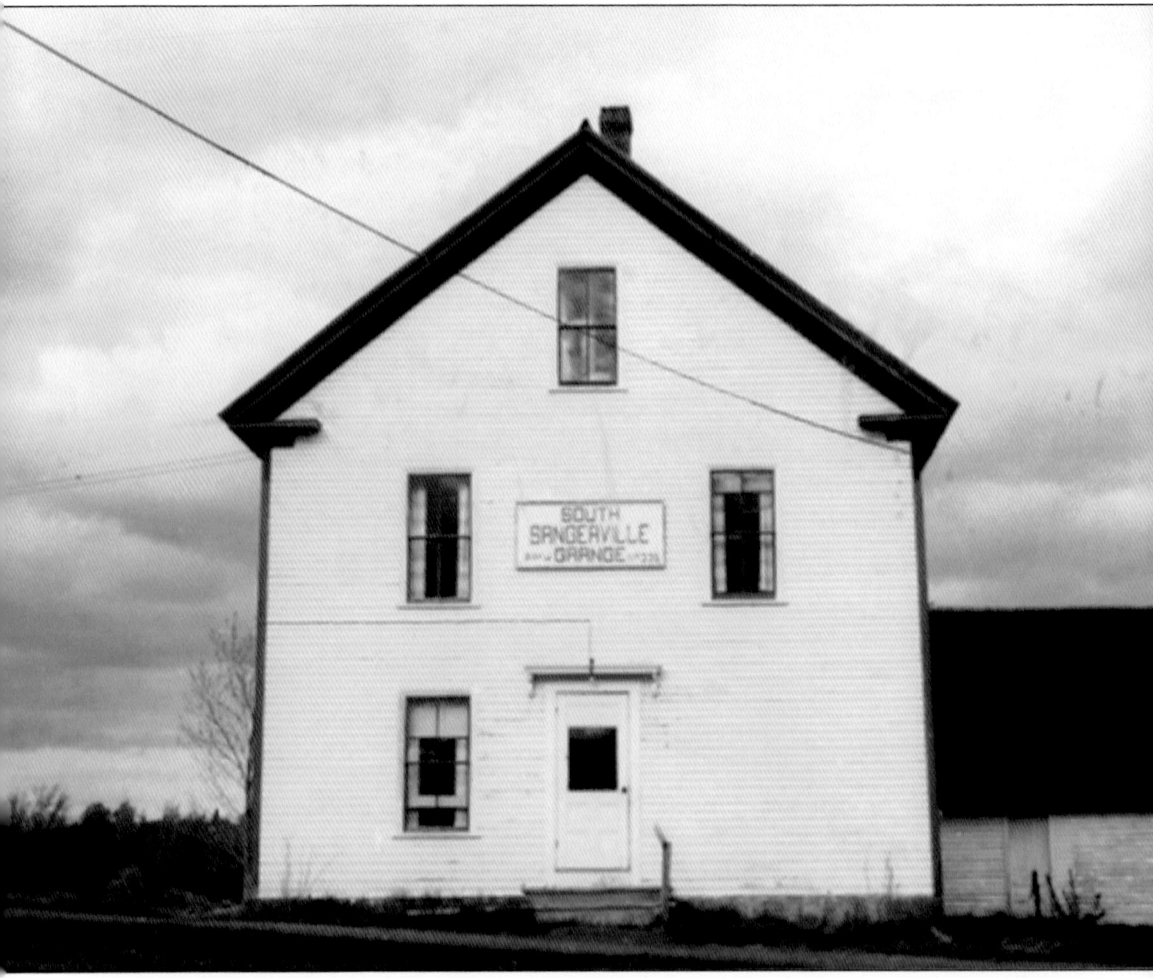

The South Sangerville Grange was organized in 1896 and met in the Gilman Corner Schoolhouse until 1898, when its present hall was built. The hall was not used in the winter when members met in the schoolhouse, which was closed in 1943. The town sold the school for $1, and the purchaser donated it to the Grange. It was then given to the Sangerville Historical Society. (Courtesy of Sangerville Historical Society.)

Eight

Some People to Remember

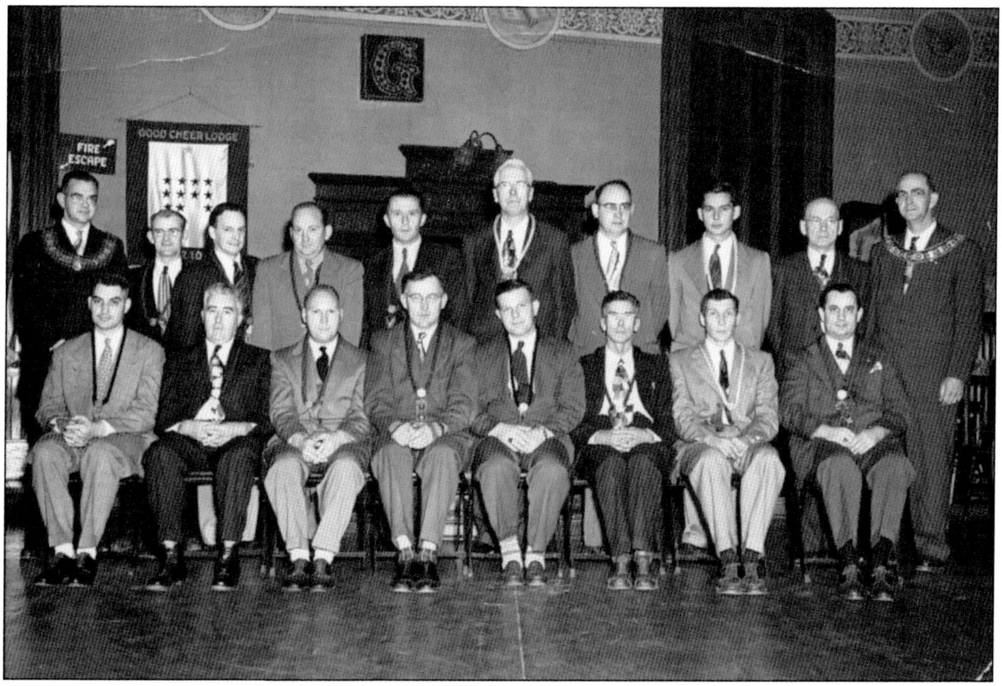

Some of the members of the Mount Kineo lodge of the Masons in Guilford are shown here in the late 1940s, although the occasion for the get-together is unknown. From left to right are (first row) Donald Rowe, John Willey, Maynard Ridley, Fernald Hamilton, Elwin Sargent, unidentified, Herbert Pulkinen, and S. Leslie Moody; (second row) unidentified, Roy Garland, Harry Pearson, Burchell Ronco, Henry Curtis, Ralph Weston, ? Olson, Thomas Blake, Ernest Farris, and Ralph Chapman.

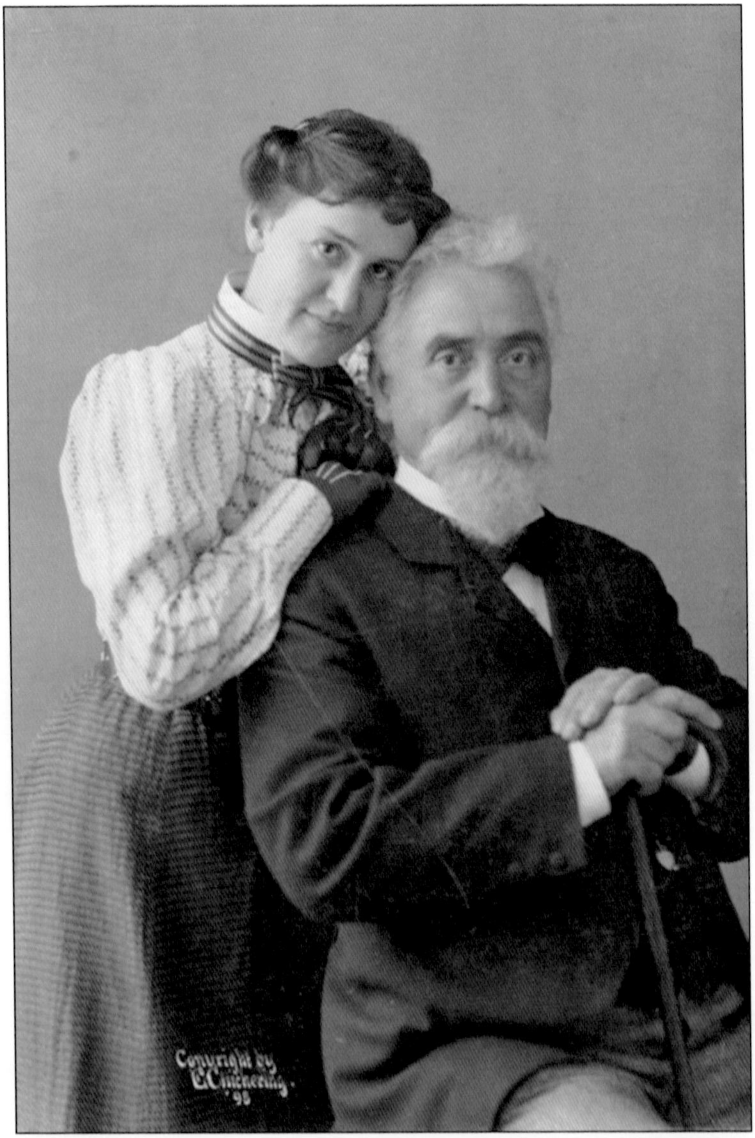

The most famous person to emerge from Sangerville was Sir Hiram Stevens Maxim, shown here with his granddaughter. Born at Brockway Mills on February 5, 1840, he had less than five years of formal education. His father was a skilled carpenter and mechanic and passed along his skills. By 1876, Maxim applied his great talent to perfecting an incandescent lightbulb. On October 4, 1878, he applied for a patent; however, Thomas Edison applied the next day and application was granted, earning him Maxim's lifelong animosity. Maxim formed the U.S. Electric Lighting Company, which later became Westinghouse. In 1881, he sailed for Europe and never resided in the United States again. His most famous invention was the Maxim water-cooled machine gun. He built his first working model in only 13 months. To improve its efficiency, he and his brother Hudson developed smokeless gunpowder and further refined the manufacturing process of the gun, which was used extensively during World Wars I and II. After becoming a British citizen in 1900, he was knighted by Queen Victoria in recognition of his many inventions and the value of the machine gun in the Sudan and at the battle of Omdurman. He died in 1916. (Author's collection.)

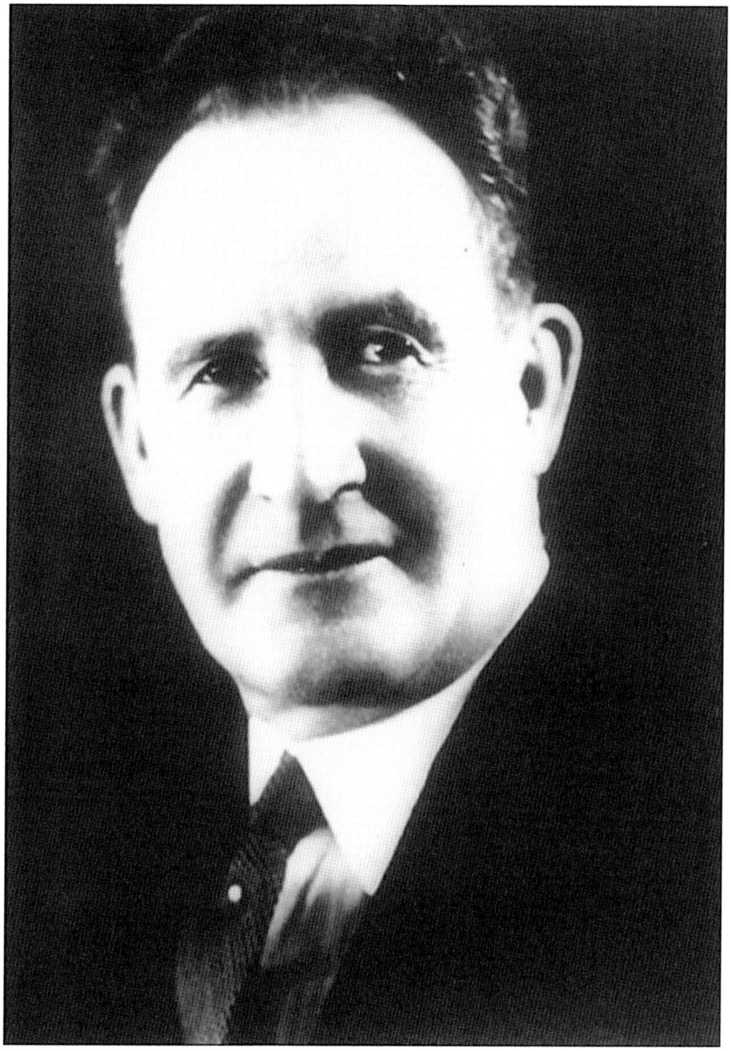

Sir Harry Oakes was born on December 23, 1874, at the family farm on High Street in Sangerville. Believing his five children would receive a better education from Foxcroft Academy, Oakes's father purchased a farm on the outskirts of Foxcroft. Oakes attended college and two years of medical school before becoming interested in prospecting, first in the Klondike and later in Alaska, Canada, California, Australia, and the Philippines. A small man of around 135 pounds, he was strong and carried a pack weighing 85 pounds when prospecting. Finally, after 14 years of lean times, Oakes staked a claim near Kirkland, Ontario, which became known as the Lake Shore Gold Mine. It turned out to be the second-richest find in North America, and he became a multimillionaire, at one time earning $60,000 a day. In 1923, he married Eunice McIntyre of Australia, and together they had five children. To avoid heavy taxes, he moved to the Bahamas, which had no income tax, and gave up his Canadian and American citizenships. He built a mansion there and maintained others in Niagara Falls, Ontario, and Bar Harbor, where his family usually summered. In 1939, he was knighted by King George VI in recognition of his philanthropic work. On July 8, 1943, Oakes was murdered in his sleep. The crime was never solved. It is suspected that it was engineered by organized crime because of his resistance to gambling on the islands. He is buried in the family mausoleum in Dover-Foxcroft. (Courtesy of Sangerville Historical Society.)

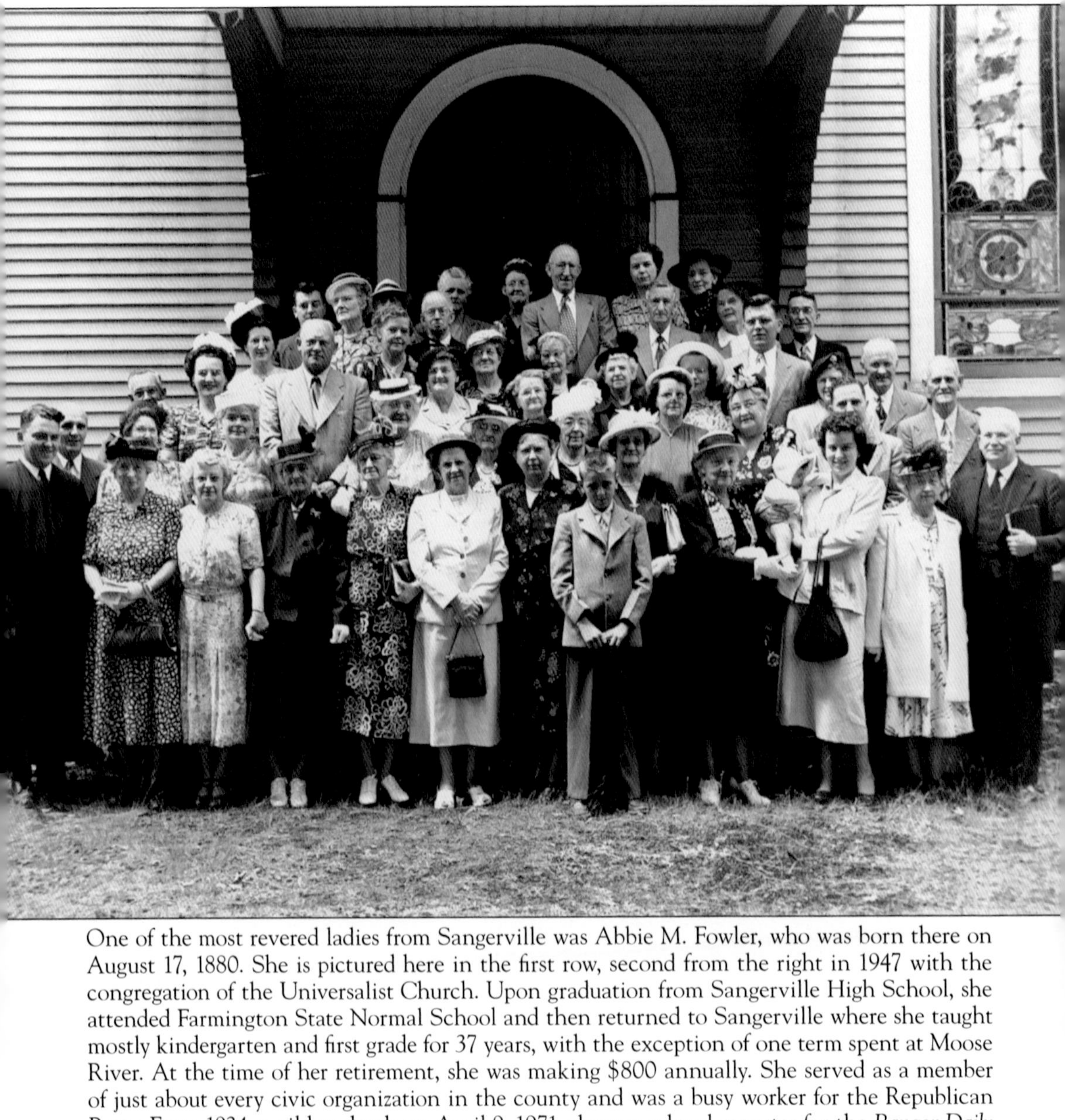

One of the most revered ladies from Sangerville was Abbie M. Fowler, who was born there on August 17, 1880. She is pictured here in the first row, second from the right in 1947 with the congregation of the Universalist Church. Upon graduation from Sangerville High School, she attended Farmington State Normal School and then returned to Sangerville where she taught mostly kindergarten and first grade for 37 years, with the exception of one term spent at Moose River. At the time of her retirement, she was making $800 annually. She served as a member of just about every civic organization in the county and was a busy worker for the Republican Party. From 1924 until her death on April 9, 1971, she was a local reporter for the *Bangor Daily News* and three local weeklies. She retired from teaching in 1940 and opened a small gift shop in her home, which was located across the road from the schoolhouse. She was well known for tinting black and white landscapes into beautiful colored pictures. (Courtesy of Sangerville Historical Society.)

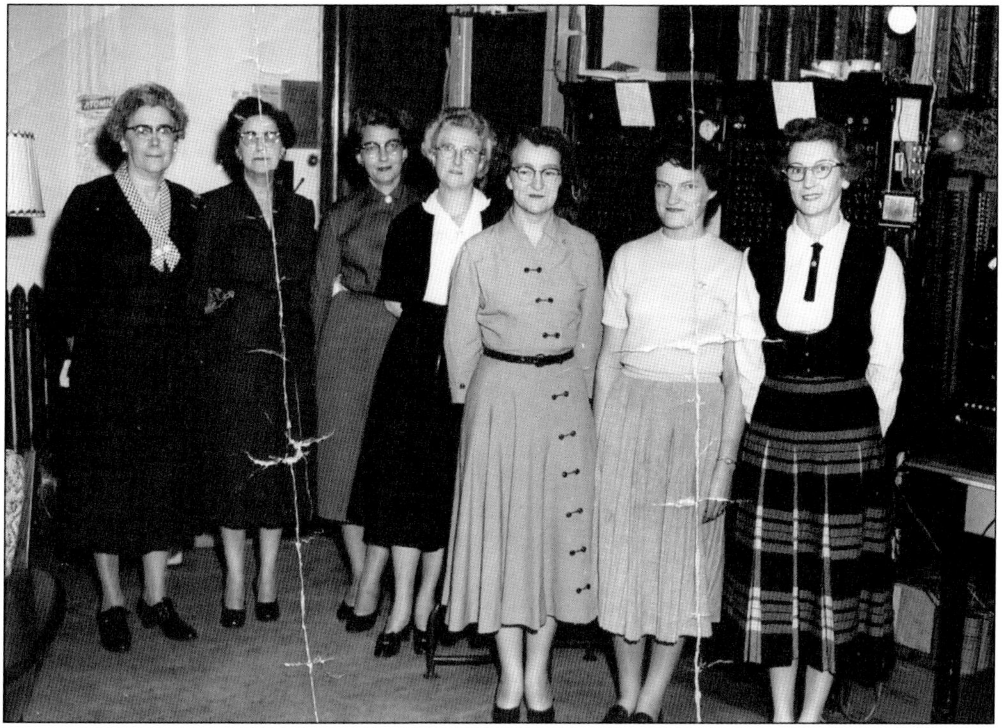

In 1950, the telephone office and exchange was located on the second floor of the Odd Fellows hall. The operators around that time were, from left to right, Hazel Moulton, Doris Lary, Betty Welts, Florence Cook, Marguerite Sawyer, Avis Edes, and Marion Crane.

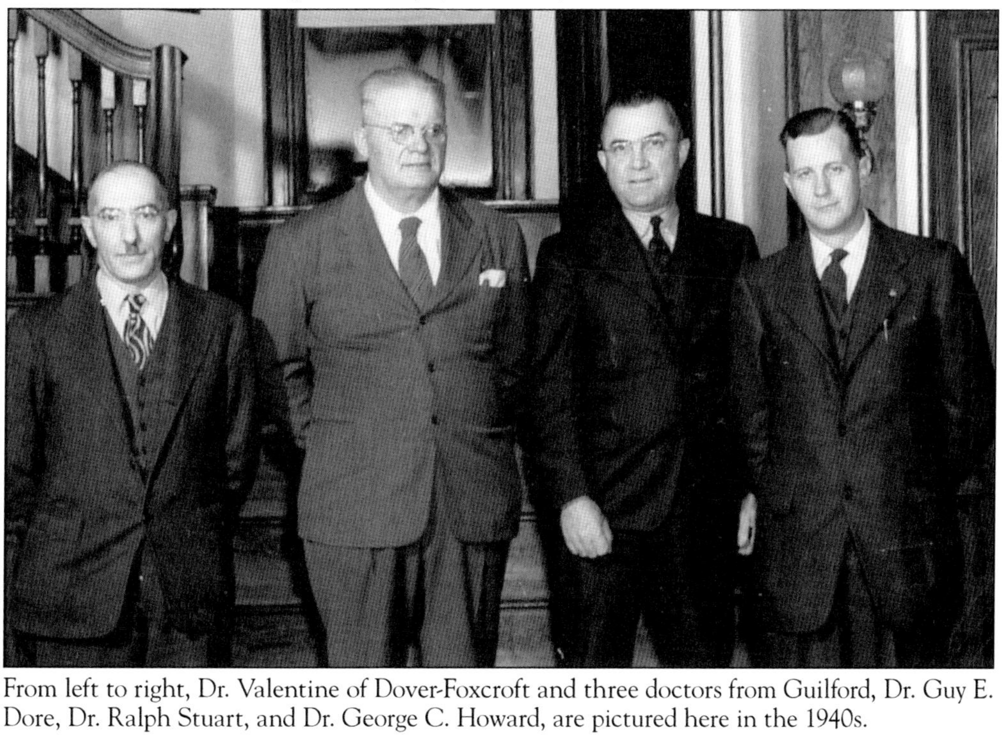

From left to right, Dr. Valentine of Dover-Foxcroft and three doctors from Guilford, Dr. Guy E. Dore, Dr. Ralph Stuart, and Dr. George C. Howard, are pictured here in the 1940s.

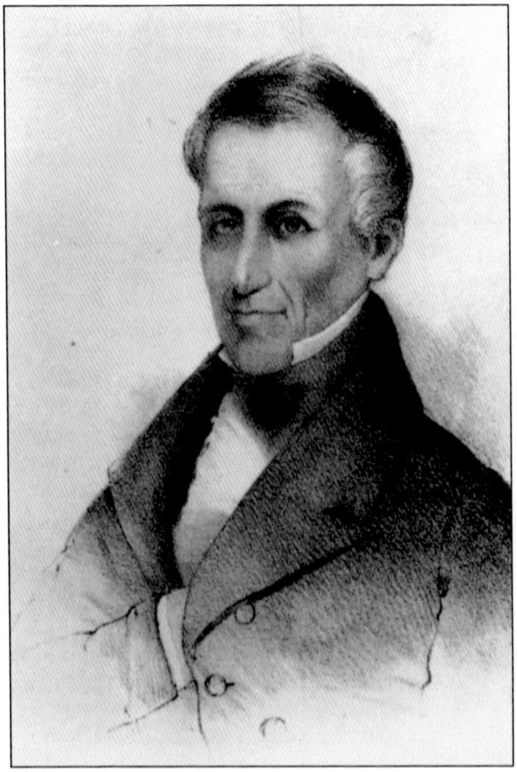

In 1809, Col. Calvin Sanger purchased three quarters of the town of Sangerville from the State of Massachusetts, and a short time later, he purchased the rest. Sanger was from Sherborn, Massachusetts, and he never actually visited the town he owned as far as is known. He financed the building of both saw- and gristmills in East Sangerville and placed his cousin Walter Leland in charge of the mills and all his land. When Sangerville was incorporated in 1814, the town was named for him. (Courtesy of Sangerville Historical Society.)

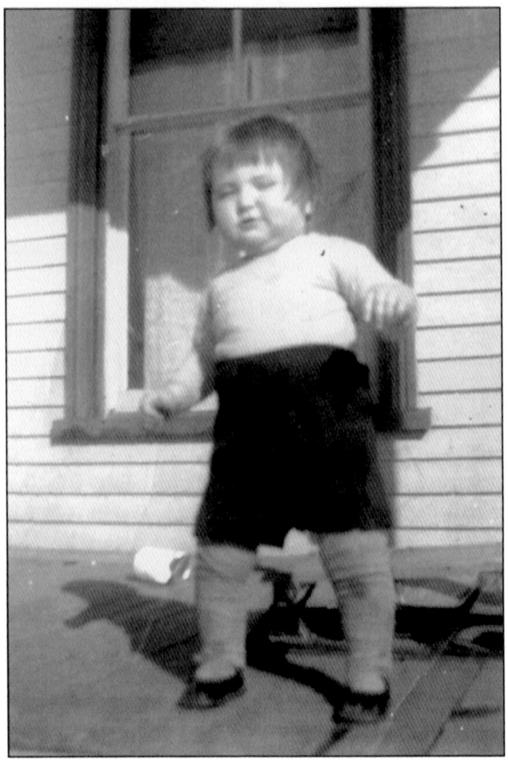

On February 5, 1938, Madeline A. Priest, third child of Guy and Nellie Priest, was born in Guilford center. Her father, being a semiprofessional boxer of some note, had a difficult time in deciding whether to train his daughter as a boxer or a sumo wrestler, but in the end, she turned out to be neither. She is pictured here at the age of 18 months, and she is now the wife of the author.

Nine

SOME INTERESTING SCENES

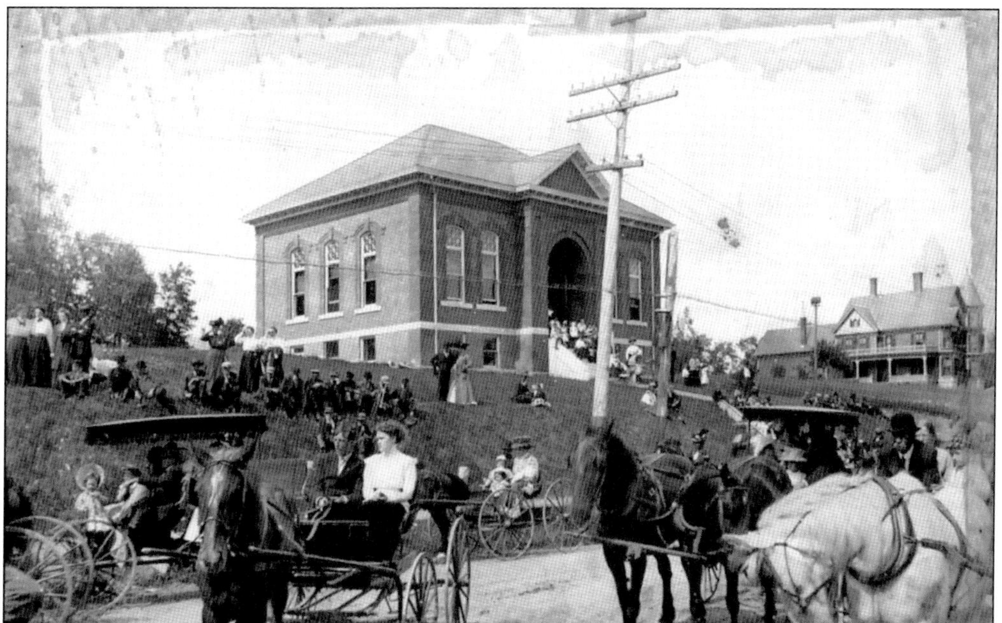

The towns and cities of Maine have always been big on parades. The occasion of the parade everyone is waiting for here is unknown, but it took place around 1912 and shows a good example of the different types of carriages people used then. The Guilford Memorial Library, sitting on the hill, was built with the help of a Carnegie grant and was completed and dedicated in 1909. Beyond the library is one of Guilford's bygone mansions, the F. S. Stevens residence built in 1891 and remodeled in 1896. The date of its demise is unknown.

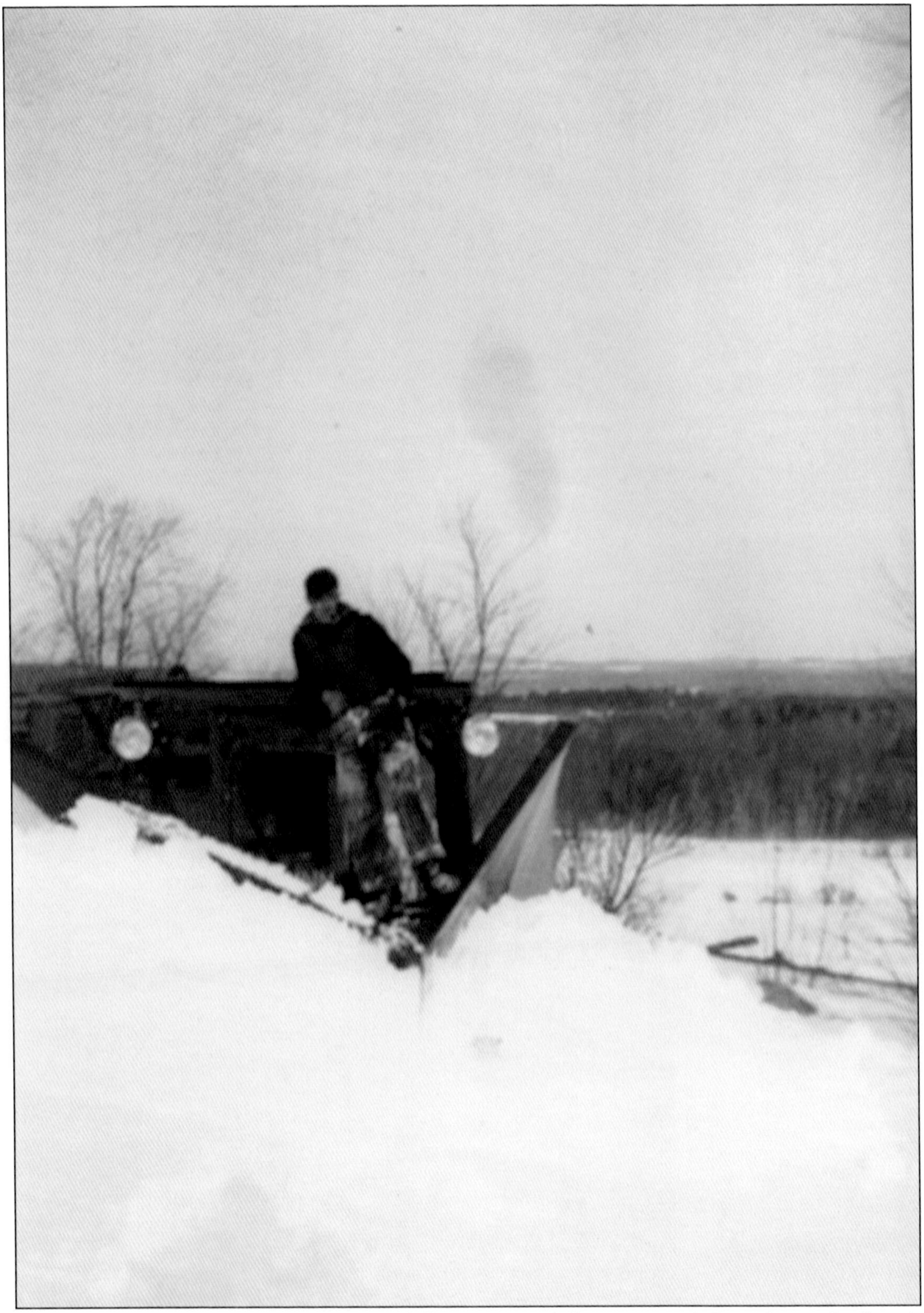

In the 1930s through the 1960s, a much different type of plow was used than those of today. A V-nose plow with wide separate wings on each side allowed a normal road to be cleared with one pass. Sometimes the snow was too much and the plows got stuck like this one did on top of Douty Hill in Sangerville in the 1940s. (Author's collection.)

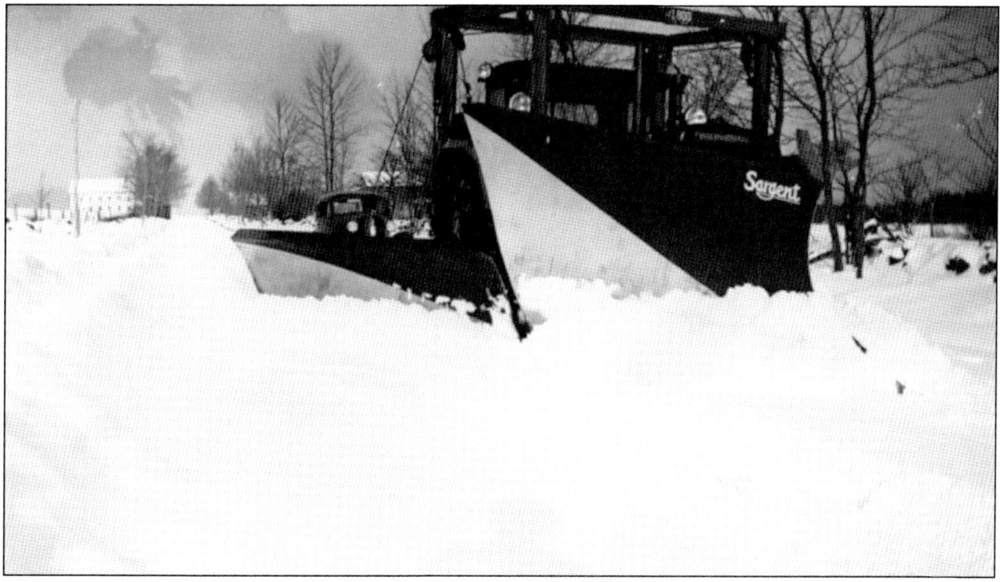

The snowfalls in the 1930s and 1940s seemed heavier than they do today, and the plows struggled to keep the roads clear. In the photograph above, Herb Harrington's rig is moving south on Guilford Center Road. In the background, the Center Grange hall can be seen. In the photograph at right, the left wing is fully raised in an attempt to push the top of the snowbank further back to make room for more.

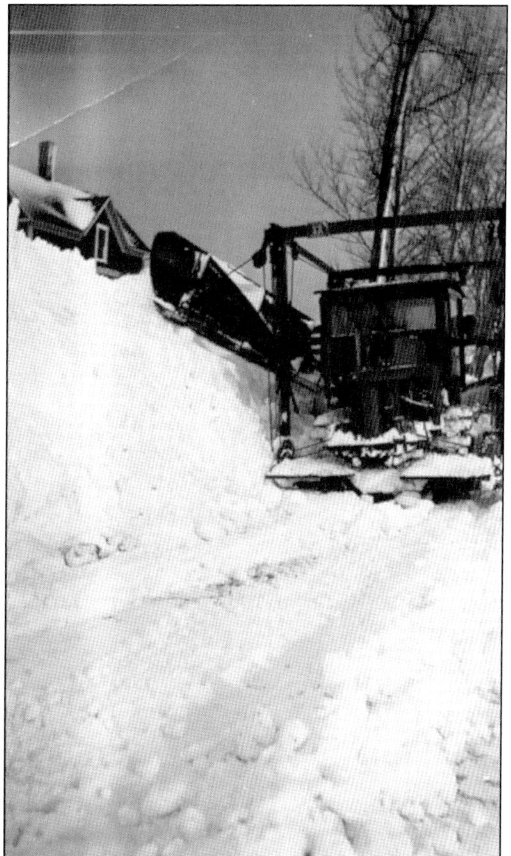

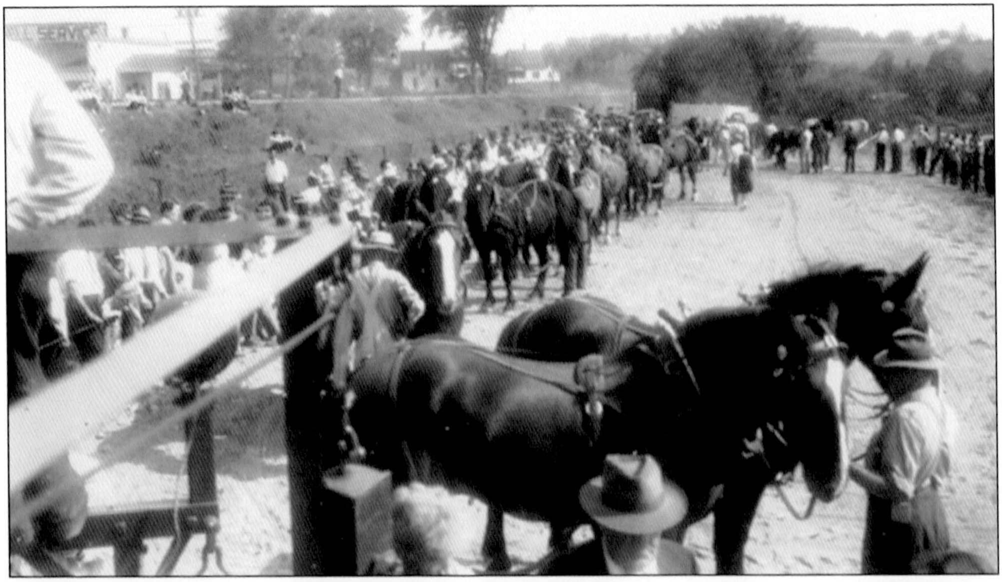

For many years up until the mid-1960s, Guilford always held a fair at the fairgrounds in September. One of the big events held was the horse-pulling contest, with teams being entered from all over the county.

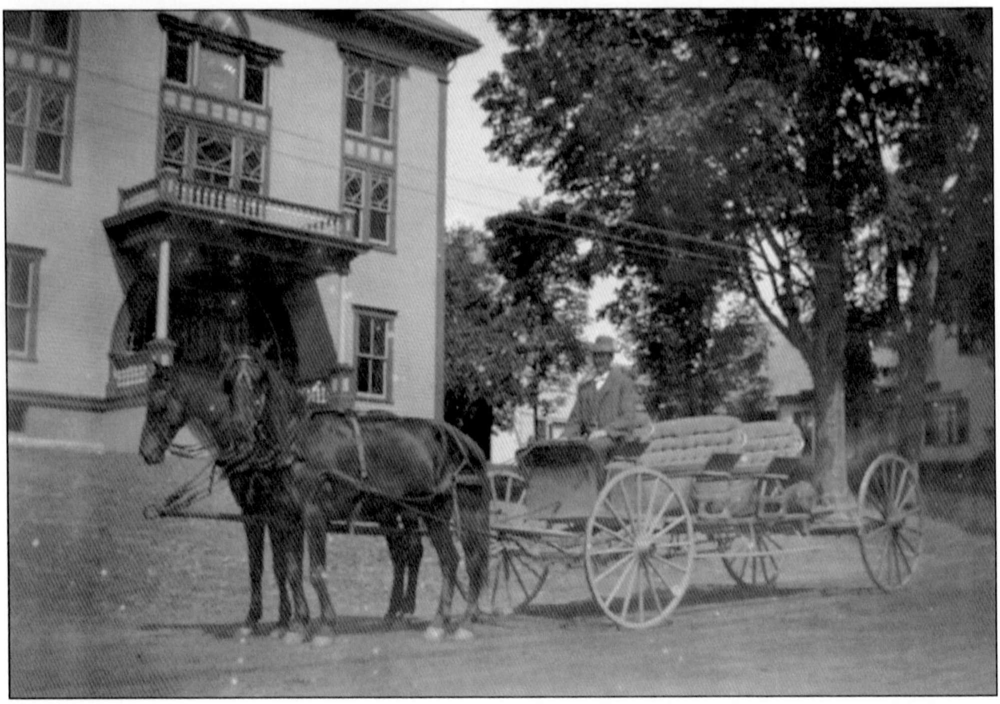

The traffic on Main Street in downtown Sangerville in the early 1900s was not terribly heavy, and if one wished to stop and look around a bit, as Bert Smart is doing here, it was okay and seldom caused a backup of other vehicles. (Courtesy of Sangerville Historical Society.).

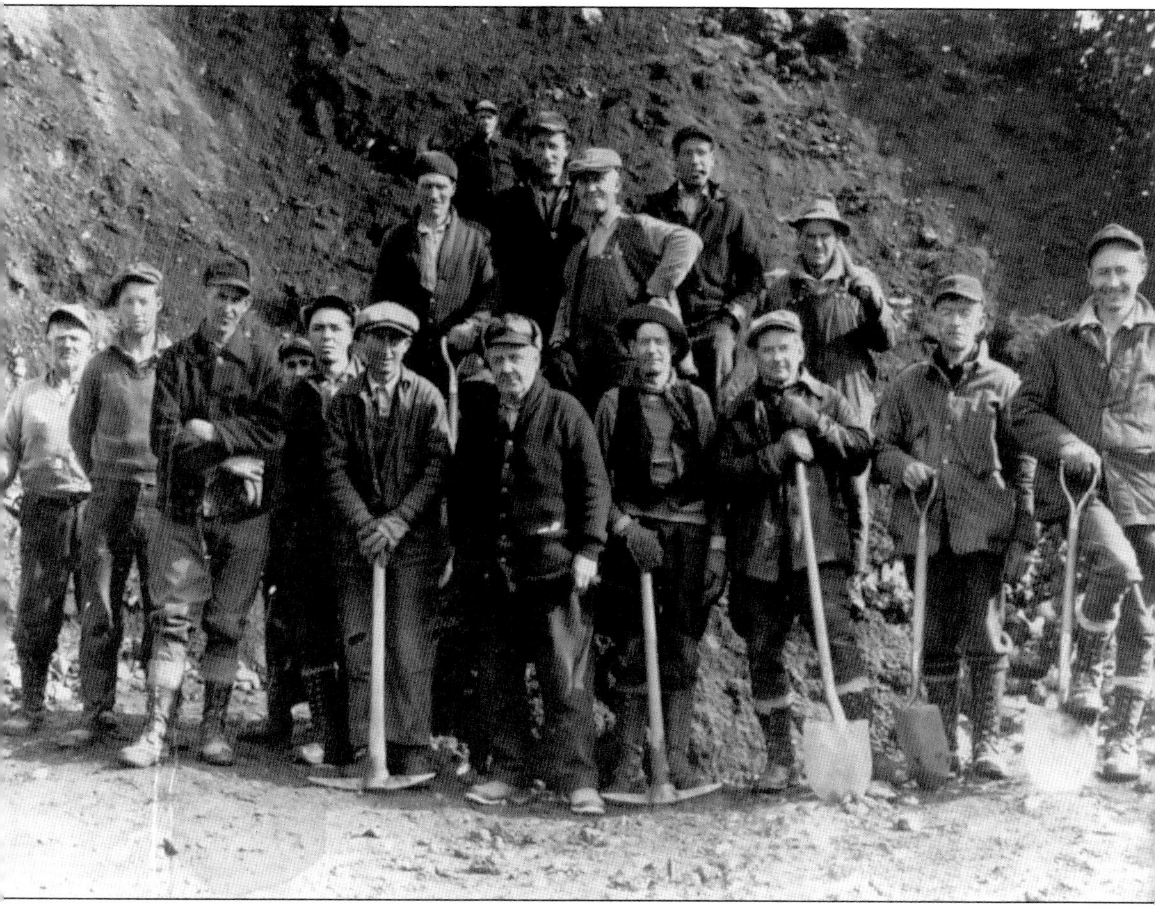

One of Pres. Franklin D. Roosevelt's Depression-era programs was the Works Progress Administration (WPA), which made work available to able-bodied men. Seen here toiling away, from left to right, are (first row) Jim Moulton, Dana Grant, William Reardon, Elmer Easler, Carroll Carle, Elwood Grant, Harold Edgerly, David Thomas, Charles Burton, Frank Bailey, and Floyd Lambert; (second row) Weldon Connor, William Edgerly, Lester Moulton, Irving Starbird, and Eugene Starbird.

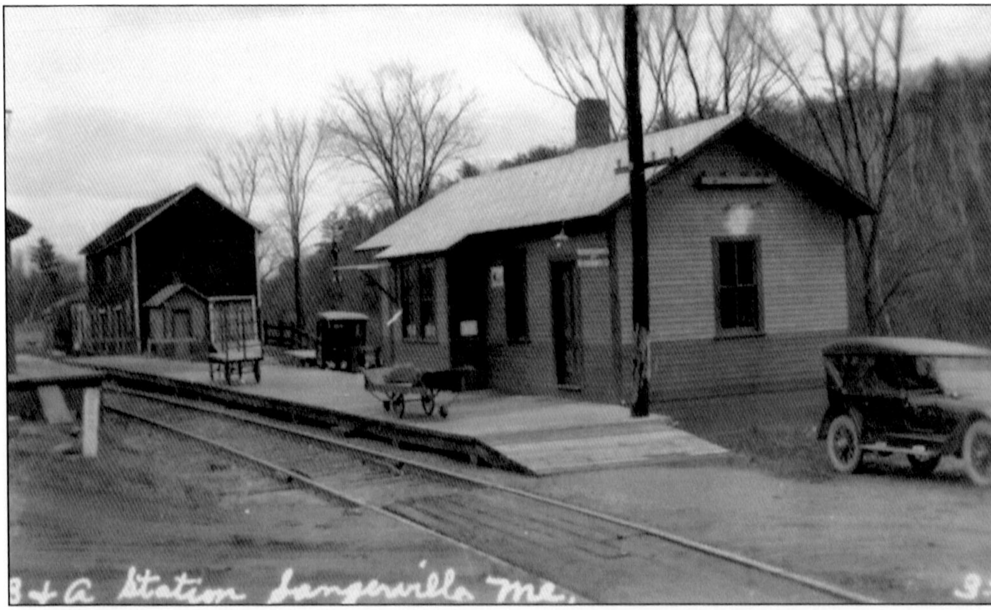

The Sangerville railroad station of the Bangor and Aroostook Railroad was actually situated on the north side of the Piscataquis River in Guilford. It was located on State Route 23 just across the river from Sangerville village cemetery. The photograph was taken around 1920.

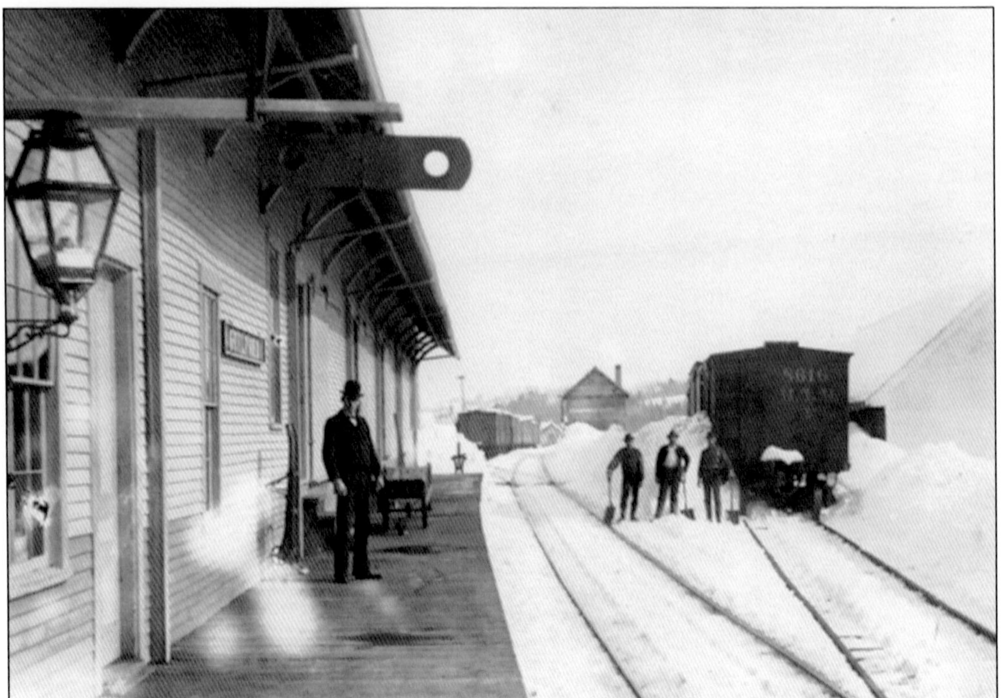

The Guilford railroad station was another mile west of Sangerville's on State Route 15 at approximately where the town tennis and basketball courts are now located.

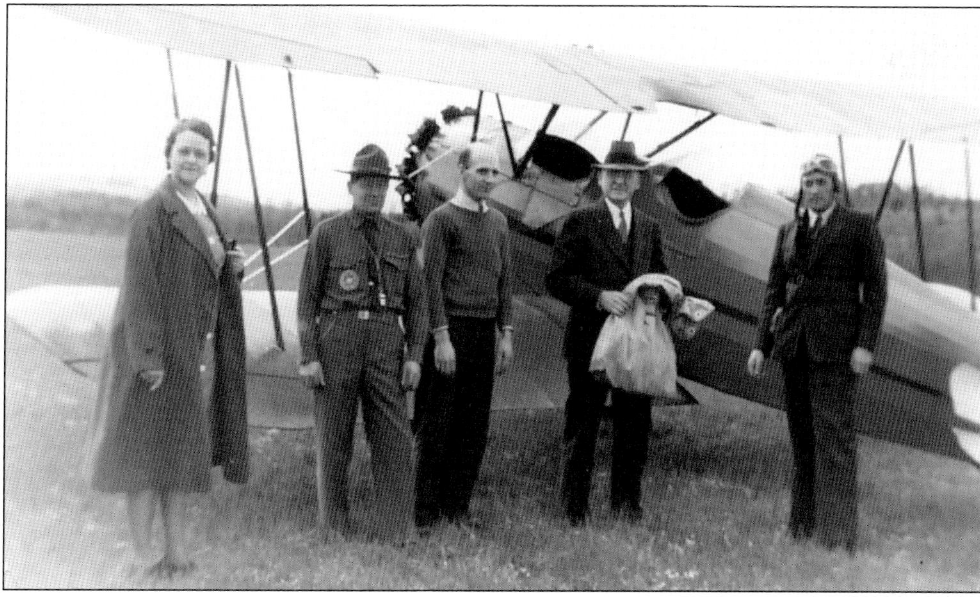

On May 19, 1938, air mail service was inaugurated in Guilford and Sangerville. A big turnout was on hand for the event, and pictured here are Ada Knowles, scoutmaster and reverend Haywood Thomas, postmaster H. Milton Edes of Sangerville, postmaster Gene Ross of Guilford, and the pilot, whose name has been lost to posterity. The planes landed in the large field on State Route 15 opposite the turn onto State Route 23. Several homes occupy this site today. There was no airport or runway here, only a grass field.

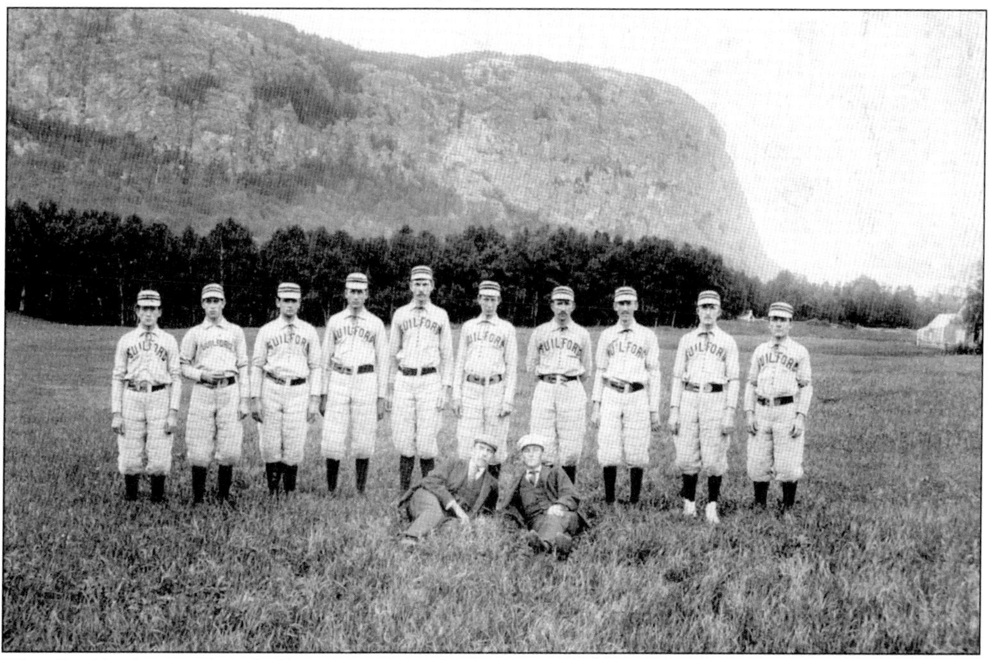

The Guilford town baseball team is seen here at Mount Kineo on August 29, 1895. Included here are (standing) Plummer Chadbourne, Frank Martin, Alton Chadbourne, Carlyle Hussey, Leland Ross, Forest Rowell, James Hudson, Arthur Witham, and Harry Katen; (sitting) Charles Turner and manager Charles Little.

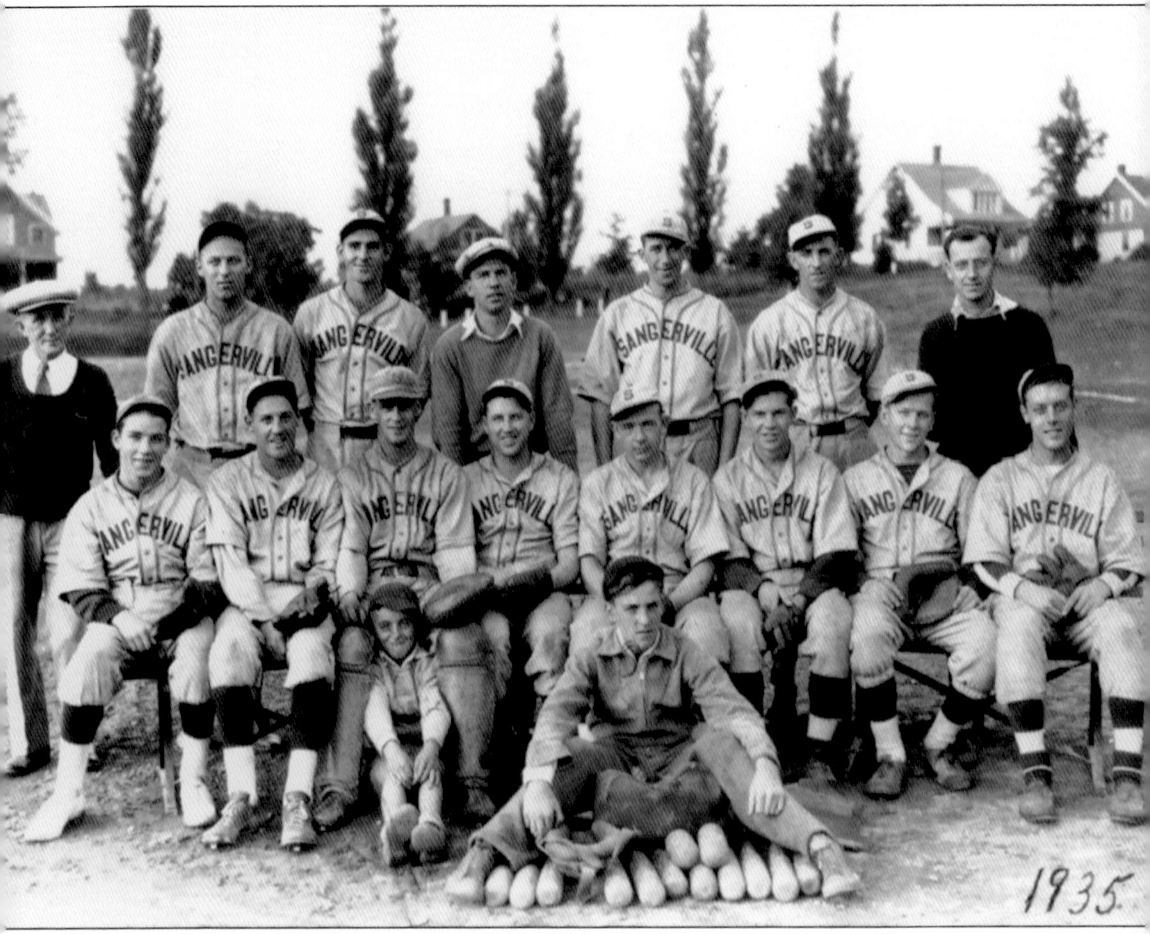

Prior to World War II, semiprofessional baseball was taken very seriously in Maine, with many towns, including both Guilford and Sangerville, sponsoring teams. The Sangerville team seen here, from left to right, includes (first row) Earl Humphrey Jr. and Kenneth Clukey; (second row) Linwood Carleton, Kenneth Coburn, Earl Humphrey, Guy Clukey, Dub Gray, Ralph Baker, Garfield Stone, and Aubrey Wilson; (third row) Tom Patterson, Winton Cobb, Maurice Pullyard, Arthur Steeves, manager Frank Dawes, George Pullyard, and James Jackson. (Courtesy of Sangerville Historical Society.)

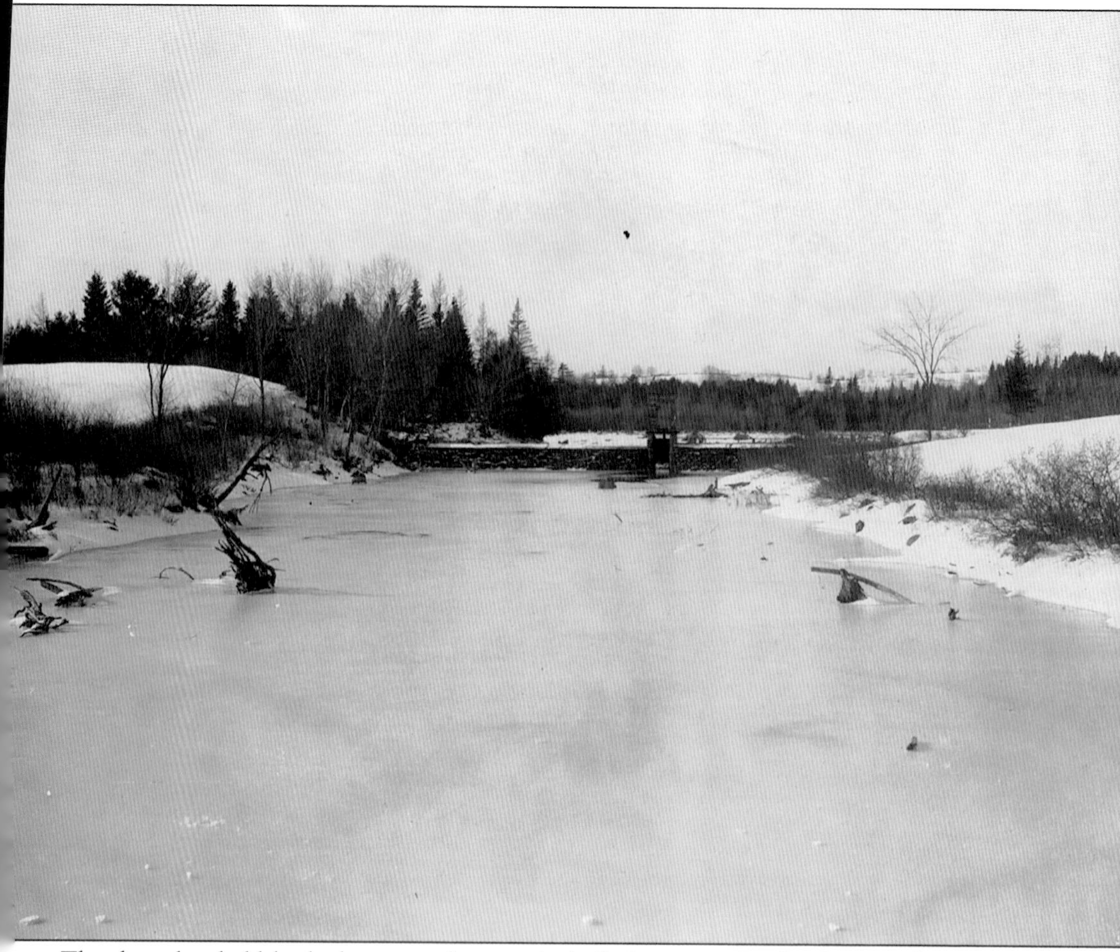

The dam that held back the water that supplied all the power for the Sangerville mills was located a half mile south of town on Dexter Road. At one time there was a small sawmill located on one side or the other of the dam. It was also known as "the ole swimmin hole" by most kids in town for it was, fortunately, located far upstream from all the sewers that once emptied into the little stream. At one time, the sluice gate in the middle of the dam was covered by a small building that was great to jump from.